Kenneth O. Morgan

Kenneth O. Morgan

My Histories

UNIVERSITY OF WALES PRESS
2015

www.uwp.co.uk

British Library CIP Data
A catalogue record for this book is available from the British Library

ISBN   978-1-78316-323-6
eISBN   978-1-78316-324-3

The right of Kenneth O. Morgan to be identified as author of this work has been asserted in accordance with sections 77 and 79 of the Copyright, Designs and Patents Act 1988.

The University of Wales Press acknowledges the financial support of the Welsh Books Council.

Designed and typeset by Chris Bell, cbdesign
Printed by CPI Antony Rowe, Chippenham, Wiltshire

In memory of my beloved parents,
DAVID JAMES MORGAN (1894–1978) and
MARGARET MORGAN, *née* OWEN (1902–1989).
Diolch o galon!

Contents

Foreword

'EVERY HISTORIAN SHOULD WRITE an autobiography.' So wrote my old mentor Alan Taylor in the foreword to his own. He argued that it would be educative in showing the fallibility of all historical sources, especially one's own memory. It is, therefore, a salutary experience for the author even if he or she gives thanks that the vast bulk of historians have not followed Alan's advice. I had for long tended to resist the suggestion of my family and some friends that I should try to compose my memoirs. It seemed at best a routine exercise to provide grist for the mill of possible obituarists, at worst the product of self-indulgence or vanity. I have, however, changed my mind. It seemed to me of wider interest to learn how a working, writing historian went about his task at a time of sweeping historical change. In this endeavour, I have followed the guidance offered in his *Memoirs* from the greatest of all historians , Edward Gibbon, that 'I must be conscious that no one is so well qualified as myself to describe the series of my thoughts and actions', and that one should aim at 'Truth, naked, unblushing truth'. Only the author himself can truthfully convey the intellectual, emotional and psychological factors that lay behind his efforts, the importance of the varied forms of evidence he chose to use, the fascinating people he met and the influence of the family, friends, colleagues and lovers he encountered along the way. In my case, I felt it was important also to spell out the ambiguities, mixed identities and divided consciousness from which I approached historical issues, a division resulting from a sense of being both Welsh and British, a commitment to radical change alongside an attachment to order and a life of peace. Like all historians, I am a hybrid within whom a variety of often conflicting impulses contend. I hope that this has given me the more sympathy as a human being in examining the characters and contexts about which I have written. At the end, I remain totally convinced that the issues on which I have worked as a teacher and a writer are of fundamental value for society, even if my judgements on them, like those of all my profession, are necessarily transient, interim statements due to be corrected in the light of subsequent knowledge. But it has given me a rich and full life, which has always been hugely enjoyable. I can only offer heartfelt thanks to those who made it so, my wonderfully loyal friends and colleagues, my wider family on both sides of Offa's Dyke and of the Channel, my extraordinary children, David and Katherine, my lovely grandchildren and my two brilliant and beautiful wives. They gave me comfort and warmth in the middle and later passages of a long life. But every story needs a strong beginning, and my awareness here is recorded in my dedication. To the generations of Morgans and Owens in my life story, I owe the greatest debt of all.

My daughter Katherine has read through my text to my very great advantage. Additionally, I am deeply grateful to Sarah, Dafydd, Siân, Catrin and their colleagues at the University of Wales Press for their help with this book. At the third time of asking, Alan Taylor wrote that he ended up with 'the almost perfect wife'. After fifty-two years with our national university press, I know I am with the almost perfect publishers.

Long Hanborough, West Oxon.
16 May 2015
K.O.M.

List of illustrations

17 The BBC General Election programme at Lime Grove studios, 31 March 1966.

18 Telling the Queen about Edwardian socialism at Stationers Hall, 26 November 1981. Jane, fourth from the left, looks very nervous in the background! Professor R. H. C. Davis is on the right.

19 With David and Katherine, lunching with Neil and Glenys Kinnock at the Campo, Siena, in 1988.

20 Jane and me at Aberystwyth in March 1989.

21 Presenting Colin Jackson for an Honorary Fellowship at Aberystwyth in July 1994.

22 With Lord Callaghan at Plas Penglais, Aberystwyth, on the University degree day in July 1990.

23 The Oxford Labour Club reunion, London, in June 1996. From left to right: (back row) Elsa Tranter; Virginia Shapiro; the author; David Marquand; Trevor Lloyd; Revan Tranter; David Shapiro; (front row) Leslie Stone; Judith Marquand; Michael Armstrong; Freda Stone.

24 Talking to EC Commissioner Bruce Millan, Brussels, in March 1994.

25 At the National library of Wales, Aberystwyth, in 1994. The Librarian, Professor Brynley Roberts, is on the right.

26 Speaking at the University of Bordeaux in 1999, with Peter Shore and Anne-Marie Motard.

27 My introduction in the House of Lords, 12 July 2000, with Lord Merlyn-Rees.

28 Celebrating my peerage with David and Katherine.

29 With Prince Charles, Katherine, Sir John Meurig Thomas and Clive Jones-Davies at Clarence House in 2001.

30 With Lord Callaghan to celebrate his ninetieth birthday at 10 Downing Street, 27 March 2002. Sir Patrick Cormack MP is on the right.

31 Speaking at the University of Bordeaux on 'The Special Relationship', 24 January 2003. I met Elizabeth for the first time after my lecture, and another 'special relationship' was born!

32 Celebrating my seventieth birthday at home, 16 May 2004, singing 'The Red Flag' with Michael Foot.

33 With my children and cousins and their spouses, celebrating my seventieth birthday.

34 My final meeting with Lord Callaghan, at Upper Clayhill Farm, 13 February 2005. Left to right: (back row) Michael Callaghan; Lord Merlyn-Rees; Lord Healey; the author; Baroness Margaret Jay; Professor Michael Adler; (front row) Lady Merlyn-Rees; Lord Callaghan; Lady Healey.

35 At a gaudy (dinner), Queen's, c.2005.

36 On 11 July 2005 with the FA Cup, after Arsenal's victory in the May final held in Cardiff.

Chapter One

A Divided Consciousness

EVERYBODY HAS A PAST, everybody has a memory. My past is the product of a divided consciousness, divided between the London of my origin and the Wales of my memory, between essentially north Wales Aberdyfi and south Wales Dolybont (just three miles away as the Welsh crow flies across the Dyfi estuary), between my sense of being an Owen and the fact of my being a Morgan. It is this ambiguity, my schizoid view of myself, that is an explanation of the way I have approached the study and writing of history, with all its multiple identities, these sixty years and more.

My historical past began in North London, in a middle-class suburb called Alexandra Park in the borough of Wood Green. I was born in a nursing home in Pellatt Grove near the tube station in Wood Green on 16 May 1934. My family lived in a small semi-detached house, number 219 Alexandra Park Road. I gather that we had a tranquil time in those pre-war years. Both my parents were state school-teachers, very modestly paid but in a profession which, in Wales, enjoyed high public esteem and which had proved an escape for many working-class Welsh people in the bleak years. In the 1930s my father, David James Morgan, who had known some unemployment in the period after the First World War, had a secure job as a school teacher in a secondary school in a working-class area of Islington. My mother Margaret Morgan, *née* Owen, had been a teacher in an infants' school who cruelly lost her job after 1931 when the National government, incredibly as it now seems, decided that married women who taught in schools should be removed from the payroll. She did not return to work of any kind until opportunities arose as a supply teacher during the war when, indeed, she occasionally taught me in Aberdyfi school. My father, as a teacher and a fine one, evidently placed much emphasis on my being able to spell and read English – though not necessarily Welsh. I have vague recollections of being on the beach in Aberdyfi – it must have been during the

Munich crisis – showing some grown-ups that at the age of four I could spell 'Czechoslovakia'. In the spring of 1939, I went to Rhodes Avenue school in Alexandra Park (the avenue so named because Cecil Rhodes had once lived there), where the headmistress, Miss Lorraine, decided that since I was so far ahead in my reading ability I should be placed in a solitary class of my own. It was not a good idea for a very shy and only child, and this decision did apparently greatly upset me. After a brief and distressing period, I was restored to the normal school class, which is what I had wanted. And that appears to have been the only crisis of my earliest years in Alexandra Park, of which otherwise I know and remember nothing.

It was Wales, not London, that shaped my memory. We were a Welsh-speaking family, my father the son of a Cardiganshire village blacksmith, the eldest of eight children, and my mother the daughter of a sailor/boatman, one of three children, of whom a younger brother had died at a very young age. Both were very devoted to their respective families in mid-Wales, and we went to visit often, usually to my mother's home of Aberdyfi with its beach and other delights for a young child. I was christened in Y Babell, the little Methodist chapel at the top of the hill in my father's home of Dolybont, in August 1934, reportedly taking exception to the event at the time. I was given the Christian names Kenneth and Owen – Owen being my mother's maiden name, which I treasure. I was an only child, but I did not mind that. To a considerable degree, my many cousins on my father's side – Gwilym, Margaret and Leri, Anne and her younger brother, David, all lovely people – made up for what, if any, sense of deprivation I felt. We and their spouses have always been very close.

My parents had met in Liverpool in the 1920s where my father had his first significant job teaching in the Bluecoat School, and where my mother had gone to visit her brother, Arthur, another teacher in Liverpool at that time. My father later took my mother to see the West End musical 'No, No Nanette', and I know that its famous song, 'Tea for Two', was always tinged with romance for my mother throughout the rest of her life. After a prolonged engagement that allowed them to accumulate some savings (not unusual in those days), they were married in a Calvinistic Methodist chapel in Maengwyn Street, Machynlleth, in the western tip of Montgomeryshire, a short distance from the Dyfi estuary. Aberdyfi is to the north and facing the estuary, whereas Dolybont is a small inland village about a mile from Borth to the south of the Dyfi. This wedding location sounds like a tactful compromise between my parents' two homes, but they were apparently married there because the Aberdyfi Methodist minister was away on holiday. The date and location of the marriage are not without interest. Their marriage date was 21 August 1930, the day on which the Queen's younger sister, Princess Margaret, was born. In those respectful royalist days, her friends excitedly told my mother that this was indeed a lucky omen which promised a long and happy marriage – and so it did, since my parents lived serenely together until my father's death forty-eight years later. The location of my parents' wedding (now an art gallery) is directly across the road from an ancient battered building, which is claimed to have been Owain Glyn Dŵr's putative Welsh parliament in 1406. It has always given me pleasure to have this link, however uncertain, with Wales's Braveheart and with this major episode in Welsh history.

My parents were quite different in personality, for all the similarity of their background. Much of this difference can be related to their respective home communities. Aberdyfi, then a straggling village with a population of around 2,500 had been a popular and quite fashionable watering place from the early nineteenth century. This was especially the case when the golf links were opened as an 18-hole course in 1892. They were much popularised by the celebrated newspaper correspondent Bernard Darwin, a grandson of the famous scientist, who sang the praises of their very varied holes. Notable among these was the short third hole, the legendary 'Cader', where a player drove into the void since the green was invisible. One of my pleasures when caddying for my uncle was looking through a rustic periscope to see if the green ahead was clear. The golf, and the convenient mid-Wales railway line, brought many more affluent visitors to Aberdyfi, most notably public schoolmaster golfers. There was quite a smart hotel, the Trefeddian, along the road towards Towyn (during the war it housed girls from a Swiss boarding school, the Chatelard), while many boarding houses on the front had a steady stream of visitors. One of them was owned by Nain, my grandmother, a happy, kindly soul with a good sense of humour. She developed a close relationship with many of these visitors who loved her and came time and again, even during the war years.

With its bathing, its swimming, its little putting course and tennis courts, and lovely walks in the hills beyond the village to such legendary Arthurian sites as Bearded Lake, Aberdyfi was a cheerful, outward looking place and great fun for children. I used to love sitting in an upstairs room in the early evening watching the changing colours of the Cardiganshire hills across the water. Another joy was walking on the beach along the shore, listening for the bells of Aberdyfi ringing out as a legacy of the legendary Cantre'r Gwaelod, the land submerged in Cardigan Bay as a result of the reputed negligence of Seithennin, a local chieftain. Seithennin, it is said, was a drunkard, a fact that led to the defences against the sea being fatally neglected and Cantre'r Gwaelod being drowned and lost for ever – a useful temperance message. I was always certain that I could hear the ringing drowned bells of Cantre'r Gwaelod from the sands in front of our house. Over the intervening years, Aberdyfi has become more affluent; British Railways provided an attractive jetty, and there are now smart restaurants, coffee bars and women's fashion shops along the sea front.

Affluence, however, has also meant anglicisation. When I last stayed in Aberdyfi with my wife Elizabeth during a holiday in 2012, I could not find a single person who spoke Welsh – everybody, it seemed, had come from Wolverhampton. Aberdyfi had gone global.

By contrast, my father's home, Dolybont (or Penybont as it was commonly called), very picturesque, was a more inward-looking place, with an atmosphere redolent of the religious revivals that had once erupted nearby. Dolybont was tiny, with a population of barely a hundred, which had to take the bus to Borth or, more ambitiously, to Aberystwyth to buy food and other necessities. It was truly a Welsh version of *la France profonde*: the postbox on the wall of my aunt's house, Tanyrallt, bore the letters VR for Victoria Regina. The village's central feature was a steep bridge that crossed the river Leri. It was next to it that my grandparents lived in Yr Efail, the forge where my blacksmith of a grandfather, Tadcu, plied his trade. He was a quiet countryman, who sadly died when I was eight after a hard life of labour. I recall him with great affection letting me use some old bellows to stoke up the fires in the forge before putting the horseshoes in for treatment. He loved to pile all his very young grandchildren into bed with him while he told some simple Welsh stories, some of which I re-told to amuse my own children decades later. I suspect that Tadcu was a man of profound intelligence for all his lack of education. Some years after his death, I found great piles of Welsh periodicals in Yr Efail, *Y Traethodydd* and *Y Genhinen*, sober monthly publications containing learned articles on literature, theology, history and much else. He would have had time to read them because his day's strenuous work as a blacksmith came to an end at around eleven in the morning. In a fairer world, Tadcu would not have remained a blacksmith for all his life. My grandmother, Mamgu, was a dignified, lovely lady always dressed in black. Mamgu and Tadcu were my main ties with Dolybont, rather than my numerous and mostly jolly uncles and aunts. Otherwise, there was much less entertainment for a boy than in Aberdyfi – indeed, on Sundays, life seemed to stop altogether. But always in my childhood, one of the great joys in life was going to sleep in Yr Efail with the comforting ripple of the Leri in my ears.

My mother, just like Nain, reflected the gentleness of Aberdyfi. A quiet modest woman of endless loyalty to friends and family, she spoke the soft north Wales Welsh of Merioneth. Where my father's Cardiganshire Welsh, used the words *gyda* or *mas* to signify 'with' and 'out', my mother would say *efo* or *allan*, as I do now. When I became a grandfather, I faced the acute dilemma of whether my new grandchildren should call me *Taid* or *Tadcu* – it is, I think, indicative of my outlook and personality that the north Wales *Taid* won out. It is an easier word for young children anyway. The vowel sounds were very different – *fo* for 'him' in Aberdyfi, *fe* in Cardiganshire. I am a *fo* man. I used to say that I grew up trilingual: English, north Wales Welsh, and south Wales Welsh. My mother, a keen pianist, had trained as a teacher in Bangor Normal College, as had my father a few years before her. She would recall the ferocious college rules to prevent the young ladies speaking to young men anywhere, redolent of the regime of the Taliban. She was rebuked, for instance, for speaking to her brother in the street at the time of the death of their younger brother, Huw. She was endlessly patient and kind, which may be a reason why she was so successful in teaching small children how to read. She spoke with great sympathy of the children of canal people that she had taught in London and of their pathetic enthusiasm for education, born of the fact that they were endlessly on the move and had no continuous time at school. She was particularly good at teaching immigrant children later on, perhaps because, like them, English was not her first language either. In the 1950s, she had remarkable success in teaching Greek Cypriot children to read, whose delighted parents showered her with little Greek trinkets as a reward. My mother's father, Owen Owen, was evidently a shy, delightful man, who sadly died before I was born in 1932 – I deeply regret that I never knew him. Among other joys, he would have taken me out on his boat into Cardigan Bay and made me less of the landlubber that I am.

My mother's family comprised unremarkable country people, with one exception: Evan Evans, my maternal great-great-grandfather. Born in Barmouth in 1779 he had been working in the field on the Ynysmaengwyn estate near Towyn to the north of Aberdyfi around 1800, when he was press-ganged into the navy. He saw fierce and active service, and fought at Trafalgar serving on HMS *Minotaur*, a ship that fought literally alongside Nelson's HMS *Victory*. Evan Evans had a tough time at Trafalgar, where three of his mates were killed, and he himself was injured in the face. He was known locally thereafter as *Boch Mawr* ('big cheek'). I still have the large musket he used at Trafalgar, and also his pension form of 1813 which states that he was to receive £10 a year for life (no negligible sum) and that anyone trying to impersonate him would be punishable by death. However, he seemed to flourish after his naval service, and is recorded in the 1851 census, which means he must have lived on into his seventies, perhaps more affluent through prize money than he would have been had he remained undisturbed in the fields of Merioneth.

My father was a more forceful personality than my mother by far. He was evidently a clever boy at Ardwyn grammar school in Aberystwyth. He liked to tell me, in his modest way, of when his sixth form class was asked by the famous schools inspector, Sir Owen Edwards (the only Merioneth man other than me who has been a history tutor at Oxford), 'Can you give me an example of perfect English style?' My father piped up, 'Cardinal Newman, sir!', which somewhat took Sir Owen aback, and was indeed a remarkable answer from a young boy, especially a Protestant. My father also went to Bangor Normal College before service in the First World War in 1916–18 following the introduction of conscription. He entered the Royal Field Artillery, in the A (Cardiganshire) Battery, and was dispatched to Egypt. So a young Cardiganshire man, who had probably never been to London, found himself gazing at the pyramids and the Sphinx. His war began at the battle of Gaza, and he ended up in Damascus at the end of 1918. He used to talk about some cultural aspects of his war years in the desert fighting the Turks, of his good relations with the Gurkhas, of his low opinion of the Egyptians (many of whom, he said, were thieving), and how he (as a virtual non-swimmer) swam across the Suez Canal. He knew a few words of Egyptian, notably 'talaheena bint' ('Come here, woman'), and I used to wonder what use he may have made of this phrase. He spoke with pride of having met General Allenby, the one military general for whom he ever had a good word. Like many old soldiers, he never mentioned any of the horrible scenes that he must have witnessed in Palestine, such as at the battles of Gaza or Megiddo, but he retained a memento of his war service in a small white circle on his left hand where a Turkish bullet had passed clean through while he was laying down telegraph wires ahead of army lines. A close friend was the Revd Jack Stephens, later both an Anglican clergyman and famous rugby back-row forward who played for both Llanelli and Wales. I recall Dad mentioning the death of his especially great friend and relative Ivor Morgan, on 19 September 1918, in the very last weeks of the war. He described this to me some forty years after the war had ended, and then burst uncontrollably into tears – it was almost the only time I ever saw this old soldier cry. I have Ivor's memorial card next to me as I write. He looks a nice, kind man too.

After the war, my father ended up teaching for some years in Liverpool, which was where and when he both met my mother and played, in 1923, in a simultaneous chess match (inevitably unsuccessfully) with the Russian world champion Alexander Alekhine. He then moved on to teach in a state school in Islington, North London. His subjects included both mathematics and science, and also English and literature. He was a quiet scholarly person of extraordinarily broad culture. Indeed, I think he was probably the ablest man I have ever known, and I was truly fortunate to have him as a father, He could occasionally be aggressive in manner, but never to me. Obviously, he was a superb teacher, much used by our neighbours to give extra-mural tuition to their children. He could seemingly do everything. He was skilled at woodwork, he could draw clever sketches, he knew all about gardening. And perhaps for that reason, I was useless at most of these – though I shared some of his talent for drawing. One of the things he made in his woodwork was a table-tennis table, and the games we played in a room off a small cellar beneath the hallway gave us endless pleasure throughout my school days. The narrow confines of our cellar meant that I always played 'ping-pong' close to the table – and so I do now, playing against my eldest grandson Joseph.

Although my father's ideas on day-to-day moral issues tended to be cautious and conservative, his opinions on many public subjects were robust. His political views appear to have moved sharply to the left during the First World War. He was thus sympathetic to Russia and hostile towards Winston Churchill, a daring viewpoint during the war years to say the least. Our house reflected some of his unorthodox interests – Marxist tracts by the Communist Palme Dutt; Union of Democratic Control material attacking lies in wartime; pamphlets from the society claiming that Bacon had written Shakespeare's plays; and, especially, papers on the putative world language Esperanto. He seems to have been naturally minority-minded. He was anti-religious but much enjoyed Welsh chapel services, where he could focus on the sermon and perhaps discuss famous Welsh preachers with the minister afterwards. His abiding interest was chess – both problems and games – which gave scope both for his mathematical gifts and his abilities as a crisp writer. He wrote a famous monthly column 'Quotes and Queries' for the *British Chess Magazine* right down to the month of his death in 1978. I was delighted in Aberystwyth, in 1995, when we appointed a History Professor who told me he had read my father's column avidly. For him, I was just the son of the famous D. J. Morgan and I was overjoyed to know it. But he combined all this with a cheerful zest for life, including a love of football and cricket which he had played as a young man and of which I also became an enthusiast. Overall, as a devoted (perhaps over-devoted) father, he had an enormous influence on me. He had no particular wish for me to make money, but he did want me to develop my mind – that in due course I became a university teacher gave him unbridled delight. I owe him almost everything. He was also devoted to his seven brothers and sisters and had an intense attachment to family, which must have been difficult for my mother and the other spouses. Several of his siblings followed the traditional Cardiganshire route of becoming milkmen in London. But my father was the only academic, and the greatest brain, within it. For him, the Morgans were a mighty tribe of biblical eminence, and he was its unchallenged elder. I do not feel that I have wanted to inherit that particular role.

As for everyone else, the tranquil tenor of our lives was totally disrupted when world war broke out in September 1939. My father had to stay with his school in Islington, later evacuated to Hertfordshire. But he insisted that my mother and I go down immediately to Aberdyfi to stay with my Nain, and I then went to the local school, Aberdyfi Council School as it was known, complete with my compulsory gasmask. I missed my father terribly during the war years – he could only come down fleetingly during school holidays. But in every other way it was a happy transition. I loved Nain and her large house, and always found Aberdyfi immensely enjoyable. When I entered the Lords, I had no hesitation in telling an initially doubtful Garter King of Arms that I wished to be 'Morgan of Aberdyfi'. The little seaport still bore many traces of its maritime past, when brigs and schooners had made it the busiest port in Cardigan Bay with much trade – coastal trade locally, and also further afield to places like Norway and Spain. My mother's father had been a part of that past before the First World War, serving on vessels that took slate from the Corris and Abergynolwyn quarries to places like Scandinavia, and returned with timber or perhaps minerals. When I lived in Aberdyfi, a notable landmark was the 'boatman's seat' on the harbour front, a haven for elderly ex-sailors, all purportedly captains, reminiscent of Dylan Thomas's Captain Cat. One prominent figure was a blind sailor who shouted at us boys as we raced along the jetty. I was told years later by my Swansea colleague, Professor Alun Davies, who gave an extra-mural class on international history in Aberdyfi, that this old man would terrorise him with loud (and unanswerable) demands for the latitude and longitude of places mentioned. The traditions of the sea were plentiful in Aberdyfi – in house names like 'Maglona' and 'Mimosa', and in monuments in the local cemetery which testified to losses through shipwrecks or other disasters. Its maritime location persuaded Kurt Hahn, with his link with Gordonstoun school, to set up the Outward Bound school there during the war in 1941, and it is still going strong. A remarkable old chap lived two doors away from us in 9 Bodfor Terrace, 'Pomona', whose owner Zoe was a great friend of my mother; he was Zoe's father, Captain Williams, a man in possession of a fine late-Victorian moustache and a colourful ship's parrot with even more colourful language. He had evidently sailed to several remote places, and held me spellbound with tales of the storms in the Bay of Biscay and of the even greater terrors of sailing 'Round the Horn', which he had done more than once. His house had ample mementoes of life at sea, including tangles of rope and lifebelts – as had our own house too, souvenirs of my grandfather's career as a man of the sea.

There were other local personalities in Aberdyfi. One was Ellis Williams, the genial ferryman who would spend his afternoons having tea in his living room looking out at the Dyfi estuary, spying through a telescope for customers in Ynyslas on the other side of the river. They would wave their scarves for him to sail over and pick them up them, which he always did. The deacons in our chapels, all shopkeepers, were much-respected big personalities – chemists, drapers, grocers and the like – with our chapel, Tabernacl, having greater prestige because the Calvinistic Methodists were the most numerous nonconformist community. I was never really a believer, though I enjoyed the Sunday School trips into the countryside. A remarkable local figure of a quite different kind was Berta Ruck, the daughter of a former chief constable of Caernarfonshire, who lived on the top floor in 'Pomona'. She was a highly successful popular novelist, who wrote scores of romantic novels which brought her to the attention of Barbara Cartland amongst others. She had the air of a *grande dame* of the late Hapsburg empire, but she was a popular figure locally. I knew her as Mrs Oliver since she was married to Oliver Onions, also a writer, who had apparently changed his surname to protect his sons. She remained black-haired and was physically remarkably energetic. Every morning when I woke up, I would look out upon the beach and see Mrs Oliver, even at seven in the morning, whatever the time of the year, doing her exercises on the shore before plunging into the chilly waters. Perhaps for that reason she lived on until 1978, dying at the age of one hundred. Down the road from us, in a huge white house called 'Craig-y-Don', was a great man I never met, Lord Atkin of Aberdovey – popularly known as 'Judgatkin'. I never went to Craig y Don – he had grandchildren whom my mother fatally dismissed as being 'stuck up' – but Atkin himself became one of my great heroes later on. His judgement in the *Liversidge vs Anderson* case, when he quoted the old Roman tag that in times of war the laws were not silent, was a great blow for civil liberties which I would refer to in the Lords when discussing the Labour Party's Counter-Terrorism Acts. I recall his funeral cortège in the village in 1944. I wish I had met his grandchildren, and certainly him.

Aberdyfi was very far from the battle zones and we felt totally secure there. I read the papers avidly and extended the knowledge of geography I had built up from my childhood passion for postage-stamps. Probably under my father's influence, I took a particular interest in the Russian front and had large maps on the floor illustrating its course; I readily absorbed, with my abiding interest in geography, names like Nivjy Novgorod and Veliki Luki. We read with alarm of the horrors of the blitz of English cities like Plymouth and Coventry and, of course, of London. I saw the latter at first-hand in 1942 when my father took me around central London – my strongest memories are of people sleeping on bunks in tube stations, and of seemingly miles of devastated rubble surrounding St Paul's Cathedral. But the war did impinge more directly, even in Aberdyfi. I faithfully carried my gasmask with me to the local school. In my Nain's home, I tried to obey the government's economy warning that we should wash ourselves in no more than six inches of bathwater; I took my school ruler with me to Nain's large Victorian bath to ensure conformity. There was stringent food rationing, of course (perhaps less severe in a country village with its own local produce), and the hazards of dark nights if you were out because of black-out material cutting out light from windows. We used to be terrified when my very aged and totally deaf Auntie Mary Jane came down the unlit village from Chapel Square to play me at tiddly-winks, which she much enjoyed. One important wartime novelty was the fact that considerable numbers of evacuees from Merseyside were brought to the town. They were taught at the separate 'National' school, and I have no recollection of any kind of conflict with them. On the contrary, more boys meant more people to play football with, while several of them learnt Welsh and added strength to the choirs of the local chapels. We had a dark-haired young girl, Phyllis from Birkenhead, a few years older than me, billeted on us. I liked talking to Phyllis in her room upstairs. My mother seemed to disapprove, believing perhaps with some justice that she was unduly 'advanced' in her social or sexual attitudes. But we did nothing more daring than discuss her girls' magazines.

More directly military, we had commandoes also billeted on us. We had two wonderful young men – Andrew, an English public-school boy, and Leslie, an immigrant I suspect, perhaps German-Jewish. They were exceptionally kind to me, allowing me to dress up in their uniforms and play with their rifles – on my ninth birthday, they kindly bought me a book about the navy in the Mediterranean, *East of Malta, West of Suez*, which I greatly enjoyed. They were, of course, among the shock troops trained to invade the Normandy beach heads, and I often wonder whether they survived, even for a week, after that bloodbath. In 1943, a most exciting development came which brought the war home even more directly. I looked out one morning and saw the beach covered with soldiers and amphibious landing craft – Ducks, Terrapins and the like. For many months, the beach between Aberdyfi and Towyn was the training area for the Normandy landing on D-Day. For small boys, this meant even more fun since the kindly men driving their Ducks would give us trips into Cardigan Bay. I reflect on this now when I often see aged wartime Ducks carrying tourists along the Thames beyond the terrace of the House of Lords. In Aberdyfi, all that survives of that particular episode are rough concrete pill-boxes scattered along the long beach towards Towyn, to ward off the alleged German threat – back in that day, my friends and I used them as bizarre and somewhat unsanitary play areas.

The small community of Aberdyfi, therefore, expanded rapidly with the evacuees and the soldiers and yet more soldiers in the nearby base at Tonfanau. The expansion happened without apparent trauma. There were dark rumours that abounded that some of the soldiers were becoming too integrated and that some of the younger local wives, whose husbands were far away on military service, were taking civilian-military harmony rather too far. My mother said they were 'a bit flighty'. A legendary figure was a dark-haired handsome officer called Captain Barnes who was socially much in demand. A frisson of excitement was caused when he took part in a local drama production and played the romantic lead. Whatever the facts, it was certainly the case that some of the servicemen took to the natural appeal of Aberdyfi – and perhaps its female residents – and settled there after the war, running sweet shops and the like.

It was, then, a safe and in many ways enjoyable war in Aberdyfi for a young child. But then, in early 1944, it all changed. My father, whose school was now back in Islington since the Luftwaffe air raids had long ceased, was anxious that we should all be back together again in Alexandra Park. My mother was very apprehensive, but my father assured us that a second front was very near and that the war would then soon be over. The first prophecy proved to be correct, but not the second. So we returned, to my great joy, to our home in Alexandra Park Road, which had hitherto survived the wartime trials. I scarcely recalled our London home at all and greatly missed the sea and my Nain , but it was good to be in the family home and have a life closer to normality. Soon afterwards, my education was fixed. I was interviewed for entry to the junior school of University College School in Hampstead. I was seen here by a genial old eccentric, Dr 'Bunny' Lake, the head of the junior school. He rambled on amiably but then asked me a solitary question: namely, the name of the stretch of water that separated Asia from Europe. With my geographical knowledge from postage stamps, that was easy and I confidently replied, 'The Bosphorus, sir.' On that sole evidence, he pronounced me to be highly intelligent and to UCS I went, with experiences that I shall describe in the next chapter.

In the meantime, the war was still very much on, and the pleasantness of our return was sharply interrupted. The belief that German air raids were a thing of the past was shattered in early June with the totally unexpected launching of V1 flying bombs or 'doodlebugs'. I still recall the terror of being at home with my mother when a V1 seemed to cut off immediately overhead, which meant that a terrifying explosion would follow in around five seconds. Miraculously it landed in the nearby Alexandra Park racecourse and there were no casualties or damage. A few weeks later, in mid-September, we were not so lucky. My parents and I were woken up during the night (we slept downstairs, under the dining room table as the government recommended) by a colossal noise. We looked into the hallway to find that, along with broken windows, our front door had been blown clean off its hinges by the blast. Remarkably, the door was not itself damaged, and its leaded glass was intact. The V1 had landed at the top of The Avenue, a mile or so away, killing several dozen people. It was a major calamity. The burnt-out shell of the rocket remained there for some years afterwards, as a grim memorial. I seem to recall that, by breakfast time, the ARP were repairing it, and that by teatime (I went to school that day!) our house seemed reasonably intact, save for boarded-up windows. But it was an anxious period. As a wartime 'scholarship boy', I took long journeys to school on the number 102 bus to Golders Green, sometimes during V1 raids. When I got there, we often had our lessons in a changing room in the school basement. Films at the Wood Green Gaumont were sometimes interrupted by air-raid sirens. I recall my mother delaying buying us a new piano, believing that our house should remain as empty as possible in case it was struck again, this time by a V2. Another hazard of this difficult time was the horrendous London fogs or 'smogs', commonplace before the Clean Air Acts, which could reduce London's road traffic to near immobility. I found them more frightening than the 'doodlebugs'.

Yet, in spite of all this, wartime in Alexandra Park had its pleasures. The neighbourliness induced by dangers from the air made people, so it seemed to my mind, friendly and cooperative. To me, whatever critical historians now conclude, this was broadly the People's War of popular legend. There was entertainment even in wartime. There were three good cinemas – the Muswell Hill Odeon being a famous instance of 'art deco' architecture – and old-fashioned music hall at the Wood Green or Finsbury Park Empires. Soon after the war ended, we had Tom Arnold's circus at Harringay (so spelt then) with the Schuman Lippizaner horses, which my father, as the son of a blacksmith, much enjoyed. There was also a cornucopia of sport, especially watching Arsenal, whom I came to support (probably my father's influence again) and who played at the Tottenham ground at White Hart Lane since the Highbury stadium had been damaged by German firebombing. The football teams of 1944–5 were a bit of a mixture – almost any eleven players who could be herded together – but the Arsenal side did include famous pre-war stars like Drake, Bastin and Male. There were also pilgrimages with my father to Lords cricket ground, which became my own particular Mecca after the war.

Even the war itself became almost enjoyable as it neared its end. VE Day was greeted with massive local celebration and a children's street party where we ate jellies and danced the hokey-cokey. Later, there were fireworks in Alexandra Park. On 8 May 1945, there was a huge show of flags in Alexandra Park Road. As a Welsh family, we could not produce a Union Jack but only a Welsh Red Dragon, which my father put up on our roof to the bemusement of some of our neighbours (one of whom asked whether the flag was in fact that of China). During the previous night, there had been a huge thunderstorm and the local vicar told my sceptical father that this was a sign from God. So my war, as a young boy, was over. It was tense, even terrifying at the time but, in retrospect, I am glad that I lived through it. It was an extraordinary phase in our history and the trauma of it a valuable corrective for a historian brought up in comfortable circumstances for most of his life, unused to reflecting on the devastating human impact of terror and tragedy.

The post-war years were for me a period of almost unbroken pleasure. This, of course, was enhanced by the surrender of Japan in July, which finally brought conflict to an end. The implications of the atomic bombs dropped on Hiroshima and Nagasaki took me – and, I suspect, most people – much time to absorb. At the time they seemed to be just one more appalling weapon in an atrocious war, not something that transformed the very meaning of war itself. The joys of life were much enhanced for my parents by the Labour landslide in the 1945 General Election. It was the first political event in which I took a relatively informed interest. I noted how, in Wood Green and elsewhere, Conservative Party posters featured not the local candidate but photos of Winston Churchill, with the injunction 'Vote National'. I could not understand how Labour, whose leaders had all served in the wartime coalition, should not be considered 'national' also, rather than sectarian and perhaps unpatriotic. I was with my father when we heard Churchill's first election broadcast with its amazing suggestion that Labour might introduce some kind of Gestapo in Britain. My father angrily responded in robust language. It was the only time that I heard him swear, albeit in Welsh. For the next six years, my parents' allegiance to 'their' government was unshakeable. My mother was not really political, but she disliked the 'stuck-up' Tories on class grounds. Her favourite was, as she called him, 'Mr Attlee' or sometimes 'Major Attlee'; her least favourite minister was her fellow-countryman, Aneurin Bevan, whom she considered too much of a class warrior. When Labour finally was defeated in 1951, my father was sure that this was the result of the malign influence of Tory press lords, Lord Beaverbrook in particular..

These years have been christened 'the age of austerity' but, for all its shortages and rationing and other private trials, for me it was a time of enjoyment about which many subsequent historians have been far too gloomy. After all, my recollection was of the war years only, and life was obviously a huge improvement on that. No-one would try to destroy our house any more. My cousin, the author Susan Cooper, has written in *The Age of Austerity* of how the years after 1945 were for our generation a revelation: 'We saw not only the first pineapples and bananas of our lives but the first washing machine, the first fountain, the first television set.' That was exactly my feeling as well. My parents were now back teaching at state schools, my mother liberated by being able to teach again after being banned in the 1930s. Our domestic routine was conventional but reassuring. We read the Liberal newspaper *The News Chronicle*, along with the evening paper *The Star*. On Saturdays, I would go and watch Arsenal or, more reluctantly, Spurs with my father or my friend Jeremy from next-door. On Sundays, as my mother cooked a large Welsh dinner, my father and I would walk down to Wood Green to buy our Sunday newspapers, *The Observer* and, for my father, the left-wing *Reynolds News*. (I never liked *Reynolds News* much because it always seemed hostile to Arsenal, which it regarded as a right-wing capitalist club owned by money-bags.) Our house had a strip of garden at the back where my father (like all our neighbours) spent many happy hours growing a variety of fruit and vegetables, and enjoyed lengthy garden-fence discussions on local and national issues with the man next-door. We also had a little verandah at the back with a good view towards Palmers Green. During the war, it had offered us a grandstand view of a V2 landing there with much loss of life.

Half a mile down the road was the most exciting local landmark – Alexandra Park, a magical, romantic territory for the young. It was dominated by the huge mysterious glass-domed bulk of Alexandra Palace with a 200-foot television mast, whose light I would always gaze at before going to bed. The Palace still survives after various disastrous fires, but it has been a spectacularly unsuccessful financial venture over the past century. Attempts to create a north London version of the Crystal Palace to the south all failed because of its distance from public transport (even though a small local railway line took passengers alongside the Palace itself). Before the war, it had been a venue for concerts, with a fine Willis organ, but most of it now lay unoccupied and unused. I never recall going inside. The Park, however, had many attractions for the young, good views of St Paul's Cathedral on a clear day, a boating lake and a football ground just below it on which the local football team, Alexandra Park, scored numerous victories and often in very muddy conditions, which perhaps gave them an advantage. One memorable winter in the Park was that of 1946–7 when massive continuous snowfalls made the snowy slopes and frozen lake of Alexandra Park an alpine delight.

Various people called round at our house, including several eccentrics drawn to us by my father's wide-ranging interests. A white-haired Russian man called by to discuss the prospects for the world-language Esperanto; a neighbour endeavoured to persuade my father of the historical and geometrical validity of freemasonry (he always failed since my father taught geometry among other subjects); some remarkable individuals came by because of my father's devotion to chess and the chess library he built up – one of them, Paul Keres, turned out to be the second-ranking player in the world and I recall his being impressed because, through my passion for stamp-collecting, I had heard of his native Estonia and could identify Tallin as its capital city.

My own interests were increasingly restricted by the pressure of homework and various school exams. I did not go to school locally and became more distant from the local community. I kept up my piano playing, going to a nice lady called Miss Helliwell for lessons and taking various exams up to Grade VI, after which I gave up. But I remained in touch with local boys (never girls in that inhibited period) via the Scout group in the Congregational Church down the road, informal football in the local 'Rec' alongside Albert Road, and playing, with modest success, for the local Alexandra Park cricket team, whose ground was located within the local racecourse, the 'Ally Pally'. As cricketers, we played such rivals as North London and North Middlesex, and also affluent Southgate three miles to the north. In the last case, there was a mild hint of class war since we humbler folk from Wood Green were particularly keen not to lose, and I do not recall our ever doing so. One of my treasured childhood memories as a 16-year-old is of playing a defensive innings beneath the stately Victorian spire of Christ Church in Waterfall Road to deny the home team victory. At the other end, we had a fine left-handed batsman called Brian Hannah, and my role was simply to stay in and do nothing else. That was my speciality as a batsman. Always, in cricket as in life, I have enjoyed playing a supporting role. The star personality at Alexandra Park, and captain of its first team, was a remarkable sexagenarian called Len Newman who had scored an immense number of centuries and once played against Don Bradman's Australians. Newman was still a pugnacious performer as an opening bat specialising, like Bradman himself, in the hook and cut shots off the back foot.

Socially, the post-war years were a transitional phase, not very different, I imagine, from pre-war. We had no television (nobody did), washing-machine or even a telephone, and had to use the phone of our endlessly tolerant next-door neighbour, Mrs Fisher, a widow – or else use a public telephone several hundred yards away. All food and clothing was strictly rationed, which could lead to disputes if the paltry quantities of meat that we received for our 'points' was deemed by my parents to be sub-standard. People also grew vegetables and fruit in abundance in their gardens, while every vacant plot of land had its allotments – a strong survivor of wartime. Many aspects of a simpler past survived. Milk was delivered by an Express Dairy van from the Muswell Hill depot drawn by an aged horse which staggered up the steep hills of Alexandra Park Road. People unquestioningly left money for the milkman beside or on their empty bottles on the doorstep: I never heard of any theft, any more than I saw violence at Highbury stadium where my friend Jeremy and I used to stand at the Laundry End (entry half-price for schoolboys – six old pence), and where order was maintained by just two policemen, one per 30,000 spectators. The sense of civil responsibility and honesty of the war years still ran strongly. We had a highly individual chimney-sweep who, as he swayed along on his bicycle, with grimy face and large brushes over his shoulder, would sing evangelical hymns loudly and greet passers-by with cries of 'Hallelujah' and 'Glory be to God'. My dear Auntie Richards, a sweet old lady, a relative of my mother who lived two doors away, opined that our chimney-sweep was 'eleven pence ha'penny short of a shillling', a characteristic phrase.

Few people had cars then. Almost everybody used public transport that never broke down (other than in 'smog'), which led to Arcadian treats such as Sunday afternoons in Epping Forest at the very end of the 102 bus route. Other local transport included trams and trolley-buses in High Road, Wood Green – the lines of the former survived for years afterwards as a hazard for cyclists. Incidentally, acquiring a Raleigh 'bike' was a huge breakthrough for me not least since I could forsake the bus, and cycle to school in Hampstead.

It was a journey of about five miles through Fortis Green and East Finchley, culminating in the glories of Hampstead Heath where the sun seemed always to be shining. I returned, wind assisted, along Bishop's Avenue (known then as millionaires and today as billionaires avenue), down Duke's Avenue in Muswell Hill, in time to listen to *Mrs Dale's Diary* on the wireless at 4.15 pm, a long-running saga of an utterly middle class doctor's wife, whose unforgettably famous line was, 'I'm very worried about Jim.' Public amenities for local citizens included the excellent central library in Wood Green, of which I was an enthusiastic user. It was a treasure-house for a bookish boy, and when I became a doctoral student at Oxford I found it had an excellent reference library as well. In 1958, before taking up my first job at Swansea, I took out manuals which taught me to touch-type, an unusual skill at that time. Wood Green Library was one of many monuments to the public-service ethos that prevailed in the post-war era.

Growing up in Britain at that period, one could not fail to be aware of the brute force of social class. After going to UCS and associating with the sons of bankers and businessmen, with far larger houses and gardens than we had in Alexandra Park, I felt we were clearly stereotyped as 'lower middle class' with my parents' profession as schoolteachers, even if in state schools, giving us a mild social bonus. My class background was revealed to the other boys in my enthusiasm for football rather than 'rugger'. I was once rebuked by a teacher at UCS for appealing to the referee for a decision and even calling him 'ref': that was 'soccer tactics', the behaviour of the proletariat we sometimes met in buses. In the class divide, Alexandra Park was a kind of no-man's land. It was far less affluent than the late-Victorian conservation area of Muswell Hill, which towered above us in more senses than one, with its Queen-Anne style, 'sweetness and light' Queen's Parade shopping centre (too expensive in my mother's view), and where even the wartime British Restaurant conveyed a sense of dignity and style. On the other hand, our neighbours also felt instinctively demarcated from traditional working-class Wood Green.

There was a distinct social boundary at the junction of Alexandra Park Road and Palace Gates Road, just alongside the high gates to the Park with their various lions and sphinxes carved on the walls alongside. That marked the class divide. Palace Gates houses were somewhat poorer, the atmosphere seemed a little 'rougher' and more hostile. In the general elections of 1950 and 1951, every house in Palace Gates displayed large Labour posters. By contrast Alexandra Park Road had a huge Conservative preponderance. I only recall two houses in our road which displayed Labour posters and, significantly, both were occupied by Welsh people – us, and a nice man across the road, the Revd Llewelyn Williams, minister of King's Cross Independent Welsh chapel, who later on became Labour MP for Abertillery. An instructive political change came in 1950 when Alexandra Park, previously part of the Wood Green/South constituency, in which Sir Beverley Baxter, a Canadian theatre critic, sat on a large Conservative majority, was yoked with Tottenham after redistribution to become an equally solid Labour and Co-op seat for many decades to come. It was one of the very few constituencies in which Labour gained from redistribution. Generally, redistribution cost Labour at least sixty seats and was a major reason why the Labour majority compared with 1945 fell from over 150 in 1945 to a mere six.

The social dynamics of the Alexandra Park neighbourhood were quite complex. The subtle social nuances were reflected in the way properties and family cultures varied between and within blocks the nearer you got to central Wood Green. There were few prefabs in Alexandra Park but they were quite numerous in Wood Green, down the road and down the social scale. But it was also a tranquil, peaceful area. Traditional hierarchies prevailed. The authority of the policeman, the schoolteacher, the football referee or the vicar survived without question, founded on custom, convention and tradition. It was also, of course, an entirely white community, solely English in speech, with exceptions such as a few Jewish immigrants (not wholly welcome even after the tragedies of wartime) and Welsh-speaking pockets such as ours, invariably schoolteachers. Local excitements were not numerous. They derived largely from institutions within Alexandra Park. There was the famous 'Ally Pally' racecourse, which brought in a miscellaneous influx of picaresque visitors on racing days. I still recall my mother's embarrassment (the product of shyness not of racism) when the flamboyant Prince Monolulu (of 'I've gotta 'orse' fame) engaged her in conversation on the bus up from Wood Green. There were also the television studios, the first in the world. They saw famous newsreaders like McDonald Hobley or Sylvia Peters catching the single-decker bus, the 211, to the Palace in the early 1950s, to the fascination of ordinary citizens, who nevertheless left them in peace. I recall my mother's excitement when she sat near McDonald Hobley on the bus and noticed that he still had make-up on his face, before departing for a journey on the tube.

Our world and our daily lives, then, were pretty self-contained and localised in those post-war years. It was still the collectivised world of wartime with a strong sense of 'pulling through together' alongside much private grumbling and patriotic prejudice. Our departures from it were invariably to Wales, especially Aberdyfi where I still had many good friends from my school days, and where I could caddy for my kindly Uncle Arthur, my mother's gentle bachelor brother, on the golf links, and where the physical delights were as appealing as ever. I had a good friend in Aberdyfi, Islwyn, the son of the coal merchant on the jetty. He was highly intelligent and well-read, but he would tell me sadly that his parents insisted that he should stay in Aberdyfi to run the family business rather than go away to study or work. I still recall the tears on his grimy cheeks as he told me this – I was happy at UCS, with strong parental backing, whereas Islwyn, an equally able boy, was condemned to a limited parochial existence. Only three times do I remember going anywhere other than Aberdyfi. In 1949, 1950 and 1951 my parents decided to go on holiday in England. It was impossible to go abroad then with countries such as France still in the early stages of post-war recovery, so we had three successive holidays in St Ives in Cornwall, Ryde on the Isle of Wight, and Folkestone in Kent. I found all of them immensely enjoyable – the thrilling coastline of Cornwall and especially Kynance Cove, Farringford Downs (including Tennyson's fascinating home) on the Isle of Wight, and the castles of Kent. An exciting feature of the last was that we somehow shared a swimming pool with the swimmers training for the annual international cross-Channel race. I recall having my photo taken with a huge Egyptian, who indeed went on to win the race; it must have been easy for him because he used to practice with 80-mile swims down the Nile. It is a slightly melancholy thought that I have hardly taken a single summer holiday in England since, and feel I know the regions of England less well than I know France. As a Welsh-speaking Welshman, I have always found England ever so slightly foreign.

More exciting still was my first trip beyond the shores of these islands in 1951, my last summer holiday as a schoolboy when I sailed from Weymouth to the island of Jersey with my elder cousin, Gwilym, and his brother-in-law. Gwilym, whom I greatly liked and admired as the first university graduate (Aberystwyth) in the family, was a natural scientist anxious to explore little mites, which apparently flourished in the rocks and beaches of Jersey. We found plenty of them (Gwilym named one – bright red in colour, the colour of Wales, Arsenal and the Labour Party – after me) and it was a cheerful and exciting time cycling around the little island and relishing the fact that the official language at that time was French, which gave opportunities to exercise my schoolboy linguistic skills. After Anglesey and the Isle of Wight, I was for the first time in my life officially 'abroad'. One particularly attractive feature of Jersey was that there appeared to be none of the dismal food rationing that prevailed at home, and treats like Jersey cream teas were readily available. For this and other reasons, I liked this place they called 'abroad' and wanted more of it. I went to Jersey again in 2014 on holiday with my present wife Elizabeth, and it was just as nice. The films, in the underground museums (located in wartime underground hospitals), of the wartime occupation and the rejoicings on VE Day reminded me of my childhood and made me emotional, though Elizabeth and I also noted that the reluctance of the Allies to send forces to liberate Jersey meant that they actually celebrated the day after VE as Jersey's day of freedom – Churchill was therefore not such an honoured figure in the Channel Islands.

My school days in Alexandra Park road came to an end in the summer of 1952 and I went up to Oxford that autumn. It was the end of a sharply divided childhood – traumatic in wartime, tranquil in peace. I continued to visit Alexandra Park as a university student in the 1950s: my parents lived there until the spring of 1959, moving back inevitably to Aberdyfi. My father retired from teaching in 1957; my mother laboriously completed her 'twenty years' to qualify for her paltry retirement pension (there was no 'equal pay' in those days). I noticed the social changes of the 1950s, the advantages and perhaps limitations that they brought. There were increasing signs of affluence, as the collective ethos of wartime gave way to individualistic consumerism. By the mid-1950s there were far more cars (my parents bought one for the first time in 1954), new blocks of flats went up on vacant sites that featured small allotments in 1945, houses all had televisions (we bought our first one, black and white of course, to see the April 1950 Cup Final in which my beloved Arsenal beat Liverpool 2–0). Church and chapel congregations fell away (I had stopped attending Sunday School around 1949, though we sometimes attended services in Welsh chapels in King's Cross, Willesden or even distant Harrow to hear the legendary aged blind poet Elfed preach). St Saviour's, the church nearest to our house, was later pulled down. Life seemed more home-based, less communal. Some local dramatic and musical groups stopped operating. Food rationing ended in 1953–4 and I could buy more than my statutory one egg per week. Large supermarkets in Wood Green made serious inroads into the trade of little local shops where we had once queued at length with our ration books. By the time my parents left, Anglo-Saxon Alexandra Park was showing signs of becoming multi-ethnic, the trend that has of course continued and increased apace ever since.

I remain profoundly grateful for my childhood years in Aberdyfi and Alexandra Park – I never found either in the least dull. Very different as they were, they provided me with a solid, comfortable base and gave life a serene quality. I learned how to write and how to think in a secure and loving family setting. Beyond the personal, it was a period of immense transformation in British life, a People's War followed by a kind of People's Peace, and my experience of it added profoundly later on to my social insight as a historian. I appreciate also having lived in that special period of regeneration after the war. It had many civic virtues on which I reflected years later when I published *Labour in Power 1945–51*. It was the first book I had written covering years through which I had lived. Many historians have written critically of that period's failures to overhaul the economy, to transform industrial relations, to rid Britain of its exaggerated beliefs of being a great power that could strut about the world stage, to see ourselves as Europeans. If you retrospectively read newspaper and other primary sources, the land no doubt appears complacent and insular from our vantage point. Many of our social issues, for instance concerning women or the treatment of children, were yet to be confronted. British social culture – conservative, royalist, class-ridden, sometimes anti-semitic, supportive of hanging – had its serious flaws.

But the achievement of rebuilding Britain after the colossal trauma of a world war, and at the same time creating a progressive version of social democracy, still seems to me immense. There was full employment, an ethos of fair shares which actually saw the impact of food rationing improve the nation's health, and the blessings of the Welfare State of which my generation was the great beneficiary. I proved to be a fortunate participant in the educational revolution after 1945, going from entry to Aberdyfi Council School in 1939 to leaving Oxford University with a doctorate in 1958, without it hardly costing my far from wealthy parents a penny; and with a National Health Service, the creation of that genius Aneurin Bevan, which transformed the quality of all our lives and made everything possible. There was also a sense of solidarity, a feeling that we really were all in it together, which I still find inspiring. The state and the public realm in all their guises were in high esteem, long before the dogma of privatisation polluted the land. My parents took pride in the fact that they were employees of the London County Council, the greatest local authority in the world. I still use my father's wooden LCC ruler for that reason, as a sign of filial respect. For perhaps the only time in modern British experience, predatory capitalism was kept in check. So, I lived through perhaps the most profound transformations in modern British history, a total war and a progressive peace, in a context of personal security and social fulfilment. Even then I felt as an 18-year-old that it had been an inspiring time and that I would like some day to become its chronicler and latimer. The best I can say about my childhood years is distantly to echo our Welsh folk troubadour, Max Boyce – I'm glad I was there.

Chapter Two

Education, Education, Education

M Y CAREER HAS BEEN that of a teacher. Like all such, I owe a great debt to those who taught me. I went to three different institutions, Aberdovey (so-named then) Council School, University College School in Hampstead, and Oxford University. All left their mark upon me, intellectually and psychologically. It was also a very instructive range of experiences since the extraordinary differences between them, in terms of geographical location obviously but even more as indicators of the huge variations of class and culture in mid-twentieth century Britain, illustrate a great deal about the contrasts and divisions within British society, then and later. My education was a bewildering mystery tour of a kaleidoscopic union-state, but for each component part of it I am deeply grateful.

I begin with my time at Aberdyfi Council School between the start of the war in 1939 and March 1944. I emphasise Aberdyfi not out of sentimental recollection but because the impact of that little school was so profound and valuable for me in every way. It was the village school which every child attended. There was no private school within at least a fifty-mile radius; probably Llandovery in Carmarthenshire was the closest. The only detectable social division came in our informal playground football games between the farmers and the villagers, when, as a village player, one had to step smartly out of the way to avoid the hobnailed boots of the farm lads. The age spread there was extraordinary: there were farm boys in the same class as me who were perhaps five or six years my senior. The school had a most attractive location, high up on a steep hill in the central part of the village, behind Chapel Square, with a splendid view of the estuary. It was very convenient for my home since it was only a short delightful walk of no more than ten minutes over Penybryn, the hill behind Bodfor Terrace, with its funny old Victorian shelter. The school had been one of the late-Victorian Board schools built after the 1870 Education Act.

It had a decent sized playground behind it, and looks today very much as it did in my time, though it ceased to be a school long ago. It was quite a crowded little school, but the influx of evacuees from Merseyside were housed in a different building, the so-called National (that is, Church) School at Brynhyfryd towards Penhelig, which I think was re-opened for that precise purpose.

There was a warmth and security in Aberdyfi school. It was reassuring to be in the same class as boys with whom I played on the beach or attended the wolf cubs, learning how to tie complicated (and subsequently useless) knots like the sheepshank and the clove hitch. There was also a link with our Methodist chapel since many of my school friends, boys and girls, attended Sunday School with me and we all enjoyed occasional treats such as trips into neighbouring hills to consume al fresco picnics. The facilities, I suppose, were limited though there were some interesting library books that I found – I recall one book about a Welsh rugby player called Black Evans. I could also borrow books from the Institute, a quaint late-Victorian institution built by the local gentry, the Corbetts, on the seafront, which had free newspapers in addition to facilities for playing snooker and table tennis. The nearest public library then, I think, was in Dolgellau, around twenty-five miles away. When my son set eyes on the school fifty years later, he was somewhat incredulous that I should have begun in so humble a place. Since it was a local state school, there was no question of anything like a playing field being available. We took our own exercise with football on a rough public field. We had some ad hoc music-making after school hours with a random collection of instruments (I took some pleasure in banging the cymbals). But what Aberdyfi lacked in physical resources, it more than made up for in human resources. The school employed a splendid group of Welsh teachers, in one case quite inspirational, whose influence has remained positive and powerful upon me for the rest of my life.

The headmaster was a genial, kindly man called Gwyndaf Morris. I remember he told me that his Christian name reflected the fact that he came from Whitland in Carmarthenshire, its Welsh name being Hendy-gwyn ar Daf (the Old White House on the river Taf). He had a bustling, slightly camp manner and was omnipresent. He took us for several lessons, mainly Geography and History, all of which had a strongly Welsh theme. He taught us about the rivers and mountains of the world, focusing on the rivers and mountains of Wales, and particularly on the rivers and mountains of Merioneth. It was good way of getting you interested and I used to go home and draw maps of the local mountain ranges – Berwyn, Aran, Cader Idris, Arenig and Ardudwy – I can still remember them all, intoned in Mr Morris's gentle accents. He also told us about the Welsh league of youth, Urdd Gobaith Cymru (founded by the father of one of my later Oxford friends, Owen Edwards) where the children wore smart white shirts and blouses and in which we as children automatically enrolled. Mr Morris was a good man, always encouraging, never unkind. I recall his sympathetic response when, to my horror, in drying my homework over my Nain's old oil lamp, I singed it. I was terrified of what his reaction might be, but he just chuckled. Another teacher was a friend of my mother, Miss Dorothy Williams, who taught us English and Welsh with great efficiency. I am afraid that one of my memories is of our being taught the history of art in Welsh from a book of famous paintings. When we came to discuss Turner's *Fighting Temeraire*, my friend Glyn Rees, son of our butcher, pronounced it very deliberately 'The Fighting Tipperary'. We all collapsed in laughter but unfortunately Miss Williams unwisely became rather cross, which made us laugh all the more.

The absolute star of my years in Aberdyfi school was a quiet lady, Miss Egwys Jones, from Llanegryn some miles to the north of Aberdyfi. While all our teachers seemed old to me, I would guess that she was in her mid-thirties. She wore glasses, had light brown hair and a beautiful smile. She taught us Mathematics, but I mainly recall the teaching of scientific matters in what was called Nature Studies in which she reflected broadly on environmental issues. She inspired in me a passion for matters in which I have subsequently taken little interest, and did so at a key period of my life. She encouraged me to go down to the beach in the roughest weather to check the wind directions, to examine the cloud formations, to examine the shells and other jetsam on the beach. I knew them all and also distinguished with confidence between the egg cases of dogfish and skate. She inspired in me a love of learning – not only in her school subjects but in everything – in a way that I have not experienced elsewhere. Apart from my father, she was the best teacher of anything that I have ever known. Like the other teachers, she taught us both in English and Welsh. She gave me the rudiments of a scholarly life because she encouraged me to pursue her subjects when I went home. Many were the times when I piled up my own maps, sketches and graphs on our kitchen table, following up Miss Egwys Jones's lessons which I found inspirational. She knew that, and regarded me always as a special pupil. Largely because of her, I was top of the form every year. Fifty years later, as I was leaving Aberystwyth as Vice-Chancellor, I heard by chance that she was still alive, but I failed to contact her; I am truly sorry for that, since I would have loved to have told her again, half a century on, how centrally important a figure she was in my life.

There was, incidentally, one other teacher that we occasionally had – my mother, who was called in as a supply teacher from time to time, and who on occasion taught me. I did not find this in the least embarrassing, since my mother was a highly competent teacher who kept good order. I felt proud to be in her class.

In April 1944 I went from the comfortable surroundings of Aberdyfi Council School to the junior branch of University College School, a famous direct-grant school in Hampstead in north London. The culture shock was enormous. There were so many things that were unfamiliar to the extent of being bewildering. UCS had the air of being a boarding school, even though it was a day school. I was astonished to be addressed by my surname, Morgan instead of Ken. It was odd to have to buy and wear a school blazer, with black and maroon stripes which made me very self-conscious. There was a school hymn, *Paulatim sed Firmiter* (Slowly but Surely), which was partly in the incomprehensible language of Latin (which had not been on the syllabus in Aberdyfi Council School). I was placed in a house called Eve after a former master; after I went to the senior school from September 1945 I entered, more incomprehensibly, a 'deme', a Greek institution of which the headmaster, Mr Walton, offered us an explanation which I found almost unintelligible.

The history of UCS was a highly distinctive, indeed distinguished one. It had been founded in 1830 by the newly created University College London in Gower Street. Its Old Boys, like me, are called Old Gowers. It moved to Hampstead in 1907 and a large statue of Edward VII is above the front entrance. Its founders were much under the influence of the Utilitarian philosopher Jeremy Bentham, and indeed one of the houses of the junior school bore his name. It was the creation of enlightened reformers like Lord Brougham, and their influence was still strong in the ethos of the school. There was no corporal punishment of any kind – transgressions by pupils met with a kind of community service called 'task book', weeding the flower beds and the like, the more effective because it was undertaken in full public view. There were no chapel or religious services – no doubt one reason why my father was eager to send me there. In the nineteenth century, it had attracted many boys from nonconformist backgrounds, and later from Jewish families. The traditions were politically as well as more broadly liberal. I once worked out that UCS had no less than nineteen old boys as MPs in the Liberal landslide election of 1906. They included such notables as John Morley, Joseph Chamberlain, Herbert Samuel and Rufus Isaacs. In my time, it was favoured by the sons of many Labour MPs living nearby, including famously Harold Wilson in the 1960s when he was prime minister. My colleagues at school included the sons of Sydney Silverman and George Strauss.

The school was in a fascinating location. When I got a bicycle in 1948, I found the ride over Hampstead Heath, with the Spaniards' Inn at one end and Jack Straw's Castle at the other, quite delightful, with fine views of north London. The junior school was on Holly Hill alongside Hampstead tube station. Next door was the still famous Everyman cinema, which I used to attend when I was in the sixth form. There were several fascinating shops nearby selling cakes and confectionery suitable for the large German-Jewish population, though food rationing throughout my school days left them much depleted. The senior school was a large, handsome set of buildings a short distance away, and I used to cycle there down Church Row and the parish church in whose yard various eminences are buried, including Gerald du Maurier and now Hugh Gaitskell. The Gaitskell family lived nearby in Frognal Gardens and I used deliberately to cycle past there in 1951 to breathe curses on poor Gaitskell, then Chancellor and apparently bent on driving my hero Aneurin Bevan out of the government. But the school's location in Hampstead added immensely to the interest and charms of being a boy at UCS.

I settled into UCS surprisingly quickly. The schoolwork was not difficult for me, so well had I been taught by Miss Egwys Jones and others. I even got the hang of Latin pretty quickly and, at the final speech day at the junior branch, I won both the form prize (by some margin) and also a prize for reading. I soon made friends amongst the boys there. They were almost all north Londoners and much entertained by my Welsh accent. Perhaps for that reason I became very friendly with another obvious outsider, a Glasgow boy, David McCallum. His family was fascinating to us all, since his father was director of the orchestra which played the background music to British films, and David thus had an entrée to the film world which we found deeply interesting. I recall his inspiring colossal envy in us one Monday morning by saying that the great and beautiful actress Margaret Lockwood had come round for tea over the weekend. I took part in a school play with David in my first year, playing Quince to his Bottom in *A Midsummer Night's Dream*, the first time I had ever performed on the stage and a very good experience for my somewhat fragile self-confidence. Later on, David went to the stage and screen, acting in a variety of B-films, playing Battle of Britain pilots and the like. In 1965 in Milwaukee airport, I unexpectedly saw his picture on the cover of a magazine listing television programmes, and I saw that he had become immensely famous playing the Russian Ilya Kuryakin in *The Man from U.N.C.L.E.* When I told the teenage daughters of the friends I eventually stayed with in Portland Oregon that I knew David McCallum well at school, I acquired instant celebrity. It was as if I had been at school with the Beatles. They told me that one reason why they adored David was that he always looked a bit ill, with a kind of consumptive 'Magic Mountain' charm – which interested me, because I recall he was quite a delicate boy at school, often absent in attendance through illness

A more enduring friendship throughout most of my life was with Roy Humphrey, a large, untidy, bookish boy, somewhat eccentric but highly intelligent with an extraordinary range of interests, whom I first met in the school playground in the summer of 1944. He was one of the few boys who lived fairly near me, at Southgate to the north of Wood Green, and we saw each other quite often as a result. Roy was to be my oldest and best friend, and a deeply loyal one. In early 2007, when he was not well, he travelled from Northumberland to London for the launch of my biography of Michael Foot. I stayed with him variously in France and near Berwick-on-Tweed. When I had to speak about him at his funeral service in rural Northumberland in late 2008, I was deeply upset. I felt as if a central thread in my life had been cut.

I was able to stay on at UCS, which my parents could hardly have afforded otherwise, because in early 1945, without much fuss, all of us who lived in Middlesex took some exams. Like most of the others, I was apparently successful and deemed to be capable of grammar-school education. As a 'scholarship boy' it meant that I would stay there, on a free place, until I left in the summer of 1952. It is only later on, as a parent and grandparent myself, that I have realised how much this must have meant to us as a family. Living in Middlesex (rather than Kent, where one of my less fortunate friends did) was one of life's really lucky breaks for me.

There were various novel features about being a UCS boy. One was that for the first time in my life I got to know some Jewish people. Jews were unknown in Aberdyfi, while in Alexandra Park there was a vague air of anti-Semitism, despite the war. I immediately got on well with my Jewish peers – as they say, some of my best friends were Jews. There were many in UCS, as in other London schools like the City of London and St Paul's, especially because there was so large a Jewish population, many of them refugees from the Nazis, in Hampstead itself and nearby Golders Green and Hendon. Whenever I see Ed Miliband on television, he reminds me of so many of my school mates. I found these Jewish boys charming, often intellectual, with an ironic sense of humour reminiscent of that of the Welsh. I recall visiting the home of a Viennese Jewish boy named George Schrager and noticing how distinctive and attractive the furniture in the house was – I saw the same style again in 1968, when I saw examples of art nouveau, the *Jugendstil*, in Vienna. My Jewish friends – one was Paul Silverman, the son of the left-wing MP Sydney Silverman – were certainly among the more memorable features of being at UCS. I had the same feeling in 1962 when I went to live in New York City, a place where people like my great friend Gerry Stearn and other Jewish academics contributed so centrally to the quality of its intellectual and cultural life.

Another new feature at UCS was more disturbing. When I arrived there in the morning there were quite often fights between the boys. A red-haired boy called Francis, seemed to be constantly engaged in them. It may be the sentimentality of hindsight, but I never recall anything of the kind in Aberdyfi school. The large farm boys were gentle and tolerant. By contrast, the scions of the aggressive London middle class fiercely defended themselves by all means available, bearing their injuries stoically for the rest of the day. Their descendants now seem prevalent in the London underground. I was never anywhere near to being one of the combatants. Apart from being a small and physically weak boy, I could not dream of hitting someone else in the face. It seemed and seems to me now barbarous and uncivilised. I have never in my life struck anyone in any way, and no man has ever struck me or come near to doing so. This outlook extends into my wider life. I am not a total pacifist – the Second World War and the American Civil War seemed to me justifiable and even virtuous, and I would have taken part. But I am instinctively opposed to all forms of violence; as a sixth-former, I had a brief period attending a Quaker meeting house in Muswell Hill. I never struck my children and, in the Lords, I joined an anti-corporal punishment group called the Children are Unbeatable Alliance. The vast bulk of the wars in which Britain has been engaged during my lifetime seem to me unjustified, even immoral, hangovers from the days of empire all the way down to Iraq in 2003. The one area of history that I have found difficult to get to grips with is military history – my favourite figures tended to be anti-militarists like Henry Richard and Keir Hardie, not to mention Michael Foot.

My days at the junior School came to an end in the summer of 1945 after four happy terms. The latter period had many moments of tension through fear of flying bombs, and my parents were often concerned about my welfare. On VE Day, the headmaster of the Senior School, Mr C. S. Walton, came and gave an emotional speech which appeared to claim that not only this war but *all* war was now over. It made an immense impression on me. We had an extra few days holiday at school. I celebrated by going with my father to see a 'Victory Test', England vs the Dominions at Lords, and saw the great Australian all-rounder, Keith Miller, hit what was said to be the biggest six ever seen at the ground, right into the top level of the pavilion, in the process of his 185-run innings.

The Senior School at UCS in Frognal was a different experience again. Walton, the headmaster, a Classics graduate of Balliol, was a most extraordinary man. An article for the school magazine would subsequently describe him as 'eccentric and deeply troubled'. The school history, chronicled for the magazine by one of my masters, Dr John Usher, says that Walton deliberately destroyed many of the school archives because he 'believed that tradition began with him'. Two years after I left the school, Walton committed suicide. His presence in the school was powerful, however, and I deeply respected him even if I could not always understand what he was trying to explain to me. The key decisions in the school came from him, the decision to call the houses 'demes' and an extraordinary idea of trying to encourage interest in the pre-school hymns by running a kind of football pool; the boys were encouraged to place bets about forthcoming hymns, their guesses assisted by clues in his morning addresses (hardly sermons). There was eventual uproar reported in the *Daily Telegraph*, among parents who objected to their children being taught gambling within the school, and some cynicism was aroused among us when the first (and perhaps only) winner of the hymn-pools was the same Dr Usher. Another personality who impressed me was the first head boy, Peter Townsend, captain of the school rugby team and, as a speech of his at the 1946 speech day indicated, a boy of unusually radical views in UCS. Later on in life, he became the pioneering left-wing sociologist who studied poverty and old age; his widow, Jean Corston, is now one of my most pleasant colleagues on the Labour benches in the House of Lords.

At UCS there was a wide range of facilities denied to many state schools, and the difference is even greater now. There was a swimming pool, tennis courts and good facilities for music and art. The school staged plays, usually Shakespeare, in the autumn, and later on staged concerts. There was also an extensive sports field a mile or two down the Finchley Road at Platts Lane, where I embarked on the unfamiliar game of rugby football. I never enjoyed playing rugby, having played football exclusively in my younger years (Aberdyfi was in north Wales football territory where the most admired team was Everton on Merseyside, because it contained some Welsh players). As a small and physically puny boy, I seemed to have no chance against much bigger boys, and rugby was always potentially violent with a risk of injury. After two or three years, a couple of friends came with me to ask Mr Walton if we could play a different game. To his credit, he did not argue at all – I do not imagine he was much of a rugby player himself – and we took up instead the indoor, but very vigorous, game of rugby fives, squash without the rackets. I became quite good at it, mainly because I was ambidextrous and could return right handed serves well with my gloved left hand, and I captained the school. It is ironic that many boys far better than I at mainstream games like rugby and cricket, where they had hundreds of competitors at university, never advanced in status; whereas I, not a great sportsman at all, was to play rugby fives for Oxford University simply because so few undergraduates played the game.

Our classes were named after letters of the Greek alphabet – mine was 'rho' – and I had a broad spread of subjects, but biased towards the humanities. I studied, amongst other things, Latin and Greek, as well as French, but not History for some reason. My father complained rightly at the relative paucity of science on my syllabus, but I did not agree with his complaints about Latin and Greek. I enjoyed Latin and Greek, both in themselves and for the light they shed on great civilisations; I worked on Latin in some fashion until I took my BA at Oxford in 1955, and am always grateful for that, and also for my instruction in Greek. They have added enormously to my feel for language and syntax, and have greatly benefited the writing of history as far as I am concerned. I enjoyed the work at school, even though I no longer won any prizes. It is fair to say that, as a boy born in mid-May, I was the youngest, as well as the smallest, person in the class. But I comfortably gained my matriculation in the summer of 1948, when I was fourteen. The only mark I recall, because it astonished me at the time, was a distinction in Mathematics. It was never my strong suit and, I suppose, a tribute to my father's private tuition.

We went off to celebrate with several viewings of Bradman's Australian cricketers who swept all before them in the tests. Don Bradman had been a particular hero of my father who had seen Bradman score a triple-century in a test match at Lords before I was born. The most exciting sporting day of my life was seeing Bradman bat for the first time at the Oval against Surrey. It was like seeing Moses return as Bradman walked with deliberate tread out to bat. There was an immense queue all around the ground, but we sat happily on the grass in warm sunshine. And the great man did not disappoint, scoring 146 quite effortlessly. The next time I saw him, he was out for 98, the only time in his career that he had been out for such a score, failing to make a century. His dismissal was greeted with complete silence, no doubt disappointment mingled with astonishment. I later saw him make 150, also at Lords, against the Gentlemen of England, a feudal relic of ancient times. I recall him and his team so vividly. When I went with my daughter to Australia in 2001, top of my itinerary was a visit to Bradman's boyhood home, Bowral, in a rural area of New South Wales. I recaptured childhood glories there by walking 'The Bradman Trail'.

The best times at UCS now began. I went into the History class for sixth-form work as I had always intended, and was gripped from the start. I had two quite excellent History teachers. Mr Rands taught eighteenth- and nineteenth-century British and European history; his method was somewhat traditional, but he was a compelling, wise and enthusiastic teacher, just right for me. Mr Rands was an old Liberal, and I recall him telling me of his excitement as a small child during the 1906 General Election when the Liberals captured his native Ipswich, early on, with the newspaper headline declaring 'Ipswich leads the way'. Election results were spread out over several weeks in the early twentieth century. The victorious MP was a famous Congregationalist minister, the Revd Sylvester Horne; Mr Rands once met his son, the radio comedian, Kenneth Horne of *Much Binding in the Marsh* fame, and asked him if he remembered his father only to be disappointed that he did not. My other teacher was a bouncy, intellectually lively man, Mr Darlaston, known to us as 'Bingo' for some reason, who taught sixteenth- and seventeenth-century history. He was full of quips – I recall the phrase '1527 sack of Rome, 1530 sack of Wolsey' – and always cheerful and stimulating. Of the two, Mr Rands clearly saw me as his favourite and star pupil, as a Welsh boy who admired Lloyd George and the Liberal tradition. Mr Darlaston, I felt, leaned towards my great friend Roy, the other leading pupil in the class, perhaps because of an innate English Conservatism beneath an iconoclastic surface. At any rate, it was always I who came out top in the end of year exams to win the form prizes. In 1950, I gained the so-called Tapson History Prize, which entailed my receiving a book award at speech day from the local Hampstead MP, Henry Brooke, later a Conservative Home Secretary. His son Peter, also a distinguished politician, is a friend of mine in the Lords, and I have told of him my one and only, if for me exciting, meeting with his father. Another teacher I should mention again was an immensely intelligent younger man, Dr John – Johnny – Usher, who taught me more Latin and also Roman history, a totally new subject to me, which I found absolutely riveting. He was quite brilliant, apparently even stronger at Greek and wrote several instructional books on the subject.

In the hands of these fine teachers, I could feel myself becoming a scholar, taking up topics of my own and giving them detailed thought. Mr Rands encouraged me to read classic works of history, and I particularly remember enjoying Lecky on eighteenth-century England, John Addington Symonds on the Renaissance and especially Gibbon's autobiography, which I found absorbing for its contrasts between self-revelation and restraint, a good model for other autobiographers. I discovered on my own initiative Élie Halévy's translated volumes on *England in the Nineteenth Century*, a work of acute intelligence and remarkable insight for a non-British author. I recall discussing Halévy's conclusions at Oxford later on with a great French scholar I got to know, François Bédarida. Among more recent works I picked up as a book prize was Trevelyan's best-selling *English Social History*, which I found readable and picturesque but rather too complacently English for my tastes.

My enjoyment of the History class at UCS owed a great deal too to my classmates – the 'Transitus', as UCS called it. It was a great joy to be reunited with Roy, and we much enjoyed each other's company despite the rivalry during school examinations. Among the others was Jonathan Penrose, the long-running British chess champion sprung from a famous intellectual dynasty, who knew my father through his involvement with schools chess. I also knew well Paul Silverman, as already mentioned, who was a good musician. The whole class atmosphere was one of friendly interaction and mutual support. I also became friendly with other boys through some growing success I had on the cricket field; I became captain of the school second XI and played occasionally for the first team, a mighty honour. We all enjoyed the coach-driven away matches when we could sing irreverent songs and whistle at girls. For the second XI, I opened the batting with a nice boy, Michael Day; he was a dasher while I was a plodder, and we had several good partnerships. To my joy, years later we caught up with each other again. He had become Sir Michael Day, a leading figure in the probation officers' profession and a fine chairman of the Race Relations Board. My present wife Elizabeth and I have had utterly enjoyable visits to Michael and his wife June in their home in Ludlow thereafter. One particularly memorable experience with my school friends was going to see the Festival of Britain on the South Bank in the summer of 1951, followed later on by a jolly afternoon at the funfair at Battersea Park further down the river. After years of bleak austerity, I found the Festival breathtaking, as did the other 8,500,000 who went there, despite the desperate attempts of the mean-spirited Tory press to deter them. I thought the Festival was a marvel of exciting design combined with a palpable sense of history and community. It was a triumph for Sir Hugh Casson, director of the Festival's Design Group, and it made you feel proud to be British. One historian has appropriately called it 'the autobiography of a nation' – what a contrast it was to the commercialised drabness of the Millennium Dome in 2000 which, unlike the stirring narrative of the Festival of Britain, did not seem to be about anything very much.

This lotus-land in the History sixth could not last for ever, and my teachers and the headmaster began to discuss university entrance. For people at UCS, this meant one university only – Oxford. My father was very excited at the thought which strengthened my resolve. Curiously, even though I was aged only sixteen years and ten months, I was put in for a scholarship at Balliol College in March 1951, and went up there full of wonder. The gigantic grey buildings were like a magic world unlike anything I had seen before. The other candidates seemed years older than me; some were in military uniform as national servicemen. All I recall of the exams is being interviewed by the dons of Balliol who listened patiently to a 16-year-old boy explaining shyly to them why, in his General Paper, he had taken the line of Aneurin Bevan in opposing the current British rearmament programme with its consequent charges on the National Health Service. Later, I realised one of the listening dons was Christopher Hill, the famous Marxist scholar, who probably agreed with me – while subsequent historians have shown unarguably that my schoolboy views were entirely correct. At any rate, Balliol seem to have liked me, but could not take me as a commoner since I was only in for a scholarship. They invited me to apply again in the winter. I wish I had done so. It would have been so stimulating to be a Balliol man, where it did not matter in the least whether you were a scholar or a commoner.

I tried again in December, applying this time for Oriel College on the headmaster's instruction. I knew nothing of any of the colleges, but my father regarded its association with the Oxford movement, including his boyhood passion Cardinal Newman, to be a positive. Oriel's alumni also included the imperialist Cecil Rhodes, but we rather passed a veil over that. This time, I felt fine about the entrance examination, including the interview, and Oriel accepted me without problems. As frequently in my life (as a Vice-Chancellor and as peer for instance) I had got in at the second attempt. The sermon on the mount should include the observation 'Blessed are the runners-up.' To my disappointment, my old friend Roy did not make it to Oxford, but disappeared into the RAF before going happily to Cambridge where he was very successful. We continued to keep in close touch.

My days at UCS were, overall, an immensely happy and fruitful part of my life. I developed intellectually and, to a degree, in self-confidence. UCS had its limitations. It was a comfortable, unchallenging place and, of course, all male. The product of a protective home and an only child, I had no confidence in meeting or talking to girls, and I feel sure that my own children have been far more sensibly brought up. My social skills were distinctly under-developed. But I was an enthusiast, academically alert, and an idealist in whom the inquiring flame of Aberdyfi school was still alive. My privileged education had reflected some of the better aspects as well as the limitations of childhood in post-1945 Britain, and I felt I could cope with the world that lay ahead.

I went up to Oxford excitedly in October 1952. It was somewhat grim and unfriendly at first sight, still caught up in post-war austerity with food rationing still very much in being. Oriel itself was a beautiful college, with a lovely front quad with Merton chapel looming in the background, and a statue of Charles I surmounting the entrance to the Jacobean hall. The second quad had an elegant and large Palladian library built by James Wyatt in the 1780s. Inside, it was less imposing, cold in more senses than one. The rooms seemed scarcely heated at all – of course, central heating was unknown at that time and open fires were, perhaps fortunately, no longer permitted. The college staff were not friendly; the Dean ominously observed in what was supposed to be a welcoming address that undergraduates were replaceable but that college servants seldom were. There was a handful of baths some distance from my room in the second quad. I shared a room – which can be a great hazard with undergraduates, given differences in taste and temperament. In fact, I was very fortunate in this regard since my room-mate was a genial boy from Kenya, Philip Allen, a cheerful outgoing character with an adventurous colonial temperament. He and I have remained friends over the generations. In 2005, it was a joy for me to stay with him in his delightful home in northern Wisconsin, and he and his wife were with me in Chicago when I heard the momentous news of the birth of my first grandchild. The food for undergraduates in the hall was frugal and of poor quality – though not for the dons, whose meals were heavily subsidised from the many bequests to the college by Cecil Rhodes. We in the lower orders watched enviously as several additional courses passed by us.

The undergraduates were largely from English public schools. Their enthusiasms focused on drunken parties (which often led to a trail of damage in the Junior Common Room) and on rowing (Oriel has always been a serious rowing college). The combination of their public school master-race arrogance and the fact that they were mostly older than me since they had largely done national service, meant that I did not find them friendly. They seemed to me to represent almost everything that was wrong in late-imperial Britain. I did not make many friends among them. Fifty years later, out of curiosity, I attended a dinner in Oriel in 2002, assuming that they must have become more agreeable over the years. In fact, I found them much the same, perhaps with a tinge of jealousy since I was now in the House of Lords. My earlier prejudices of half a century earlier were more than confirmed; some of them behaved with an imperial superciliousness. Some nice lads from the north, with whom I played in the college football team, were dismissed as 'the northern chemists'. They had little time for me. It is ironic as I look back that I have been more successful than any of them, and have advanced much further in my career. I am the only elected Fellow of the British Academy and much-published author amongst their ranks.

There were, however, some undergraduates I found both enjoyable and interesting. Nearly all of them were Americans – Oriel had quite a number of them, since the fact that Rhodes had been an Oriel man led to Rhodes Scholars and others going there in some strength. My closest friend from my first week was an astonishing man, Robert Woetzel, a Henry Fellow from Columbia University, who had been a school pupil at the Shanghai American School. He took to me right from the start, since Welsh socialists from humble backgrounds were a new experience for him, and we joined together not only socially but in setting up an undergraduate politics discussion group, the Political Study Circle, of which I became secretary. I presented him with a copy of Aneurin Bevan's newly-published *In Place of Fear* for his edification. A man of immense charm, Robert had an extraordinary range of talents, including command of many languages and great ability as a pianist. His doctoral thesis was on the Nuremberg war crimes trial, and it has a treasured place on my bookshelves. Unfortunately later on, for me and for some others, things began to go wrong. Robert became involved with the Roman Catholic chaplain of the university, and began to turn into a far less tolerant and relaxed character as result. In his later years he was to enter the priesthood, then abandon it and get married, then throw over that relationship as well. In addition, it emerged that the intense nature of his sexuality disturbed him, even giving him a crusading quality in that respect. I had never encountered this before (though it seemed rife in Oriel with our many public school boys) and had never been inclined that way whatsoever – I could readily agree with Robert in deploring the intolerance shown towards gay people (at that time it was a criminal offence), but his proselytising I found disturbing, including his hostility towards female relationships. It is possible to be intolerant either way. My friendship with him in my first two years at Oriel was intensely rewarding; after that it was almost a relief when he left. There were other Americans, too, as well as Australians and Canadians. I found almost all of them more fun and more intellectually stimulating than the lumpen mass of British public school boys.

The disagreeable nature of the undergraduates was matched by the mediocrity of the tutors. They were astonishingly poor. Having subsequently spent my entire professional life as a university teacher, including twenty-three as an Oxford tutor, I realise how very inadequate they were. The Modern History tutor was particularly dreary with apparently no interest in undergraduates whatsoever. His two or three books on political thought were equally dull. Tutorials with him were lacking in any kind of stimulation, and he was in no way up with his subject. I recall asking if I could write an essay on the American revolution the following week, which threw him. The only authors of relevant works on that topic he could come up with were Namier and Butterfield – both useless for my purposes – before adding, 'I dare say there are some American books on the subject.' His lectures in the schools on such topics as the Social Contract were simply lamentable; he could have taken plenty of tips from Miss Egwys Jones on how to interest a class. Because of him, and knowing that Oriel would ensure that he tutored me on a modern topic, I switched to a medieval special subject: Richard II and John of Gaunt. I found this subject quite fun, especially with the eccentric Professor Galbraith, the Regius Professor, running the classes (even if he was an archivist rather than a historian). The Oriel Medieval tutor was a nice man but very strange, a devout Roman Catholic bachelor, who had nuns round for tea and behaved like a small hypochondriac child unused to the world at large. His tutorials were much more interesting, but I do not recall his ever taking essays in to mark and comment on them. The rest of the Oriel senior common room sounded just as bad – friends reading PPE (Politics, Philosophy and Economics) told me their tutors were even lazier and more incompetent. The Provost, Sir George Clark, was a famous historian of the seventeenth century, but I never met him once in six years in the college. It is astonishing to me that Oxford dons, supposedly the cream of their profession, should have been so lethargic as teachers. The strength of the Oxford teaching method – the highly personal tutorial system – depends entirely on the quality and enthusiasm of the tutors. If they are lacking, the rationale for Oxford's form of instruction collapses. All in all, Oriel seemed more like a backwoods seminary of mid-Victorian days than a modern educational institution.

Much later, a very nice man and my contemporary, Peter Collett, got me involved a bit with the college once again and, in 2002, they generously made me an Honorary Fellow. Under the lead of two quite excellent Provosts, the Revd Ernest Nicholson and Derek Morris, and with the stimulus of having women as well as male undergraduates, Oriel is quite unrecognisable from the dreary place I experienced, and obviously dynamic and academically successful. My wife Elizabeth and I have hugely enjoyed chamber concerts in the college library. Oriel is now splendid. What a pity it was not like that in my time.

My pleasures in Oxford during my undergraduate years, though, were far from negligible. I enjoyed playing football once again, for the Oriel first XI. I had one full season with them before I sustained a knee injury after a bad foul. In that season, I recall that Oriel scored 69 goals; of these, 61 were scored by a Yorkshireman called Denis White who went on to play for the university. I scored two, and was thus second highest scorer. I well remember the first ever goal I scored for Oriel; a corner kick came from the left, I swung at it with my weaker left foot and missed, it hit me on the right knee-cap and shot into the net. It was a feat that neither Messi nor Maradona ever achieved, and I tried unsuccessfully to pretend that it was deliberate. On the intellectual side, I attended a variety of lectures which seemed to me brilliant and what I really needed in Oxford, by people like Asa Briggs, Christopher Hill, Hugh Trevor-Roper, and the incomparable and deeply entertaining Alan Taylor who always lectured at nine on a Monday morning in the schools to show that he could draw in the crowds. Also, out of curiosity, I listened to the great socialist G. D. H. Cole, now an elderly man (this aroused the massive scorn of the Oriel chaplain who, quite unexpectedly, invited me for tea for some reason). I also joined the Oxford Union as a life member and attended many of the debates, hearing many of the leading politicians of the day. But I was always an observer, listening in awe to the mighty presidents of the time, such as Patrick (now Lord) Mayhew, and my friend now, Bryan Magee. I also heard many great figures at the Labour Club – Attlee, Dalton, Morrison and, most memorable of all, Aneurin Bevan, whose sparkling oratory overcame his evident disdain at being in Oxford at all. There were also memorable concerts in the town hall (Oxford has no proper concert hall to this day) which I attended with an Oriel friend, Herbert Chappell, later to be a major figure in the music world at the BBC. So life was not that dreary.

My undergraduate years came to an end with my taking my Schools examinations in June 1955. Despite my unsatisfactory experience of Oxford, I wanted to remain in academia and applied for a doctorate. My proposed research area was on the Liberal Party of Gladstone's later years. I had long been fascinated by the variety of groups, social, cultural and ethnic, that the party spawned after the Irish home rule split of 1886. Then I noticed that Wales was prominent among the issues involving disestablishment of the Church, education, land reform and modified forms of devolution. That excited my mind, even though my topic was a pretty hazy one at first. My Modern History tutor was predictably discouraging, but I decided to ignore his views. I began my long vacation in 1955 wondering if it would mark the end of my time as a student. Others in Oriel convened in noisy post-schools parties, but I just went home as soon as I could. I had had more than enough of Oriel and its braying philistines, and went down to dear old Aberdyfi once again to commune in the real world.

The start of that vacation was, I suppose, the low point of my aspirations. By the end of it, my life had completely turned around. Without realising it, I had embarked on a long upward progression with hardly a setback, which has been the story of my life over the past sixty years. My schools gave me what I had been hoping for – perhaps significantly, my marks in Medieval History were stronger than in Modern History. Oxford would now take me as a doctoral student, and my scholarship from the taxpayer would cover not only all of my fees but effectively all of my maintenance costs as well. More important still, I had now a very clear idea of the trajectory of my proposed research. That July, I called on Professor David Williams, the Professor of Welsh History at Aberystwyth, in his eyrie at the top of the tower in Laura Place, which I later got to know so well during my time as its vice-chancellor in Aberystwyth. I spoke with Professor Williams for a long time, perhaps for a couple of hours; he had the quiet country air of his background in Welsh-speaking Pembrokeshire, but he was obviously a man of broad culture. He also had a noticeable tic in his eye, which speeded up when he was excited. He had written on the ideas of French *philosophes* prior to the 1789 Revolution, while he had also worked on American history at Columbia University. He was very much a devotee of the eighteenth-century Enlightenment and the cult of reason. The most striking feature of his room was a bust of Voltaire on his desk. His own work was on early nineteenth-century Wales, notably two marvellous books on John Frost and the Rebecca Riots, the latter a model of how local history should be written. But he took an immediate interest in my proposed research and in me personally. He remarked to me at the end, 'Really, Kenneth, your subject is Wales in British Politics.' And so a song was born and a career was forged. That was the most important academic conversation I had with anyone in the whole of my life, my Damascus road. I remained close to dear old David for the rest of his days (sadly crippled later on by the onset of extreme Parkinson's Disease). He was a decisive influence on my early career as a young historian and, without question, the great mentor in my journey of academic self-discovery. I owe him almost everything.

So I returned to Oxford full of enthusiasm and confidence in October 1955. The second phase of my time there was as fulfilling as my first had been disappointing. The university offered D.Phil. students of the modern period almost nothing. There were no lectures or seminars for graduate students, and little opportunity for me to meet other graduates students – to be truthful, there were very few of us at that time. I recall lectures by Professor Wernham, a nice man but a mediocre scholar, about state papers for Britain in the sixteenth century, in which he almost desperately offered a reference to the Council of Wales and the Marches, which was of course of no interest at all to me. But I supplied my own energy and motivation now. I enjoyed Oriel much more too, and made some delightful new friends – notably David McKie, later on to be deputy editor of the *Guardian*. It was now that I became especially friendly with another Christ's Hospital boy, Leslie Stone (of whom more anon). I was happy with my friends, and also with my supervisor R. B. McCallum, Master of Pembroke College, a genial Scotsman and author of the first Nuffield election studies on the 1945 General Election, who was always very encouraging. He knew next to nothing of late-nineteenth-century Welsh politics, other than about Lloyd George, but he had an instinctive feel for late-Victorian and Edwardian Liberal culture, which was very helpful. It was a world he knew at first hand. He came from Paisley and well recalled the famous by-election of 1920 which saw Asquith return to the House of Commons after the debacle of the 'coupon election' of 1918.

Nowadays, graduates have to take a preliminary course on such matters as statistics and the technology of libraries, even the ethics of research. I appreciate the value of some of that, but I am glad that I did not have to do it. I got straight on to my thesis, white hot with enthusiasm. Within a month, I was under the great dome of the reading room of the British Museum looking at the papers of Mr Gladstone. I found them totally absorbing, not least because, as I suspected, Wales loomed quite high among his interests. His sly evasions on disestablishment of the Welsh Church, to which he finally committed himself, in principle at least, around 1885, were in themselves marvellously illuminating. I also found myself totally absorbed in his appointments to Welsh bishoprics, not a topic I could have imagined I would ever have studied, but full of political as well as ecclesiastical significance. In the meantime, I immersed myself in the sources for Wales itself in that period, down to and beyond the First World War. The fact that hardly any Welsh historian had previously written on these matters, or indeed on the Welsh relationship with the First World War and its aftermath, was all the more exciting. I was happy to pursue my own pioneering research on religion, the land, education and other manifestations of radical protest in Wales, and to note also the very fascinating contrasts with Ireland with whom the Welsh Liberal Cymru Fydd (Young Wales) movement claimed affinity. There were also extraordinary personalities to explore – ministers of religion and bishops, editors and journalists, educationalists and *littérateurs*, lawyers and councillors, miners' agents and coalowners. Among the politicians, Lloyd George seemed a towering figure practically from his entry into parliament in a by-election in 1890; but even more attractive in some ways was his colleague Tom Ellis, a cultural nationalist and idealistic intellectual of much force. Many other powerful Liberal political figures came to my attention – men like the lawyers Sam Evans, Llewelyn Williams and Ellis Griffith, and the maverick D. A. Thomas, the coalowner, Lord Rhondda.

My enthusiasm for my thesis reached a new level of passion when I started work at the National Library of Wales, high up on Penglais hill overlooking

Cardigan Bay. I stayed variously with my two auntie Annies at Dolybont, taking the hourly bus to Aberystwyth. In the National Library, where proceedings seemed to be conducted almost entirely in Welsh from ordering manuscripts to getting tinned pears and evaporated milk for lunch, there was an abundance of marvellous resources. There were huge boxes for a variety of Welsh Liberals which it seemed no-one had ever looked at before – Tom Ellis, D. R. Daniel, Bryn Roberts, Llewelyn Williams, Ellis Griffith, the almost daily correspondence of Gladstone's friend, the Englishman Stuart Rendel, with A. C. Humphreys-Owen. Lloyd George's papers were not available at that time, but I had masses of other material to go on besides them. (Here, incidentally, being an Oriel man proved to be unexpectedly helpful, since Rendel had been an undergraduate there, taking a poor degree in 1856, and the excellent college library had his printed diaries.) I also soaked myself in newspapers, in English and in Welsh, and in parliamentary reports of all kinds. For the first time, I was in love, not with another human being, but with this inspired generation of Welsh politicians and public personalities. I knew what I wanted to do with my life, and I loved what I knew.

My thesis, therefore, progressed rapidly. I was happy as I never truly had been before. In addition, life at Oxford had its own stimulation of a kind I had never known either. At Oriel, I had encountered another lifelong friend, Leslie Stone, a determined working-class Londoner with strong views on socialism (for) and religion (against), extraordinary knowledge of American politics, and a shared enthusiasm for Arsenal football club. That came to be a important bond between us, as Leslie's views later on drifted to the right, and kept us always close. One poignant match we saw was that between Arsenal and Manchester United (the latter winning 5–4) just before the Munich air crash. Several of the United team, notably the brilliant wing-half Duncan Edwards, were making their last appearance as events transpired. Leslie took me with him into the Labour Club (I had joined the Labour Party on my twenty-first birthday in Wood Green in 1955), and I then made a number of important and brilliant friends of a kind I had never met before: David Marquand at Magdalen, a wonderful scholar and public intellectual, and my dear friend over the past sixty years; Revan Tranter at Pembroke, a laconic Yorkshireman of far-left views, still a great friend even though he lives in California; and Brian Walden of Queen's, later an MP and television interviewer, a complicated man but the finest orator I ever heard. Walden came from a shabby terrace in West Bromwich and I recall going with him to see Arsenal play the local Albion in the cup, the match resulting in a draw; he could, one felt, easily become prime minister. These and others became my treasured intimates.

Our social centre was the Oxford Union where we had lunch and attended the debates. I also found the Union valuable for my thesis because it was open on Sundays, uniquely for Oxford, and I could work on *The Times* before dining with friends in some greasy cafe. The Labour Club was enjoyable in many ways – and also historic, because many of the New Left people, including major intellectuals like Raphael Samuel, Peter Sidgwick and Stuart Hall, joined our ranks after leaving the Communist Party following the Russian invasion of Hungary at the end of 1956. I also had two terms editing the Club journal *Clarion*, a new experience which I found most enjoyable, not least taking it round to sell in famously right-wing colleges like Christ Church and Trinity. There were always plenty of gifted people anxious to write for us – the identical twins David and Michael Armstrong were prominent among them. A particularly appealing feature of the Labour Club was the LPG, the Labour Party Group of party activists who met on Sunday mornings at Somerville College. It was, of course, a women's college but my recollection is that even here women played their traditional silent role of being pleasant makers of coffee for us men. The Oxford Labour Club of that era has been an enormous power-house in our cultural and intellectual life ever since. People who dominated their professions thereafter would turn up – Jeremy Isaacs, Philip French and Marilyn Butler (*née* Evans). For myself, the opportunity to cross dialectical swords with these clever people gave me a sense of self-confidence I had never previously known; at school, I had dreaded speaking in public.

There were more practical issues to involve the Labour Club as well. Foremost among these was Suez when the invasion by British and French troops horrified us. I recall marching and handing out leaflets (greeted with predictable hostility in Oriel, I recall). There was also a powerful meeting in the Oxford Union opposing the Suez venture, chaired by the venerable Lord Beveridge. There was at that time a kind of atavistic patriotism, which made protest an uncomfortable experience, but we did what we could and rejoiced in the failure of Suez and the departure of Eden. Our pet slogan had been '64–5, Sack Eden' (referring to the adverse vote against the Suez invasion in the United Nations). Some of these protests were even comic. One Labour Club member went to London to daub slogans on the Bank of England and succeeded in doing so – but then, sadly, he became transfixed by the artistic quality of his handiwork and the police arrested him, paintbrush in hand. Suez had its follow-up in February when several of us went down to campaign for the Labour candidate Niall MacDermot in the North Lewisham by-election. When we got there, to our dismay we told firmly by the Labour agent that we should on no account mention Suez, because the bulk of the electors supported it. We were told to hold forth instead on the iniquities of the Rent Act, of which we knew relatively little, but we won the election anyway. At any rate, Suez was an important phase in my political upbringing, as for many others. It was a shameful post-imperial conspiracy of deceit and dishonour, and I could not imagine that I would see Britain behave so badly again. But, in 2003, this time in Iraq, that was precisely what we did.

Apart from the Labour Club, I should mention another society I enjoyed greatly, which annoyingly often met on the same evening. This was Cymdeithas Dafydd ap Gwilym (the 'Dafydd'), the society for the Welsh-speaking students at Oxford, which commonly met in Jesus College. It is a famous and prestigious body in the social culture of Wales, set up by a group of distinguished intellectuals back in 1885. I joined it to bring my Welsh back up to speed (my parents had, rather sadly, stopped speaking to me in Welsh when I began at Oxford). I found it great fun as we read papers to each other – I read one, which was said to be the most left-wing the society had ever heard. There were several delightful people there – all men, inevitably. The *caplan* (chairman) was Owen Edwards, the grandson of the famous Sir O. M. Edwards, who became a great friend and went on to a most distinguished career first as a television presenter and then as a director of BBC Wales. Others whom I recall with much affection were Bedwyr Lewis Jones (later Professor of Welsh at Bangor), Owen R. Jones (later Senior Lecturer in philosophy at Aberystwyth), and Gwilym Jones (later Professor of Theology at Bangor). They were a gifted group of people, and I have happy memories of standing in Turl Street in front of Jesus College at around ten in the evening singing the Welsh national anthem loudly while missiles and abuse were hurled down from the Englishmen in Exeter College above us. In the autumn of 1985, a PPE pupil of mine at Queen's, Guto Harri, later a famous broadcaster and journalist, asked me if the fellows would allow us to hold the centenary dinner of the Dafydd in the college hall. I managed to achieve that, after getting the private support of the Provost, Lord Blake, in advance, even though it meant relocating two elderly dons from the hall to a neighbouring room for that evening's meal, which was a serious matter. We had a great time, with Owen Edwards addressing us, and I was delighted to see that my own generation of the 1950s was especially well represented. It was a memory of happy times, part of my rediscovery of Wales after the Oxford undergraduate years.

By the autumn of 1957, my thesis was going well and I was writing furiously. The D.Phil. was supposed to take three years but it looked as if I would finish it before that. The uncertainties of the job market now beckoned, when I then had an enormous slice of luck. The spectre of national service loomed larger throughout the Oxford years. I had just hung on, hoping against hope that it might be brought to an end as many politicians forecast or demanded. In early 1957, with the Duncan Sandys White Paper on Defence, that is exactly what happened under the Conservative Party. I then faced a medical examination and felt properly apprehensive, since men were still being conscripted even if in fewer numbers. I tried to make what I could of my football knee injury, but salvation came from elsewhere. My doctor had mentioned that I had had a temporary ear infection, with very unpleasant discharges earlier in the year, and it was still somewhat inflamed. This clinched it, and shortly afterwards I had a note saying that I was Class 3 in my medical, and unfit for service in tropical areas. Shortly afterwards I was told that I was excused national service altogether. Richard Viner's excellent book *National Service* (2014) says that making the medicals more severe was a way of running numbers down in the final period, and I was clearly a beneficiary of that. I was, as I have said, very close to being a pacifist, and national service would in any case have been a horrible experience, to judge from Viner's book. Furthermore, national servicemen were not in fact taking part in warding off any alleged Russian threat to our shores, but rather fighting post-imperial wars against colonial peoples in Malaya, Kenya and, particularly in 1957, in Cyprus. My sympathies would have been invariably with our adversaries, and I contemplated whether I would have the determination or courage to be a conscientious objector (it seemed unlikely that I would have been accepted as one since it would not have been on religious grounds). In fact, it never happened. I avoided both possible prison and the harshness of the military life, and was twenty-four (not twenty-six) when seeking a job. It was one of the truly fortunate things that happened at that key stage of my life. I have never had any ear trouble since.

So I went serenely ahead to finish my thesis. I was examined in May 1958 by none less than Professor David Williams of Aberystwyth, and Pat Thompson of Wadham College, later a close and wise friend when I was a don at Oxford. I was very nervous beforehand, and my nerves were not improved when David mentioned some factual errors in my first chapter. That was not surprising, since my knowledge of Welsh history was relatively slight and my thesis was primarily a study of Westminster parliamentary politics and its hinterland. But the rest of it appeared to be fine, my treatment of Gladstone's attitude to Wales arousing especial interest. I was given to understand that I had passed. A few weeks later, I took my degree in the Sheldonian Theatre in the finery of a scarlet Oxford doctoral gown. In fact, I got my MA the same afternoon, since I had finished my thesis so rapidly that I did not need to complete the required number of years for that formal degree, which nevertheless made me a full member of the University and its Congregation. My parents were present in the Sheldonian Theatre for the ceremony, and it was in all ways a highly emotional afternoon. The examiners had even suggested that my thesis be published as a book, so a great range of pleasant prospects opened up. I celebrated with my parents, who had supported me so selflessly over the years, by taking them to see *My Fair Lady*, which had just opened in Drury Lane with Rex Harrison, Julie Andrews and Stanley Holloway – a marvellous evening. My mother loved the music, my father enjoyed the fact that it was by his great hero, George Bernard Shaw.

Kenneth O. Morgan

My formal education, taking me from Aberdyfi to the Sheldonian, was over. At the time, I cannot say that all of it was wholly enjoyable. There were always examinations to pass, hurdles of one kind or another to surmount, problems of grappling with my shyness and lack of self-confidence. My nerves were frequently on edge. But I had stayed calm enough when it mattered, including when things had gone wrong the first time. Most important of all, I now knew what I wanted to do with my life, if the opportunity came my way. I now had to find a job, anywhere, and that was far from easy. The expansion in the size and number of universities advocated in the Robbins Report a few years later had not yet happened, and lectureships or similar posts were scarce indeed.

Then, after weeks of uncertainty, I saw in the Wood Green library newspaper room an advertisement in *The Times* for a humble research post at University of Wales College Swansea. I knew nothing of that institution, nor of Swansea either, but armed with recommendations from Mr McCallum and Professor David Williams I sent in my application. I travelled down to Swansea by train, taking in the dilapidated industrial tips of Landore just before we got to Swansea station. It was a wet evening with a dense sea mist, and I had no idea that Swansea was actually on the sea at all. The next day, when the sun shone and Swansea Bay glistened, I had my interview with an ebullient genial man I identified later as Professor Glanmor Williams, head of the History department, along with Professor Fulton, Principal at Swansea, and one or two others. I recall nothing at all of the interview, but I did note that there were no other candidates. I was told immediately afterwards that I had got the job, and I then got to know Glanmor Williams a little bit better. His warmth and enthusiasm told me at once he would be a marvellous person to work with. His wife, Fay, a kind, delightful lady, I also met, and she arranged lodgings for me in the town. So, suddenly, everything had fallen into place.

My new position was a lowly one indeed, Research Fellow (temporary) for Welsh Social History at the princely stipend of £600 a year. For me, it was riches beyond compare. I knew that I wanted to continue the original research that had so thrilled me at Oxford and bring it through to publication. Furthermore, I wanted to work in a lively academic environment, preferably one as unlike Oxford as possible, and to strike out anew as a teacher, if I was good enough. And I would now do that in my beloved Wales. In Aberdyfi, to which my parents were about to retire, my job, humble though it was, brought enormous acclaim from neighbours, a product of the overwhelming Welsh enthusiasm for learning and scholarship. They were right. I sensed that I had found the platform for the life for which I had always been striving. Swansea simply looked and felt perfect. I thought from now on it would be happy ever after, and so it proved.

42

Chapter Three

History-making:
A Welsh Historian

IT WAS AT SWANSEA that I learned how to be a historian, and became confident in my ability to write and teach history. There was an almost tangible atmosphere of intellectual and personal comradeship amongst my fellow historians that I found deeply satisfying. Yet, when I first went there, it was a bit of a surprise. After the crowded historic monuments of Oxford, I found a very small institution of 800 students, set in a public park, which felt more like a school than a university. I got there, not via the classic grandeur of The High in my former university, but by walking across Brynmill Park, a pleasant green oasis which featured a small menagerie to distract me on my morning stroll. But the University College, as it was then, had a wonderful location. It was set in Singleton Abbey, a late-eighteenth-century Gothic building, the home of Sir Hussey Vivian, a Victorian industrialist and one-time Liberal MP for Swansea, who featured prominently in my thesis. To my joy, I discovered that one famous episode from my researches had taken place right there, when in June 1887 Gladstone, as guest of the Vivians, addressed a mighty procession of perhaps 50,000 Welsh Liberals gathered below and proclaimed the need for Irish Home Rule. The newspapers noted that he was interrupted by a cry of 'Home Rule for Wales', but that did not appear to distract the Grand Old Man as he surveyed the throng, with Swansea Bay in the background and distant views of Devon and Somerset.

Swansea encouraged a sense of togetherness, a feeling stimulated by its smallish Senior Common Room, the Vivians' former living room, into which the academics crowded at coffee or lunch time. And a sense of community was certainly conveyed by my wonderful new colleagues. Glanmor Williams, tiny and voluble, was a remarkable personality, a Labour-voting miner's son full of the warmth of his native Dowlais. I once met his mother, a gentle old lady. He was a quite wonderful head of department, dynamic, endlessly sympathetic and encouraging to younger colleagues, but also a very fine scholar in himself. He was working on a history of the Welsh Church during the Reformation but became so absorbed by the medieval antecedents that in 1962 he published an immense volume on the pre-Reformation Church, which no less an authority than Dom David Knowles pronounced to be 'a great book'. Glanmor's great friend, and a precious colleague of mine too, was Ieuan Gwynedd Jones, whose research was now focused on Welsh politics prior to 1868. That was the starting date of my own research, so our interests dove-tailed with an almost magical perfection. Ieuan was a lifelong friend thereafter, the gentlest, most generous scholar I have ever known. A most remarkable personality was Neville Masterman, with whom I shared an office for a time. His interests spanned the Christian socialist John Malcolm Ludlow, and the Welsh national leader Tom Ellis, so we had endless fascinating discussions on their ideas. However, since Neville's father was C. F. G. Masterman, Lloyd George's close ally in passing the New Liberal social reforms of pre-1914, but who had quarrelled with him during the First World War, we tended to steer clear of the Liberal Party split of 1918 to avoid splits of our own. I did once meet Neville's impressive mother, Lucy, a grande dame of Edwardian Liberalism and, I noted, like most women a huge fan of Lloyd George herself. It was a great joy to me in November 2012 to join in the Swansea celebrations of Neville's one hundredth birthday. Another Englishman was a more angular character, an economic historian, Walter Minchinton, who had been a candidate for the Swansea chair when Glanmor was appointed. He took a negative view of the Welsh and their climate, but he was a Labour Party member and for that reason it was thought that I would be a suitable room-mate. Two of the others were English; David Walker, a medievalist who was also an Anglican canon, and Muriel Chamberlain, another new appointment whose specialism was nineteenth-century international history, both very nice people and fine scholars. Then there was Bill Greenway, a delightful, modest medievalist, whose career was blighted by poor health and who actually died in his late twenties, a huge tragedy.

I also got to know people well in other departments, especially Jack Lively and John Rees in Politics, and Graham Rees in Economics, while my membership of the staff cricket team had the huge benefit of getting me to meet some scientists. The best-known member of the staff at Swansea was Kingsley Amis, whose famous novel *Lucky Jim* was not based on Swansea – it contained, of course, the memorable phrase 'History speaking'. However, his second novel, also made into a film, *That Uncertain Feeling*, was set in the Swansea public library. I met the handsome (married) woman who was supposedly the model for the glamorous heroine, played in the film by Mai Zetterling. Amis was not a hard-working colleague, but he used to entertain a friend and myself on Friday lunchtime by reading out some absorbing tit-bits from the tabloid newspapers which would relieve our fatigue and raise our spirits. I once went canvassing with his wife, Hilary, a beautiful woman who, unlike her husband, had serious and strongly socialist views about politics, on such issues as comprehensive schools; I liked her more than him. I should mention, too, some other important scholars I met elsewhere in the University of Wales: in Aberystwyth, remarkable historians like Gwyn Alf Williams and Richard Cobb, both of them geniuses in their way; and the delightful Professor Charles Mowat in Bangor, who shared a common enthusiasm for Lloyd George.

In my first year, I was something of a fringe figure, travelling much to Cardiff Public Library in pursuit of my research. But Glanmor was keen to give me some lecturing experience, starting with seventeenth-century Europe for some reason. My first lecture ever was on Gustavus Adolphus in Sweden and, to judge from my surviving notes, it must have been terrible, far too long and detailed. I know that, like many young lecturers, I was terrified of drying up before time. But, by the end of the year, my notes were halved, I was far more relaxed, and I felt I held the attention of the students. The next year I was fortunate that Walter Minchinton went to the United States and I took his place as temporary lecturer. I worked very hard that year, writing up dozens of brand-new lectures, mainly on British history but also including a popular course on The Modern World. This featured my first venture into American history, which subsequently became a major part of my work as a history teacher. Then, after I had the unnerving task of having to apply for my own job, Swansea appointed me to a full assistant lectureship. I now had a tenure post. My stipend had also risen to the heights of £750 or so. In addition, I was made sub-warden of a men's hostel, Neuadd Gilbertson, in Clyne Park, a mile or two down the road. Thus, I had free accommodation and food, so I felt almost affluent. Around the same time, I took over my father's car (I had passed my test in 1955), and now enjoyed a far more expansive lifestyle. Three years later, I became a senior lecturer on the strength of publishing two books, and felt more comfortable still.

In addition to the university, I greatly enjoyed Swansea itself. The 'ugly, lovely town' of Dylan Thomas's childhood had been destroyed by the Luftwaffe, but, even in its somewhat bleak rebuilt form, it had much to entertain with its cinema and cafes, and the glorious Gower peninsula nearby. Its proximity to Cardiff made for a fuller life still. At various times, I met several of Thomas's most intimate friends, the composer Daniel Jones, the painter Alfred Janes, and the delightful reclusive poet Vernon Watkins, who worked, extraordinarily enough, as a cashier in the local branch of Lloyds Bank. I also bought second-hand books and prints from Dylan's haunt, 'Ralph the Books', in the Uplands near to the university. A major factor in making me feel at home in Swansea was my active membership of the Labour Party. I lived in St Helen's Ward, one of the relatively few Conservative areas in the town; one of my fellow members was perhaps my ablest student at Swansea, Donald Anderson, who went on to get a first-class honours degree and became a Labour MP, and is now a colleague of mine in the Lords, fifty-five years on. I liked my new Labour comrades, not least the aged Joe Davies, secretary of the Swansea party, who had been its very first secretary back in 1916. People always agreed to his suggestion that the minutes be read 'seriatim', possibly because they did not know what it meant.

In the General Election of October 1959, there was a large Labour meeting in Brynmill school, the main speaker being the shadow Colonial Secretary, James Callaghan. I had to chair the meeting as chairman of the ward party, and arrived hot and breathless. The first words addressed to me by my future biographee were 'Take it easy, take it easy', and we went on to have a great and enthusiastic meeting. I felt certain that after this we must hold Swansea West, a marginal seat but, in fact, the elderly Labour MP Percy Morris was narrowly defeated. It was a valuable, if disappointing, lesson for me in political prediction. It was also a first opportunity to meet Jim Callaghan as I did often again as president of the student Labour Club.

Swansea was fun in every way. On the staff cricket team, I opened the batting with a delightful man, David Sims, a colleague in English and a close friend of Kingsley Amis. When I ran him out one day, he was forgiveness itself. I recall our opening the batting on a flattened-down coal tip at Llansamlet, east of Swansea, on a warm sunny day, and each of us hitting many fours which left the fielders hot and exhausted as they climbed back uphill after retrieving the ball. Our reaction, I fear, was *schadenfreude*.

The students were overwhelmingly Welsh and products of the local grammar schools, almost all Labour, different in social class from students at Oxford, but many of them manifestly very able. In many cases, they were from families in which no-one had experienced higher education before – a feeling with which I identified – and they demonstrated both huge respect for their teachers and passion for their studies as a result. They were glad to be there, in contrast to the cynical student mood widespread a decade later. It was difficult to place all their very similar Welsh names; two had identical names and had to have their home towns attached. Many of the girls were dark-haired and very pretty, curious to explore the reactions of a young male lecturer. The students included some unusual characters. I recall a Chinese boy called Wing Hong Ng, the son of a Chinese laundryman in Caerphilly, who sat in the front row of a large first-year class taking beautiful notes in Chinese ideograms, starting at the foot of the page and working up. I recall he was a left-hander which added to my interest. At the end of the term I asked to see his notes, which were indeed a work of art and elevated my mundane lectures to a graphic beauty.

I had other most enjoyable experiences with Swansea students beyond the History department – I still recall the amazing scented magnolia just outside my bedroom window at Neuadd Gilbertson. As I have said, I was president of the student Labour club, where the committee included some of my own History students. More unexpectedly, I acquired some celebrity as a performer in student debates, where my version of Oxford Union humour seemed to go down well. As a result, I was made the Swansea adjudicator in the *Observer* mace competition and travelled with the Swansea team to debates in Swansea itself, in Cardiff and in Bristol. As it happened, our team was very strong with two of my own bright pupils, Donald Anderson and Paul Wilkinson (later to be an international authority on terrorism). I had the pleasure of, quite objectively, proclaiming their sucesses on several occasions. They made it, I believe, to the final. For a bachelor, only two or three years older than the students themselves, it was great fun, added to my self-confidence as a public speaker, and made me feel that dear old Swansea, like the Glasgow of legend, belonged to me.

My main concern at Swansea, though, was to continue work on my thesis, improving and expanding it for possible publication. I worked on this with much determination, in Cardiff public library on local newspapers, on the same in the Swansea public library, reading *The Mumbles Weekly News* and *Gower News* and *Llais Llafur* (Labour Voice), the first socialist newspaper in Wales, edited by Ebenezer Rees, the grandfather of my Oxford friend, David Marquand, in Ystalyfera at the top of the Swansea valley. There additionally was always my spiritual home, the National Library of Wales, made very accessible by my parents moving in retirement to Aberdyfi in early 1959 and then to Aberystwyth itself in 1962. A particularly memorable experience in my research came in the summer of 1959 when I worked on the papers of a notable Welsh Liberal MP, Sir Herbert Lewis, who had died in 1933. They were kept in his beautiful Jacobean home, Plas Penucha in Caerwys, near Mold, and I was the guest of his kindly daughter, Mrs Kitty Idwal Jones. She was not only amazingly hospitable but also fascinating to talk to about the high noon of north Wales Liberalism in her girlhood. The Lewis papers are now safely in the National Library, but it was extraordinary to work on them in his own hearth and home, amid the beautiful countryside of the Vale of Clwyd. Later on, in 1969, Arthur Marwick invited me to make an Open University film called 'The Historian at Work', based on my *Wales in British Politics*, designed to show how historians went about writing a book. We went with a television camera crew back to Plas Penucha, where Mrs Idwal Jones was still in sprightly form. I asked her if she could show the cameramen the four-poster bed in which I slept when working in her house. She looked baffled. She assured me that she never had a four-poster bed. So I had made up the whole thing – a salutary lesson regarding sources for any historian.

My main work was now trying to build up my essentially parliamentary study of Welsh politics between 1868 and 1922 with far more work on the sub-structure within Wales itself. I worked in immense detail, especially on local politics and social movements in the period 1880–1914; sometimes, I think it is the only aspect of history that I really understand or know about. I felt I could hear them speak, anticipate what they would say, and what their complicated personal relationships would be like. Lloyd George in particular emerged as a significantly different figure when the local dimension was being considered, a more consensual figure indeed. I thus embarked upon the idea of writing a short book on him to mark the centenary of his birth in January 1863, focusing on his origins in Wales and what this meant for his career. I reacted contemptuously to Keynes's notorious biographical sketch which saw him as 'rooted in nothing'. I felt rather that he was rooted in the Welsh rural community, one incomprehensible to an elitist Cambridge don, but all too vivid for someone of my background and experience. This work fitted in very conveniently side by side with research on my bigger book which, following my momentous conversation with David Williams in 1955, I had already decided to call *Wales in British Politics*. I felt that my book would be significantly stronger than my thesis in having a robust first-hand analysis of Welsh politics, society and culture, and that the first chapter in particular would be very much better than that of the thesis.

The other major dimension that I worked on – and, of course, one that was most congenial to me – was that of the relationship of Welsh Liberalism with the rise of labour and of the Labour Party in particular, which had been only a fringe consideration in my thesis. I found the early challenges from the labour movement in Wales to be absorbingly interesting, perhaps all the more so because the source materials were those accumulated by working people (whose descendants might therefore lose some of them) rather than the carefully ordered archive of Liberal lawyers and businessmen. Labour in Wales emerged as strikingly different in culture from that in England, with a surprisingly strong tinge of national consciousness before the First World War, and also much involvement with popular religion. One feature I noticed was the effect of the religious revival of 1904 upon Labour pioneers, and the impact it had upon their rapid transition to socialism. Many key early socialists – men like Noah Ablett, Arthur Horner and later James Griffiths, S. O. Davies and Ness Edwards – had been active nonconformists, many of them keen to enter the ministry. Then the revival came, ironically to drive them out of the chapels but also to give them a passionate social and moral commitment to rebuilding their world as it was. My book, therefore, reflected the Labour connection in a way I had not really done in writing my doctoral thesis, and was much stronger for it. I was confident about this when it was accepted for publication by the University of Wales Press at the end of 1961. Further, it would be printed by

Oxford University Press, who had also wanted to publish it; so, in a way, I had the best of both worlds.

This wonderful news that my work was to be published was part of a wider process of which I was aware within myself of greater sureness in pronouncing on historical themes. This was enhanced by invitations to speak to local historical groups, schools and other bodies. I now felt confident about holding forth in public in a way I had never done in Oxford – particularly because Welsh audiences are always seemingly enthusiastic and full of questions, often dressed in their Sunday best as if they were listening to a chapel sermon. The only other place in which I have found this kind of electric response was Newcastleupon-Tyne in 2006, where the audience, also largely working class, was very similar in culture, and even in accent. Throughout my eight years at Swansea, my lecturing ventures were often memorable. One episode I recall around 1964 was an extramural class I gave on modern Welsh history in a Carmarthenshire mining community called Pontyates, where the local pit was still working. I recall very pleasant coffee sessions with some wives afterwards, obviously highly intelligent and with a zest for learning but, as usual, casualties of our class and gender prejudices as far as education was concerned. They told me, wryly, of one famous citizen of Pontyates, of whom I had indeed heard – Mandy Rice-Davies, of Profumo fame, who died in 2014. Perhaps the most memorable lecture of all that I gave was in early 1965, when Glanmor Williams got me to speak in Merthyr Tydfil on 'The Merthyr of Keir Hardie'. On equal billing, Gwyn Alf Williams covered 'The Merthyr of Dic Penderyn', Ieuan Gwynedd Jones 'The Merthyr of Henry Richard', and Joe England the most recent period. Glanmor, a native of the town, was in the chair. The sense of local communal engagement I felt in Merthyr that night was electrifying, and I know the other lecturers felt the same. The transactions were published as a highly successful collective book by the University of Wales Press in 1967, and it is one of my most treasured memories as a historian.

If lecturing was one important part of my development as a Welsh historian, a more long-lasting one now was taking place in Swansea. Glanmor Williams had in 1960 launched a new grey-jacketed journal, *The Welsh History Review*. It included my first significant publication on 'Gladstone and Wales', expertly typed out for me by my dear cousin Anne. The new journal made an instant impact and, in 1961, it was decided that it should appear twice a year. As a result, Glanmor asked me if I would act as his assistant editor, which would include such details as preparing lists of articles on Welsh history that had been published each year. I was most honoured to be asked and found the task absorbing, not least working ever more closely with Glanmor himself, whom I had come to recognise as a really great man – as scholar, impresario and public figure. Later, in 1965, as other duties at Swansea increased his burdens, he asked me if I would succeed him as editor. Again, I was delighted to do so, and the Board of Celtic Studies, after murmurings about my youth, consented to appoint me. I invited my recent Swansea colleague, Ralph Griffiths, a distinguished medievalist with whom I shared a flat in the Mumbles at that time, to serve as assistant editor. All went strongly thereafter. We kept up a high rate of productivity as editors of *The Welsh History Review*, making sure that it was published promptly on 1 June and 1 December, seeking out distinguished young scholars as authors (people like Rees Davies, Geraint H. Jenkins and Martin Daunton, all future Fellows of the British Academy) and occasionally working out special thematic numbers. We edited the journal for the next thirty-eight years, making a total of forty-two for me, more than half my present lifespan. I believe *The Welsh History Review* has been an immensely important publication in the cultural and social life of Wales. As my editorship went on, through all the years at Queen's, then at Aberystwyth, and finally well into my retirement, I sensed how enduring its importance was. This was not least because at least half our material covered the later-nineteenth and twentieth centuries, on which very few had previously written other than myself, rather than focusing on the earlier reaches of history in the medieval period before the Act of Union in 1536. The Welsh historians seemed to be quicker off the mark in this respect than the Scots, at least so it seemed to me when I wrote later on Keir Hardie, though subsequently such great Scottish scholars as Tom Devine have emerged. Further, in my view at least, the influence of the journal, entirely scholarly and non-political though it obviously was, has had a far wider effect. It encouraged the view that the Welsh had had a continuous past right down to yesterday, and that their history had not petered out at the time of the Tudors. If you believed you had a past, then you might also feel that you had a present and a future. *The Welsh History Review*, therefore, I see as a subterranean, non-political force that led to the achievement of Welsh devolution. I consider editing the journal between 1961 and 2003 to be probably the most important thing I have done in academic life. In its way, it changed the world. I trust that future obituarists, if such there be, will keep that in mind.

My life, though focused on my activity as a Welsh historian, was not confined to Wales alone. It had wider points of stimulus. In 1960, I went with Glanmor to attend the International Historical Congress at Stockholm, a most enjoyable event involving a viewing of underwater exploration of the great ship *Vasa*, which had sunk on her maiden voyage in 1628 in Stockholm harbour through fatal ballast distribution. What was most depressing to encounter, however, was the ideological ridigity of Eastern bloc historians who scarcely contributed as scholars at all. The worst were the East Germans, who seemed to be there for no other reason than to spy on each other. I proceeded on my way with an international group to Finland, where I was equally impressed by

◄ Figure 1 *Tadcu and Mamgu from Dolybont.*

► Figure 2 *Nain and Taid from Aberdyfi.*

◄ Figure 3 *My father, left, in 1916 at Bedford Camp during the First World War, with his great friend Ivor Morgan.*

▼ Figure 4 *My parents' wedding day, 21 August 1930. From left to right: Owen Owen (Taid); my mother; Mary Owen (Nain); my father; Elizabeth Jane Morgan (Mamgu); Thomas Morgan (Tadcu); the officiating minister.*

▲ Figure 6 *The author aged eight months in January 1935.*

◀ Figure 8 *Our family home at 219 Alexandra Park Road, London.*

▶ Figure 9 *Our former home at 11 Bodfor Terrace, Aberdyfi (photographed in 2005).*

▲ Figure 10 *With my parents on the beach at Aberdyfi, c.1947.*

▲ Figure 11 *The Alexandra Park cricket Colts, 1949; I am seated fourth from the left in the front row.*

▲ Figure 12 *The History Sixth, UCS, in 1951. From left to right: (back row) C. Cowland; Roy Humphrey; David Macmillan; Mr Rands; Peter Roscoe; David Drown; (front row) Geoff Brown; Mr Darlaston; the author.*

▲ Figure 13 *With Philip Allen (and a cat) at Christ Church meadows, Oxford, in 1953.*

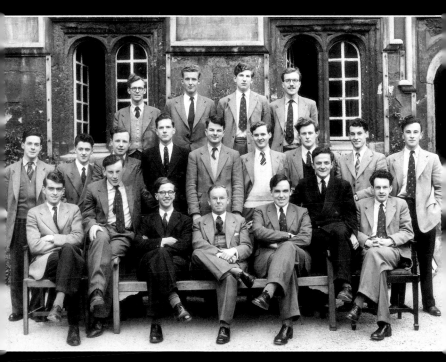

▲ Figure 14 *Cymdeithas Dafydd ap Gwilym at Jesus College, Oxford, in 1957.*

▲ Figure 15 *A publicity shoot, teaching at Neuadd Gilbertson, Swansea, in 1961 (where gowns were never worn for teaching!).*

Figure 16 *Staff and students of the History department at Swansea in May 1964.
From left to right: (front row) Neville Masterman; Dr Muriel Chamberlain; Professor Alun
Davies; Peter Stead; Professor Glanmor Williams; Mrs Thomas (departmental secretary);
Dr Walter Minchinton; Revd Dr David Walker. I am in the middle row, on the extreme right.*

Figure 18 *Telling the Queen about Edwardian socialism at Stationers Hall, 5 November 1981. Jane, fourth from the left, looks very nervous in the background! Professor R. H. C. Davis is on the right.*

▲ Figure 20 *Jane and me at Aberystwyth in March 1989.*

▲ Figure 21 *Presenting Colin Jackson for an Honorary Fellowship at Aberystwyth in July 1994.*

▶ Figure 22 *With Lord Callaghan at Plas Penglais, Aberystwyth, on the University degree day in July 1990.*

▲ Figure 23 *The Oxford Labour Club reunion, London, in June 1996. From left to right: (back row) Elsa Tranter; Virginia Shapiro; the author; David Marquand; Trevor Lloyd; Revan Tranter; David Shapiro; (front row) Leslie Stone; Judith Marquand; Michael Armstrong; Freda Stone.*

▲ Figure 24 *Talking to EC Commissioner Bruce Millan, Brussels, in March 1994.*

the maritime charms of Helsinki and the physical charms of the blonde Finnish girls. I much enjoyed visiting Sibelius's former house – he has long been perhaps my very favourite composer; his seven symphonies, his violin concerto, his folk sagas, such orchestral suites as the immortal *Karelia* and *Finlandia*, I adore them all. They have a special appeal to Welsh people, I think (with Lewis Valentine's Welsh words for the hymn 'Finlandia' sometimes considered as a second national anthem). One of my companions in Finland was a lively man, L. G. Pine, editor of *Burke's Peerage*. Every evening at dinner we somehow got into fierce arguments about socialism, capital punishment, fox-hunting, empire or other issues, which became nightly entertainment for our American, Canadian, Rumanian and the inevitably silent East German colleagues, unaccustomed as the latter were to free speech. Pine and I always ended as the best of friends, and I liked him. But some time afterwards he wrote to me out of the blue saying that he had rethought his entire political philosophy, starting with a book that condemned blood sports (which he had defended in Finland), and that he had now concluded that I was totally correct on almost everything! This remarkably humble retreat cannot have been mainly due to my own powerful logic, I am sure, but it was nice to think that my strenuous endeavours on behalf of truth and justice had perhaps found at least one distinguished convert. Or, as Aneurin Bevan famously said, 'This is my truth, tell me yours.'

In the course of 1961–2, I felt I would like to look academically further afield. I had handed in my big book, and also completed my little work on Lloyd George. What I now wished to pursue was modern American history, especially reform movements in the United States prior to Roosevelt's New Deal. I had been interested in this ever since my talks with American graduate students at Oriel in the past. I was also struck by the affinities and contrasts between the American Populists and land reformers in Wales and Ireland. I had read more and more on post-Civil War American history, and brought it into my lectures on international history, especially the Modern World course. Glanmor and his new professorial colleague, Alun Davies, were anxious that the Swansea syllabus should be extended in this way, and obtained a grant to add substantially to the holdings on American history in the university library. So they gave me every encouragement to apply for a scholarship or some other award to spend a year in the US. The whole idea had excited me for some time. It seemed to me that a visit to America, which my friends Leslie Stone and David Marquand had already undertaken, was a kind of modern equivalent of the Grand Tour of the eighteenth century. I was also an active member of the British Association of American Studies, and was given some good advice by Herbert Nicholas, a specialist on American matters at New College who was friendly towards me as a fellow Welshman. I then obtained an award which would have sent me to the University of Pennsylvania, and that would have suited me fine.

But then came an even better offer, a well-funded fellowship from the American Council of Learned Societies to spend a year in Columbia University, that celebrated Ivy League citadel situated in central Manhattan, to work on the connections between American and British reform movements between 1870 and the end of the First World War. My director of studies would be no less than the mighty Richard Hofstadter, author of two wonderful monographs which I admired intensely, *The American Political Tradition* and, more relevantly, *The Age of Reform*, covering the Progressive movement between 1880 and 1914. I was thrilled beyond measure. I had travelled abroad only relatively little hitherto, to France, Germany and Scandinavia. Now the Big Apple, and the wonders of the US as a whole, which I had recently read about in a book by my later friend, Bryan Magee, *Go West Young Man*, lay before me. I felt it was a colossal opportunity, and so it proved to be. If I matured as a scholar at Swansea, at Columbia I matured as a man.

I arrived at New York harbour at the end of July 1962, after a five-day voyage on the SS *United States*. The only notable event aboard ship was that I won a table tennis competition. It was a noisy, brand-new vessel, which demonstrated some of the more blatant features of American capitalism: most of the deck area was reserved for first-class passengers (rather like on the *Titanic*) and the rest for cabin class (including me), with the lower orders in steerage, hopefully being able to look out of the portholes or get a whiff of ozone while the band played 'Nearer my God to Thee'. My porthole, at least, did afford me a breathtaking view of the Manhattan skyline in brilliant morning sunshine. The importance of being at Columbia was impressed upon me in my very first conversation. The immigration official, after making me open all my luggage on the dirty quayside, was disturbed by the possibility that I might be carrying seditious literature and shook his head angrily when he spotted the title *Age of Reform*. At first I thought they would not let me in, but then, in desperation I mentioned that Richard Hofstadter was a very famous author at Columbia. The man's attitude changed completely since, apparently, his niece or nephew was at school at Columbia, so all was well in the end. I found a small apartment on 111th Street, just three blocks down from Columbia, my landlady being an elderly Jewish widow, Mrs Sebba, and rented a typewriter from a nearby store. Columbia was still deep in its summer vacation, so I took the opportunity to do some basic sightseeing in the great city in very hot, humid weather. Then, after Labor Day, in early September Columbia opened up for business and I began work.

I shall detail in chapter 9 my reactions to living and travelling in America, which was an unforgettable experience – and I did travel an enormous amount that year. In New England, I visited Yale and lectured at Brown, in Rhode Island. In the Houghton library at Harvard, I found some fascinating manuscript material on American radicalism at the turn of the twentieth century: I also had the great pleasure at Harvard of getting to know Rhodri Morgan, the son of my friend T. J. Morgan, Professor of Welsh at Swansea, who was studying for his master's degree. I spent Christmas, delightfully, in Minneapolis with distant American relatives, where I survived temperatures of –27°F. I attended two conferences, the American Historical Association at Chicago (where someone offered me a job in the lift, in the passage between the ground and eighth floors) and in Omaha, Nebraska, the Mississippi Valley History Conference, where I first met a delightful, voluble Irishman, Owen Dudley Edwards, whom I later persuaded to write a fine life of Eamonn de Valera. Our first meeting was over a lunch that lasted five hours, a triumph of Celtic eloquence on both sides. At Easter, I went with a friend driving around Virginia, visiting Civil War battle-fields like Bull Run, Chancellorsville and Fredericksburg, and seeing the homes of Washington and Jefferson, and colonial Williamsburg. Finally, in the summer with two good friends, I made the great drive across the country over about three weeks, down to Miami in Florida, then four amazing weeks in Peru taking in Macchu Pichu, and finally across the beautiful south and west, through New Mexico, Arizona, Utah and Nevada, ending up in San Francisco. The ACLS, a most enlightened body, gave additional grants for travel. It added enormously to my understanding of American civilisation, and I am deeply grateful to them.

The year 1962–3 was most eventful not only in terms of my mobility, but also in terms of the political background. The US appeared at its most self-confident and affluent when I arrived. Serious background troubles were suggested in my first few weeks when I joined many Columbia students in a demonstration in support of James Meredith, a black student who had been forcibly kept out of the University of Mississippi where he had been enrolled. The state governor, Ross Barnett, or his officials, turned dogs on the demonstrators, and there were fatal casualties. Race relations were an ominous backdrop throughout the year. Even more alarming was the Cuban crisis in October, where the prospect of world annihilation suddenly seemed close at hand. The records now suggest that people had every reason to be anxious, since it took all the efforts of the Kennedy brothers to keep at bay the more bellicose military chiefs. It was the nearest the west came to nuclear war in the post-1945 period. I have always thought that President Kennedy handled the crisis quite brilliantly, and US Defense Secretary McNamara also showed up well. I was terrified at the time, and inquired about flights to take me back to Swansea. After a week in which New York seemed eerily quiet, almost frozen in terror, the Russians agreed to withdraw their missiles from Cuba (after a political trade-off in Turkey, revealed much later), and there was a mass sense of overwhelming relief. I was glad to see Kennedy moving down Fifth Avenue on Columbus Day in mid-October, greeted enthusiastically by the Democratic voters. The latter months of my year in 1963 saw the huge civil rights protests by black Americans, and the emergence of Martin Luther King as their charismatic champion. Kennedy responded cautiously here, but the spectacle of the Washington March of 28 August, shown on television, was quite thrilling. I still have the badge I wore in sympathy: 'For Jobs and Freedom.' All the time, there were rumbles of disquiet about the course of American policy in South Vietnam, without the passionate conflicts of later years. So, historically, it was an absorbing if often alarming time for a historian to be in the US.

But my year was primarily about Columbia. I did an enormous amount of work mainly in the brilliant Butler Library, which was open seven days a week, a joyous novelty for me. But, of course, I also came into contact with many of the faculty – my own indeterminate status as 'Senior Student' gave me a shared office in the History department, but also qualified me to have free tea as a graduate student, and also join the Student Union with such heterosexual attractions as ten-pin bowling.

I did come into first contact with the great Richard Hofstadter early on. Although he was personally very pleasant, I did not get as much out of our meetings as I had hoped. This was partly my own fault, since I was unduly diffident about giving my fledgling thoughts about American history to so distinguished a scholar. But, in addition, Hofstadter, like many of his colleagues, concentrated on his writing outside Columbia and seldom came into the university. I found him a fascinating, complicated man. He had a difficult background. He had been a member of the Communist Party as a young man, and was half-Jewish; on both counts he fell foul of the demagogic populism of McCarthyism. This underscored what he wrote about the darker, racist side of the Populist Party of the 1890s, as he saw it, and the links he claimed to detect between McCarthy and the crusader for the monetisation of free silver, William Jennings Bryan. This came out in a book he produced while I was in Columbia, *Anti-Intellectualism in American History*, in which the phobias and prejudices of supposedly radical movements like Populism figure prominently. As a result, he received a really severe critical review for the first time, by Christopher Lasch, in the *New York Review of Books*, which was started up during a lengthy New York newspaper strike in the early months of 1963 – this critical review apparently shook Hofstadter. Even so, this book, admittedly not his best, contains many brilliant passages and is hugely thought-provoking. Even though I wish I had known and seen him more, I still think of him as one of the truly great men I have met. How could a Freudian historian who wrote of the 'paranoid style' in American history or the 'psychic crisis of the Nineties' fail to be captivating?

There were other splendid scholars in the Columbia History department, which was especially powerful on US history. William Leuchtenburg gave brilliant lectures on post-1865 history, and was also a charming, approachable man. Bob Webb was a wise and agreeable British historian – I noted that he invited me to lunch on the top ('professors') floor of the highly stratified, multi-layered Faculty Club. A lovely man, whom I felt was as able as any of them, was Bob Cross, a historian of religion who had written rather less than some colleagues. He ran a most interesting staff seminar on modern America, focusing each week on an important book. I spoke successfully on C. Wright Mills's *The Power Elite*, and really felt myself to be a true Columbia man after that.

But mainly, my stimulus came from far younger people. There were many exceptionally able junior colleagues in or around the History department. One was Paul Noyes, a charming and brilliant historian of nineteenth-century Europe, who had written a thesis on the 1848 revolution under A. J. P. Taylor at Oxford, where Paul and I first met. He and his delightful wife, Helen, were amazingly kind and hospitable throughout my US sojourn. There was Bob Dallek, a historian of US foreign policy and later author of fine works on Lyndon Johnson. Most important was Gerry Stearn, a roly-poly Jewish student of Progressivism, a man of endless wit and wisdom, and an important figure in making my year at Columbia so enjoyable. Even the critical Professor Hofstadter found Stearn interesting. His ironic, mordant sense of humour reminded me of the Jewish boys whose company I had so enjoyed at school at UCS. He was part of the extraordinary Jewish presence in the education, music, press and politics of New York City, its motor as a cultural centre. He enjoyed good-naturedly satirizing his own Jewish community, and we used to reflect on the cultural resemblances between the Welsh and the Jews, outsiders both. Gerry was one of my closest friends thereafter, and it was a terrible blow when he died suddenly of heart failure in his late thirties. I still keep in touch with his family, and recall our numerous cheerful meetings – from breakfasts in nearby drug stores to seeing the home team wallop home runs at Yankee Stadium in the Bronx – with the deepest affection. One intriguing experience we had was our friendship with Viktor Malkov, a rare Russian scholar apparently bent on demonstrating that the US authorities were deliberately preventing him from working on the F. D. Roosevelt papers in Hyde Park, even when the people there wrote him a warm and friendly letter of invitation. It was the height of the Cold War, and Viktor reflected that atmosphere. When we invited him out to dinner in the mid East Side, we noted that he ate absolutely nothing, save for scraps of bread. Evidently he had been told to trust nobody, not even a Welsh visitor as alien as he was. He revealed himself only in showing enthusiasm for Russian chess grand masters like David Bronstein, who were Jewish like him. There were also some wonderful British friends that I made at Columbia, a Russian historian Roger Pethybridge, later to join me at Swansea, and Robert Maclennan, a Scottish graduate law student, later a long-term Labour and then SDP MP, and now an important colleague and friend in the Lords, whose friendship and wise counsel has added lustre to my life over many decades since.

It was, then a memorable time at Columbia University, and I felt enriched in every way, despite the hazards of life in New York, which I shall refer to later. I was there for thirteen months and benefited enormously from being in what I still think is the most foreign country to which I have ever been. As it happened, I was to go there again, two years later, after Bob Cross invited me to teach summer school in 1965. I taught two courses: a survey course of British history from the mid-eighteenth-century to the early twentieth, and a specialist course on social reform and British politics 1886–1914. Columbia sympathetically put me on at eight in the mornings in the Law School, before the humidity became impossible. I had some enjoyable colleagues, including a lively medievalist from York, Gordon Leff, and the famous historian of the French revolutionary crowd, George Rudé, then at an Australian university because he had been kept out of jobs in Britain through political prejudice. Gordon and George were both Communists so, for once in a while, I found myself the most right-wing of the British visitors. I also got to know my delightful namesake, Roger Morgan, then at Aberystwyth, a European historian and political scientist. We encountered each other because the Columbia postal system sent each of us the other's mail – including, embarrassingly, our pay cheques. I made up for it by taking Roger with me on another pilgrimage to Yankee Stadium, his first ball game. My teaching at Columbia that summer was great fun. The students, and there were many of them, were responsive and enthusiastic, if not always quite *au fait* with what they heard. After my lecturing one morning on the taxation details of Lloyd George's People's Budget of 1909, a lady called Diane shyly came up to me afterwards to ask, 'Please, Professor Morgan, what is one and tuppence in the pound?' She and her husband later invited me and all the class to dinner at their apartment, a very cheerful affair. They had a piano, but it turned out that I was the only pianist present, so I banged away at various American popular songs, including, I recall, 'The Lady is a Tramp'. After that, it was across America again, via Chicago, South Dakota, Salt Lake City, Yellowstone National Park, ultimately to stay with friends in Portland, Oregon – but that is a later story. It was all a fantastic adventure.

Yet it was not an academically productive adventure in the way I had hoped. I found out all kinds of fascinating connections between US and British political reformers between 1870 and the end of the First World War. In many cases, Britain was the leading inspiration, in social work (Hull House, for example), in municipal government (the LCC and Birmingham, for example), in adult education (Ruskin College, Oxford, for example) and the whole policy spectrum of the New Liberalism. It was a vivid period of the transatlantic relationship which I felt had been inadequately dealt with by previous historians, because neither in the US or in Britain did they know enough about the other countries. I wrote some academic articles on my subject, among the best I have written. I went on to write some powerful reviews on Progressivism and other themes in the *Times Literary Supplement* and other journals. It enormously enriched my teaching, especially at Oxford, where I taught a favourite course on Industrial America and Political Reform, and later Franklin Roosevelt and the New Deal. But after my year, I felt I still had much to do. This would mean repeated visits again and again to American archives, which would be financially and personally difficult. It would also divert me fundamentally from my research on modern British and Welsh history in which I was still passionately interested. In the end, a splendid book was written exactly on my chosen topic, *Atlantic Crossings* by Daniel T. Rodgers (1998). It makes kindly reference to my scattered writings on the topic in the foreword: in my vanity, I think I could have written an equally good book. But, in the event, I decided to stay as a British historian rather than jump ship and become an American one. As my old mother used to say in Aberdyfi, you have to be one thing or the other; especially, perhaps, in the harsh competitive world of modern academia.

When I returned to Britain in September 1963, it was academic achievement not academic neglect that awaited me. A little-known young man before I went to Columbia, I came back and found myself famous – or at least famous in Wales, which may not be quite the same thing. While in Columbia, my first two books had appeared. In February, my little book on Lloyd George as a Welsh radical had appeared and attracted a surprising amount of attention. That was partly because mine was the first favourable work on Lloyd George that had appeared for many years, at a time when his reputation as a political wrecker and personal philanderer was at its lowest ebb. One early and sympathetic reviewer was Oxford's Max Beloff, an old Lloyd George Liberal himself in his younger days (he actually voted for the famous Oxford Union motion on 'King and Country' in 1933), and always a warm supporter of mine until his death. But the main reason for my new celebrity was the publication of *Wales in British Politics*, an extended and much stronger version of my thesis. It appeared while I was in Lima, in Peru, on 18 June 1963 – Waterloo Day. It was nearly our Waterloo as well, since I foolishly decided to celebrate by taking my two friends, Graham and Barbara, to dinner in a Chinese restaurant in downtown Lima. Even worse, we drank it down (not for long, alas!) with Peruvian champagne. The results were predictably horrible and we were in bed for three days with severe food poisoning. But things could only get better, and when I got back to my parents' home in Aberystwyth I found the book had received dozens and dozens of glowing reviews from such senior academics as Max Beloff and Charles Mowat, politicians like Goronwy Roberts, and young intellectuals like David Marquand. Life would not be the same again.

Wales in British Politics has helped to define my career ever since, not only as a historian of Wales but in my work as a scholar and in public life more generally. It is of note, I think, on three fronts. It was part of a wider debate on popular Liberalism and its ability to withstand the challenge of Labour, and was thus often compared in its conclusions with Peter Clarke's fine book *Lancashire and the New Liberalism* and Paul Thompson's work on radicalism and labour in London. In each area, the experience of Liberalism seemed to be significantly different: for instance, in Wales, unlike Lancashire, the New Liberalism of social reform hardly seemed to exist, despite the presence of Lloyd George. Additionally, in later years my book helped in wider consideration of Britishness, and the different experiences that Scotland, Ireland and Wales brought to the idea of Great Britain and a United Kingdom. The advent of devolution in 1997 and, even more, of the Scottish referendum on independence in September 2014, gave my book an apparently continuing relevance. In Wales, a further major element was emphasised – the rise of a revived sense of nationhood, not marked by conflict and violence as in Ireland where the theme was exclusion from the British polity, but a dawning view, political, social and cultural, of the need for reassertion of the national identity of Wales on the basis of equality rather than exclusion. Here the movement goes on, given new impetus by the advent of governmental devolution after 1997, which was only a minor, intermittent theme in the Wales of post-1868. It was an aspect which most excited attention, even in the Oxford History School, which was solidly based on three compulsory courses on English history, with Wales being thrown in with the Channel Islands and the Isle of Man in a kind of peripheral dustbin. I think it is this aspect that has helped to change the perspective of history in the past fifty years, and encouraged many brilliant younger scholars in Wales to carry the cause of national self-discovery much further forward.

A number of varied opportunities now opened up. I somehow ceased to be the shy introverted young bachelor and only child that I had been before I went to Columbia. I had a richer range of requests to lecture. One enjoyable one was to the Balliol College History Society, the Devorgilla, where I went to speak about Lloyd George, taking along my very gifted Swansea research student, Peter Stead. I discovered that the officers of the Society were largely Welsh, which probably accounted for my invitation. Dai Smith, later Professor of Swansea and chairman of the Welsh Arts Council among many other things, was to be an inspirational friend, academic colleague and comrade on the left for the rest of my life. Gareth Williams was to be an important Welsh history lecturer on the staff at Aberystwyth when I was Vice-Chancellor. During the drinks break after my Balliol talk, someone – possibly the irrepressible French historian, Richard Cobb (ex-Aberystwyth), or possibly even the future Governor of Hong Kong, Chris Patten – took down a portrait of Asquith from the college hall and placed it behind me, Someone else – possibly the alleged spy and convicted drugs trafficker Howard Marks – then found a Welsh rugby rosette, bearing the timeless slogan 'Cymru am Byth', and stuck it on Asquith's lapel. The resulting prolonged hilarity made the remainder of my meeting distinctly more informal.

Another new venture was being asked by Anthony King, another ACLS fellow with me at Columbia, to take part in the Nuffield College election surveys, of which he was now joint editor with David Butler. I worked on Swansea West, where I lived and whose politics I knew well from the Labour Party. It was a most intriguing constituency with an old Labour working-class core and an affluent Consevative suburban fringe. The Conservatives had rather unexpectedly captured it with a very small majority in 1959. This time, as I could predict, Labour won it with a significant swing of 3.2 per cent, and Alan Williams (who died in late 2014) was to remain its member for the next forty-six years and would become Father of the House. In the next election of March 1966, since David and Tony were anxious to cover safe seats as well as the marginals, I wrote on Rhondda West with Peter Stead, who did most of the work. In effect, there was no campaign there at all, merely local encouragement of the predictably Labour voters in the pubs and clubs. 'North of Pontypridd they've just stopped thinking', one Conservative agent observed lugubriously. The strong Plaid Cymru showing in a by-election there shortly afterwards was at that period totally invisible. All this added some diversity to my work as historian by turning me into a kind of political commentator.

What took up a particular amount of my time, in my new-found celebrity after my book, was that I became a regular television performer. BBC Wales was in its infancy and I was asked to write and take part in a series on the University of Wales in the winter of 1963–4. It was all very informal, rather slapdash, but immensely enjoyable, with programmes put on in a disused chapel in the Newport Road in Cardiff. On the strength of that questionable success, the BBC then asked me, through the then editor of news and current affairs, Alan Protheroe (a brisk military man with a sharp, original mind), to become the Welsh general and local election commentator. I took to this with much zest, and my bulging files of newspaper cuttings, leaflets and other material are still of value for me in my never-ending research. In the exciting election of October 1964, in which Harold Wilson very narrowly became Labour's prime minister with a three-seat majority, I had ample opportunity to sound forth to the Welsh viewers. I interviewed a beaming Jim Callaghan who had just increased his majority tenfold in Cardiff South. I also quizzed the defeated Conservative in Cardiff South, Ted Dexter, captain of the England cricket team and a most improbable choice as a parliamentary candidate. He was known as the arrogant 'Lord Edward' to the cricketing press, but now he was deeply crest-fallen, almost crying, shaking his head and saying that it was all his fault. I felt genuinely sorry for him and I think we talked mainly about cricket. I continued to do a great deal of television on historical and political topics, and became well-known for it among the Welsh viewers. When in September 2014 I took part in a programme 'Week In, Week Out' in Cardiff Castle, the lady producer was astonished when I told her I had appeared in the very first programme of that long-running current affairs series in 1964. This period in the mid-1960s was my version of being famous for fifteen minutes, with elderly chapel-goers patting me on the back and Welsh-speaking schoolgirls asking me for my autograph and, of course, it did not last.

The high point was the March 1966 General Election when we were all in the Wood Lane studio in London. I felt very nervous, not helped when a famous BBC Welshman, Huw Wheldon, greeted us by saying that the worldwide audience was around 250 million. I was terrified of all those people seeing my electoral map of Wales spin around on its axis like a children's toy, especially since I was placed near the great Robin Day on the programme set. But the wheel did not rotate, we got by and, indeed, on the Friday morning, after about three hours' sleep, there was real opportunity since the great mass of results had been declared, and the producer asked us all to fill in the time down to closure at five in the evening as best we could. There were a few Welsh results to come and I made the most of them. I spoke on Brecon and Radnor at length, discussed Labour's first-ever victory in Cardiganshire, starting with Gladstone in 1880, and then had the delight of informing the viewers that the Labour victor over Peter Thorneycroft in Monmouth, Donald Anderson, was a pupil of mine at Swansea. I continued to be the Welsh BBC's main election commentator until October 1974, usually in the entertaining company of the excellent and fluent broadcaster, Vincent Kane. I did a variety of other programmes too, including a two-part series for HTV on Wales and the First World War in 1964, which I greatly enjoyed, and ad hoc commentary on the US presidential election of 1964. I am told I then coined the Welsh for 'white backlash' – *adwaith gwyn* – my only contribution to enriching the language. I probably invested too much time and energy into this television work, but it gave me added confidence as a communicator, and I think added zest to my very full programme of lecturing at Swansea, where the rapidly growing numbers of students were as warm and enthusiastic as ever. My lectures on American history seemed to go especially well. Decades later, former students would recall such quotes as the trade union leader, Sam Gompers, declaring 'What does Labour want? More!' The only thing on which I had to cut down was my cricket, which I found too time-consuming for a full-time historian and broadcaster. I did, however, give a broadcast from an ancient chapel vestry in Aberystwyth on 14 July 1966 on the Ten O'Clock BBC programme, to tell the world of Gwynfor Evans's by-election victory for Plaid Cymru at Carmarthen. I was playing in what was to be my last staff match for Swansea against Aberystwyth, and I may have been one of the few broadcasters ever to do my piece on the air wearing cricket pads. I went back to the cricket once the broadcast was done and actually managed to score a few runs.

It seemed that I would stay on happily at Swansea, making my niche in Wales ever stronger. I was now senior lecturer and quite well off. Glanmor Williams was as inspirational as ever as head of department. We had been joined by a number of young colleagues, mostly Welsh and all very able. They included my learned flatmate, the medievalist Ralph Griffiths, and Rees Davies, a most gifted medievalist also, with whom I was to work in Aberystwyth and Oxford (where he held a distinguished chair) and who brought lustre and warmth to my life until his awful death at a relatively young age. Others were Prys Morgan, Rhodri's brother, a Tudor historian of remarkably wide culture and a superb lecturer, and John Davies, an eccentric, unpredictable, strongly nationalist historian of Wales, and a man of very keen intellect. Swansea had made itself the new dynamo of history in Wales, particularly well-known for its 'younger generation of Welsh historians' (of whom, at the age of thirty, I was the doyen) and attracting sixth-formers from all over Wales away from the old stronghold of Aberystwyth. I remained active myself as a scholar, lecturing to all and sundry, editing with Ralph Griffiths *The Welsh History Review*, which went from strength to strength. One unusual little volume that I wrote at this time was on the history of the movement for disestablishment of the Church in Wales, which was finally achieved in 1920. I had long been fascinated by the political implications read by Victorian religious controversialists, or even Giraldus Cambrensis, into such arcane matters as the legal origin of Welsh tithe or the impact of Norman Conquest on the Welsh dioceses. This originated, in fact, by my being asked to give a radio talk on the subject, and I felt the rich material I uncovered was, so to speak, too important to go waste. As the only living author of a work on this arcane subject, I was able to correct the statement on the Gay Marriage Bill in the Lords in 2013, where the government draftsman did not appear to know that the Welsh Church was not established. Swansea in my world was also closely linked with Cardiff, to where I frequently sped in my small Morris car for radio or television broadcasts, and also for socialising. Predictably, New York had considerably reduced my shyness and inhibitions with young women, and I had acquired for a time a charming and beautiful dark-haired girlfriend from Carmarthenshire whom I had met in my publishing activity. It came to a predictable end, but left pleasant, long-lasting memories.

I might have added another dimension to my deep roots in Wales since my political involvement with the Labour Party became ever stronger after *Wales in British Politics* was published. I was active in the Swansea Party over many years. I actually had an extraordinary first meeting with Neil Kinnock in 1965. I was dining out with my girlfriend and Rhodri Morgan suggested that I stay with him and his friends in Cyncoed; he told me that he had left the keys under the crazy paving and there would be no problem. When I arrived at the house around midnight, I was confronted by at least a hundred pieces of crazy paving. Then I saw that a bedroom window was slightly open and, being young and athletic, I started to climb in. At this point a policeman approached and quite reasonably asked me what I was doing. With, I suppose, innate pomposity I replied irrelevantly that I was a Senior Lecturer at University College, Swansea. Such was the Welsh regard for higher education that the policeman replied, 'Thank you, sir, I'll help you in!' I got in, and collapsed into the nearest bed. Some time later, another man jumped in and with furious oaths then jumped out on to a sofa. For the benefit of scandal-mongering journalists, therefore, it is of historical record that I was once in bed with the future leader of the Labour Party, unplanned, and for approximately one second. The next morning we became properly acquainted at a well-known left-wing watering hole called *The Arcade*. My friendship with Neil has flourished in more orthodox fashion ever since. He has been a good and loyal friend, notably when I became a widower, as well as an inspirational and brave political leader.

But Swansea, not Cardiff, was the hub of my Labour world. I served on the Labour Association and on some local government committees as a co-opted member. One of my memories in Swansea was the annual dinner in 1961, addressed by Hugh Gaitskell. CND was strong in Swansea and Gaitskell received a pretty cool reception with few standing to applaud. I did stand up, even though my sympathies had always been with his rival Aneurin Bevan (whom I had heard make a final, utterly memorable speech at the Swansea Elysium cinema in the 1959 election). I thought Gaitskell had been treated unfairly and discourteously. Later, I went up to him, which he seemed to appreciate, and talked to him about Labour support in the university. Gaitskell had tended to seem remote and dogmatic on the public platform but, as in 1957 when I also spoke to him at Oxford after a Labour Club meeting, I found him very pleasant, an attentive listener to the immature views of the young. I was very sad when he died in January 1963, a week or two after I had dined with the Noyeses and with Gaitskell's elder daughter, Julia, who seemed sanguine about her father's health at that time. In 1966, my connection with the Labour Party seemed to advance to a new level when I was seriously approached as a possible Labour candidate in the by-election in Carmarthen following the death of Lady Megan Lloyd George. It would not have been a good idea. I was far too sensitive and unused to life's harsher side to be an MP, and I would have been a failure. In the event, I would have always been known as the man who lost

Carmarthen for Labour; it was, after all, not a Labour citadel like the Rhondda. The eventual, inevitable Labour loser was to be Gwilym Prys Davies, much later a wise and cherished colleague in the Lords. But in fact, I rejected the thought after about five minutes for a very simple reason. I was no longer going to be in Wales. After eight deliriously happy years in Swansea, I was moving on.

I had not thought of leaving Swansea at all. I was immensely happy there and felt a deep bond of loyalty to Glanmor and my other lovely colleagues. But when I saw in the papers an advertisement for a post as Fellow and Tutor (Praelector in Queen's) at The Queen's College, Oxford, my heart skipped beat as they say. I knew it was the post of the distinguished Labour historian Henry Pelling, whom I had found as a friendly face during my time as a research student. Despite my distinctly mixed experiences at Oxford, I was obviously aware of the rich array of talent and academic resources at my old university which I knew so well. Glanmor Williams showed enormous generosity of spirit in that he certainly did not want to lose me but also felt that it would be an upward step in my career. So, shortly before appearing on the BBC election programme in late March, I went to Queen's for interview. It was a curious occasion. The appointment was made entirely by the college, who would pay two-thirds of my salary, the university paying the rest with a Common University Fund lectureship. Later on, when I was appointed, the History faculty was overjoyed that I could and wanted to teach American history, since I would add 25 per cent to their woefully small strength. The Queen's tutors made no response at all to my efforts to rouse their interest on this point – there was some mention of American tourists, I recall. However, we focused happily on British history in which I would succeed Henry Pelling. The main interview before the Queen's governing body was led by the Provost, Lord Florey, who had received a Nobel prize for his work on penicillin, and whose bust I saw decades later in front of the university buildings in his native Adelaide. He displayed the quiet modesty of the really great man. There were several gifted other candidates, but perhaps my acquired confidence in front of the television cameras made me sound more persuasive or plausible. At any rate, I was told a day later that I had got the job. I spent half a day thinking about it and then accepted. A major new chapter of my life commenced.

I often wondered in subsequent years whether I had made the right decision. I was supremely happy in Swansea – more so than in my early years at Queen's – and it seemed a major psychological disruption at the time. I thought about it with more seriousness in the next two or three years when I was in effect offered chairs first at Cardiff, then at Bangor. But, from this distance, I am certain that Queen's was the right move and that my abilities as a historian were enormously stimulated by the Oxford experience. I retained all the good things about Swansea; I kept my friendships there and my close connections with the History department. In 1985, I was to become an Honorary Fellow, and my French wife loves going down to that magic place now, especially to the rocks and beaches of the Gower. I continued to edit *The Welsh History Review* with Ralph for nearly another forty years. I certainly kept up my interest in Welsh history even as my research interests focused now on the wider British and transatlantic scene. I was to write three major books on Wales in later years. They were *Rebirth of a Nation* (1981), my most personal book written with my father's help, spanning a hunded years from 1880 to 1980, *Modern Wales* (1995), a collection of already published essays, a kind of *festschrift* to myself on my retirement from Aberystwyth, and very recently *Revolution to Devolution* (2014), which contains much new writing and links current developments, devolution, the centenary commemorations of the First World War, and the debates over Europe, with key movements and personalities of the Welsh past. I have always found it rewarding to work on Welsh and British history side by side, adding comparative insights from American history, also European, and especially now French. Wales and its history, which now loom far larger in the public mind than when I began in the 1950s, inspired my initial thoughts and gave me a sense of command as a writer. It was the staff and students of Swansea who gave me a special home and intellectual excitement. How I would translate all of that to the far bigger academic pool of Oxford was the challenge that lay ahead.

Chapter Four

History-making:
A British Historian

I STARTED AS FELLOW and Praelector (that is, tutor) at Queen's at the beginning of October 1966. I was appointed to two faculties, Modern History and Social Studies. In the latter I was a Politics tutor but teaching political history, British and international. Queen's had some contradictory aspects, but it was just about the perfect place to study and teach history. There was a strong tradition in the subject. My three amazingly different predecessors were Lord Elton, a right-wing historian of modern France who was an adviser to Ramsay Mac-Donald and tutor to his son, and who became a National Labour peer; Edmund Dell, later a government minister under Wilson and Callaghan in the 1970s in economics departments, who was then (in 1946) a declared Communist; and my immediate predecessor, the eminent labour historian Henry Pelling. The fellowship in 1966 was thus strong in the subject, with three full-time fellows including myself. In addition, the Provost from 1969 was another historian, the leading historian of the Conservative Party and author of a brilliant life of Benjamin Disraeli, Robert Blake, a kindly man who became a great friend. There were junior research fellows who were also historians – notably Malcolm Vale, an expert on medieval Gascony with whom I went on a wonderful summer holiday in the Dordogne in 1967, and learnt all about the Hundred Years' War. Most helpfully, there was also a secretary, Pat Lloyd, to type out the books of such fellows who actually wrote them. She was Welsh, which meant she could cope with the place-names of some of my own works.

In addition, a particular joy for me was the presence every year of a distinguished American scholar as Harmsworth Professor of American History. The Harmsworth in my first year at Queen's was a warm and friendly man, T. Harry Williams, with whom I built up a particularly close relationship. Later, in 1972, he invited me to lecture at his own university, Louisiana State at Baton Rouge, which was marvellous. I stayed at his elegant home and was amused to see that, since he had written two famous books on *Lincoln and the Generals* and *Lincoln and the Radicals*, it was named 'Lincolnand'. The Queen's undergraduates were friendly and unpompous, and I liked them. Queen's was, unusually for Oxford, very much a state school college with many coming as Hastings scholars, from grammar schools in Yorkshire and Cumbria. One of them in my first year, Roger Liddle, the son of a railway worker in Carlisle, is now one of my Labour colleagues in the Lords after a distinguished career in Brussels. When closed scholarships were ended in Oxford around 1980, it had the unfortunate inegalitarian effect of making Queen's more of a southern, minor-public-school college for a time. In 1966, therefore, I found myself plunged from teaching in the fastnesses of voluble west Wales into the cannier culture and humour of the North of England, which introduced me to such novelties as the northern pronunciation of Aristotle ('Arry Stottle). And the Queen's library, a jewel of English baroque dating from the 1680s, had astonishing holdings on all aspects of my subject and was in itself a huge resource for anyone with a serious interest in history.

Still, Queen's in 1966 was an odd place in some ways. I lived in college as a bachelor for six years and felt it to be variously a glorious gilded cage and a glittering prison with little privacy. One curiosity was that the head porter, a former policeman, felt it to be his duty to ward off as visitors any young woman under the age of, say, thirty. A don's bachelordom should be preserved at all costs. I enjoyed an amazingly comfortable existence in an age of affluence, eating and drinking well in a glorious building designed by the great Nicholas Hawksmoor, with an incidental building by Christopher Wren in the Back Quad. At the weekends, I liked to spend time alone in the great library, perusing such works as the Shakespeare first folio, once owned by David Garrick, or a copy of Camden's *Britannia*, the possession of the astronomer Edmund Halley, a Queen's man. In the senior common room, hung a famous fifteenth-century portrait of another Queen's man King Henry V. When I saw an exhibition at the Palace Gallery in 2014 on the early Hanoverians, I noticed it made much of the talents of George II's wife, Queen Caroline, whose statue in the cupola above the Queen's entrance on the High Street I gazed on from my rooms. I felt sorry that Queen's, a jewel of Hanoverian architecture, did not get a mention.

But for a resident fellow, it was still a somewhat mixed existence. I discovered the eccentric side of Queen's on my very first night when, on a Sunday evening in an empty hall before the start of term, I found myself dining with two elderly fellows who apparently hated each other – they addressed conversation animatedly to me, showing a keen interest in the culture and topography of Wales, but said not a word to each other. The fellows generally were a mixed bag, several of them brilliant and world-famous scholars, a few sadly aware of the failure of their academic careers; some eloquent prima donnas, others silent and subservient. One of my two history colleagues was John Prestwich, a great authority on the Norman conquest, appointed as a young man in 1937 when he was twenty-three. His wife, Menna, was Welsh, from Carmarthenshire, and in time she became a great friend and champion. We shared a common interest in the French Huguenots, one of whom I was later to marry. When Prestwich retired in 1981, we appointed as his successor a brilliant young man, John Blair, an Anglo-Saxon historian with great knowledge of archaeology and a man of great warmth; he married a Finnish lady, which confirmed the view I had formed back in 1960 of the fine qualities of the land of Sibelius. The modernist was a most remarkable and gifted human being, Alastair Parker, originally appointed as a specialist in eighteenth-century agriculture who had turned into a leading authority on appeasement and the diplomacy of the 1930s. The son of a butcher from Barnsley, he adopted a new name (he was christened Alan) along with the air of a raffish refugee from the Hellfire Club of George II's time. He was deeply conservative about college policy, yet also a man of strongly radical, Old Labour views on politics. He famously had an eye for attractive young girl pupils: when we went canvassing for Labour at election times on the Blackbird Leys housing estate, a mixed area indeed, I noted how more effective for the cause was Alastair's chatting up of young Caribbean housewives compared with my boring little homilies on the Health Service. Alastair and I took some time to get to know each other but, from around 1980, we developed a deep and affectionate friendship. Each of us would have said the other was his closest friend in Oxford. I wrote his obituary in the *Independent* in 2001, with tears rolling down my cheeks.

My PPE colleagues at Queen's were all powerful scholars. Two were fellows of the British Academy. Geoffrey Marshall, Politics tutor and a great expert on constitutional law, was a laconic product of Blackpool and a fine footballer in his youth; his greatest pride came from having trained for the Blackpool club at the same time as the immortal Sir Stanley Matthews. Jon Cohen, a good friend, was a very sharp Jewish philosopher, a bracing presence on the governing body. The Economics tutor was Nicholas Dimsdale, a quieter, thoughtful man who was related to J. M. Keynes. All three had apparently backed me strongly in my appointment, against some opposition elsewhere; none of them was a Conservative. Other fellows with whom I was friendly were Brian McGuinness, the Greats philosopher, an authority on Wittgenstein; and Allen Hill, a genial Northern Irishman of much my own age, who had to struggle with Cold War formalities to get married to a charming Hungarian lady. Equally amiable was Martin Edwards, a Lancastrian Mathematics tutor and a good cricketer. Another interesting character was the Fellow in Theology and college chaplain, the Revd David Jenkins. At the time, since he had so few students, he was made Domestic Bursar to deal with the catering deficit; he succeeded in doubling it.

Later, he became Bishop of Durham and a major controversialist, defending the Durham and other miners during the 1984 miners' strike, and then causing dismay in his Church by casting doubt on such key tenets as the Resurrection and the story of the empty tomb. Apparently, during his time at Queen's, he put in much time working in youth clubs and engaging in good works generally. He was certainly a good man, a man of conscience.

But not all the fellows were as amiable as David. Indeed, I had been warned before I went to Queen's that its governing body was a quarrelsome one. So it proved. There was a formidable Senior Tutor, a Scotsman, Iain Macdonald, with fierce prejudices on matters academic, political and especially ethnic. As it happened, he was friendly to me since he liked the Welsh as a rugby-playing people and claimed to be an old socialist – 'My father played snooker with Jimmy Maxton.' But you had to be wary. As a proud Macdonald, he still resented what the Campbells had done to his people when massacring them at Glencoe in 1692. An early guest of mine at dinner in Queen's was a Scottish friend, Alec Campbell, history fellow at Keble and a specialist on American history. Macdonald was insistent on knowing what my guest's name was which, of course, he knew perfectly well. The governing body was stormy in my early years: one of the many gifts of Robert Blake, Provost of Queen's, was the ability to restore peace and harmony before the Grim Reaper gave us some assistance in that respect. But it was not all conflict. In my very first term, the fellows agreed to build the Florey building in St Clement's, from designs presented to us by the eminent architect James Sterling, famous for the rather similar design of the *Neue Staatsgalerie* in Stuttgart. It was an arresting project, but badly constructed – too cold in winter, too hot in summer, and with poor sound-proofing. Most undergraduates disliked living there. There was subsidence, and to date there have been repeated efforts to repair it or even knock it down altogether. The Queen's governing body voted the project in during my first term, which was Michaelmas Term, and when I had no vote, so I claim no responsibility at all for the troubled history of the Florey Building.

In addition to working as teachers, dons usually undertook college posts in helping to run the college (Henry Pelling had been much criticised for declining to do so). As a bachelor living in college, inevitably I became in 1967 college Dean, in charge of student welfare and discipline. For almost the next year, I enjoyed the pleasant tranquil life, with much socialising, that had been the privilege of deans since Queen's was founded in 1341. Then, in 1968, there began a wider explosion – violent troubles on American campuses with deaths at Kent State; 'les evenements' in Nanterre and the old Sorbonne, which almost brought the regime of Charles de Gaulle crashing down; demos and sit-ins at many British universities, notably Warwick and the London School of Economics where a university porter died. Oxford was fairly tranquil by comparison, but there were some mass protests even there. Some were about such reasonable points as the inadequacy of the university's disciplinary procedures, of which I had had some experience as a student myself, but others were copycat responses to utterly trivial or even false charges of the university having secret files or resisting having a student's union. Queen's had the problem of being next-door to All Souls, a college which took no undergraduates and was understandably a target for the demonstrators. The proctors urged me to be watchful lest it be occupied, and I promised them that if I saw people with ladders and grappling irons walking through Queen's I would take action. Queen's was not one of the more militant colleges – inevitably Balliol led the way – and the fellows complimented me for this, undeservedly. It was suggested that I be offered a silver cigarette case by way of thanks; as a non-smoker, I declined.

But the atmosphere changed and relaxed informal procedures by the Dean became difficult for a time. I lived alone in college and could often feel defenceless at weekends, with no campus police or other assistance. It was a strange feeling for me, as a lifelong man of the left, to suddenly become a target of the radical young, a symbol of 'repressive tolerance' and the authoritarian side of university life. In the end, I got fed up with it all and resigned as Dean a few months ahead of time. I regained student respect afterwards by agreeing to join thousands of undergraduates in sitting down on Iffley Road rugby pitch to stop a university match against the all-white South Africans. In the event, the police wisely called the whole thing off. The students also learned that I took part with a girlfriend in a demonstration at Trafalgar Square against the Greek Colonels, where we were addressed by Melina Mercouri of 'Never on Sunday' fame. The student troubles petered out – they were part of the rebellious youth culture of the 1960s. There were some improvements that followed, notably in student provision and disciplinary procedures. But, in general, these self-indulgent student disturbances were harmful to the universities: they made them look out of control and ripe for the Thatcherite counter-attack in the 1980s. Oxford students in 1968 lived in gilded comfort, their maintenance costs part-financed by the taxpayer, compared with students almost everywhere else outside Oxford and certainly with students now. Their behaviour helped to lead to a long-term diminution of the universities' essential freedom from political control.

In addition, to being a college tutor, I was also a lecturer in Oxford University. I thought a good deal about this aspect, especially after experiencing my Queen's interview at which the university was not represented. It seemed to me the most important part of my job was to contribute, as teacher and very much as author, to Oxford's wider strengths. I noticed that when I was asked what my work was, whereas colleagues would usually refer to their college affiliation, I would reply 'university lecturer'. The History faculty as such did not impinge greatly on my life, but I took my lecturing for the university very seriously. I gave successive courses on Lloyd George and British Politics (a hugely attended series as I shall mention below), the ILP and British Politics, the Attlee government, British political history in the period 1945–80 and, finally, a survey course on British history from 1867 to 1964 – much as I had done in Swansea, and which the students seemed to need. I also took university seminars on American history and gave a regular course on US reform movements from 1870 to 1920. I greatly enjoyed it all – no doubt it appealed to my theatrical sense and, on occasion, my lectures even ended with applause, a rare event for laid-back Oxford students. The particular pleasure for me was that I was lecturing to an intelligent audience precisely on the issues on which I was doing research for various books, which was most valuable for me in clearing my mind. Some of the other members of the Modern History faculty were too eccentric or introverted to become close colleagues. But, by the mid-1970s, there had assembled a group of brilliant younger scholars of my own age or thereabouts – Ross McKibbin of St John's, a trenchant Australian; Philip Waller of Merton, a man of particular warmth; Brian Harrison of Corpus Christi; two women colleagues, Jose Harris of St Catherine's and Janet Howarth of St Hilda's. The university dimension was always central for me. I hugely enjoyed the staff seminars at All Souls, and spoke frequently to them. I found them the most intellectually stimulating thing I did at Oxford, though I did disapprove when some colleagues tried to make it a lions' den ordeal for lecturers from other universities (especially Cambridge). I felt it was good of visiting lecturers to come at all. When I returned to Oxford after retiring from Aberystwyth after 1995, I found that these excellent seminars, predictably, had been cancelled by the faculty.

My most cherished colleague of all was Colin Matthew of Christ Church, whom I first met when he was working on the Liberal Imperialist political group as a graduate student, and who went on to be the brilliant editor of the *Gladstone Diaries*, editor of the *Oxford Dictionary of National Biography*, and one of the most influential historians of his generation. He was also an active member of the Labour Party and a wise and fascinating human being. I felt desolate when he died young, and was deeply saddened at his memorial service in Christ Church in 2001. I went home from that service wondering how to respond to the personal and professional loss of Colin, and then reflected that, although I had completed twenty-two of the twenty-three articles for the *Dictionary of National Biography* that he had asked me to write, I had delayed writing the last one – a 23,000-word entry on David Lloyd George. I immediately went upstairs and typed out on a blank piece of paper, 'David Lloyd George was born at New York Place, Manchester, on 17 January 1863.' It was the least I could do. A week later, my entry was done and my promise to poor Colin fulfilled.

At Queen's as at Swansea, I regarded myself above all as a researching, writing historian. My academic interests were now on the move, from a prime concentration on Welsh history to wider British historical themes. I continued to work on Wales, and studied some different aspects of modern Wales, including anti-war movements before and beyond both world wars. A new edge was given to my work on modern Wales by the unexpected surge in strength for Plaid Cymru, which not only captured Carmarthen through Gwynfor Evans at the 1966 by-election, but also shook Labour to the core by coming close to winning further by-elections in Rhondda West and Caerphilly. The theme of Welsh home rule, or at least devolution, dormant through most of the years from the 1870s down to beyond 1945, seemed suddenly aflame, with the prospect of changing the basic course of the history of Wales and the unity of the United Kingdom. The process reached its climax with the Scottish independence referendum in September 2014 and is still far from over.

But it was political and ideological change in Britain as a whole that now gripped me. I was focused on the many issues emerging from *fin de siècle* Britain – the 'strange death' or renewal of Liberalism; the kind of challenges posed by the rise of Labour; the crises in the party system during the First World War and its aftermath; and the specific role of Lloyd George as a catalyst, an inspiration and an agent of destructive change. A huge boost, therefore, was given to me and others when the Beaverbrook Library opened for business in St Bride Street, just behind Fleet Street, in the summer of 1967. For the first time, the papers of David Lloyd George, Bonar Law and, indeed, Beaverbrook himself, were available for research. There were only around eight tables in the Beaverbrook Library, so I booked myself in for six weeks once the long vacation began. It was memorable in every way, a delightful place to work, well-lit and air-conditioned, which was a blessing in the hot summer of 1967. The Honorary Director and presiding genius was Alan Taylor, whom I now got to know well for the first time. He was omnipresent, asking people what they were working on and making terse comments on the documents being read. He was also an excellent, enlightened guardian of his material, true to his own public declarations. Genuine scholars could cite and publish what they wished free of charge; commercial outfits would be charged all the market could bear. In many ways, I think this period was the professional high-point of Alan's brilliant career (he remained at the Library until it was closed in 1975), and I was fortunate to be around while he was there. The other personnel were also notable: there was Rosemary Brooks, the archivist, a warm-hearted woman in poor health who did not long survive; there was Mr Igo, a tiny bow-tied former *Express* journalist, who brought round the boxes of papers; and there was Veronica, Alan's blonde-haired secretary, whose effect seemed partly to distract the readers from their studies, which she did most successfully. The library was open for just six hours, from ten in the morning until four in the evening, so I usually skipped lunch to dive into the sea of paper.

It was an invigorating, liberating experience. The Lloyd George papers, on which I focused my attention, mainly dated from 1916 when he became prime minister and Frances Stevenson started organising his papers. There was a rich array of correspondence with all his political contemporaries. I found his correspondence with fellow Liberals to be of especial interest – people like Christopher Addison, H. A. L. Fisher, Edwin Montagu, and the 'Coaly Lib' whip Freddy Guest. Above all, his correspondence with Churchill, especially after 1918, was riveting, memorable both on issues (such as Russia or Ireland) and even more so on their personal relationship. At that period, Lloyd George's Liberalism was still marked; as Churchill himself ruefully observed, it was a question of 'master and servant', with Lloyd George very much the dominant figure in Britain if not the world at that particular time, though Churchill comes out of it well too. The Lloyd George papers were the prime source on all this, and I was captivated by them.

The Beaverbrook Library was more than an academic resource, however. It became a Mecca, almost a community, as Chris Wrigley has described. It was an excellent place for international networking, and I made important friends there. One was John Grigg, later Lloyd George's excellent biographer (the son of Edward Grigg, one of Lloyd George's political secretaries). There was Maurice Cowling, the formidable leader of the Peterhouse historians in Cambridge; he was as remote from me in historical method and political out-look as it was possible to be – he was the high priest of 'high politics', while I was champion of the 'low' – but we became good friends, nevertheless. There was also Michael Fry, a Canadian specialist on Lloyd George's foreign policy, who later kindly invited me to lecture in Canada in 1972. Again, there was the delightful Chris Wrigley, working especially on Lloyd George's work at Munitions and with the trade unions. Then there were Cameron Hazlehurst, a very able Australian and a somewhat controversial character who published a fine volume on Lloyd George's first year at war, 1914–15, who for a time was a research fellow at Queen's; and Stephen Koss, a sociable and produc-tive American scholar from Columbia University, now embarking on a series of monographs on Liberals politicians and the press. There was a problem with Cameron and Stephen, however. Cameron, against my advice and apparently Alan Taylor's, had included in his book a very lengthy detailed passage of crit-icism of Stephen, whom he claimed had misinterpreted some key documents on the formation of the first wartime coalition under Asquith in May 1915. But he did so at such length that offence was caused. Both Cameron and Stephen thought of me as their closest British academic friend and, indeed, I much liked them both; but they also used me as an anvil upon which to smite the other.

I recall suggesting to Stephen that he might like to meet Ross McKibbin in Oxford; he replied dourly, 'I don't like Australians'.

Perhaps the most memorable part of the activities at the Beaverbrook Library was the seminar at which library-based scholars read papers around their research. I gave a talk early in 1969 on Lloyd George's Coalition Liberals, those Liberals who went with him after the peacetime coalition was formed following the General Election in December 1918. In broad terms, my line was that they were a much more significant and worthy group of politicians than previous writers had concluded, a view that I still hold. The session in the library seemed to go well at the time, and Alan, in high spirits as a result, took me for a memorable dinner to a riverside restaurant called the *Samuel Pepys*. On the way, he took me around St Paul's, and demonstrated his considerable knowledge of architecture *en route*. I was, however, able to correct him on one point, when he showed me an old Dutch-style Welsh chapel which, he assured me, was now closed for worship. I was able to inform him that it bore a sign 'Gwasanaethu'r Sul', meaning Sunday services, which much amused him. My talk later appeared in a volume *Twelve Essays*, edited by Alan in 1971, and the article was praised in reviews. It was taken as the work of a new generation of unknown young scholars, even though I was myself thirty-seven at that time and had published five books. It did, however, include the work of other historians younger than me, people like Paul Addison, who would soon announce themselves as important historians. Another result of my work at the Beaverbrook Library was that Alan got me to translate some Welsh passages in letters from Lloyd George to his secretary and mistress Frances Stevenson, letters than Alan himself was due to edit. They were almost all cloying terms of endearment and, disappointingly, revealed nothing scandalous. Alan's edited volume appeared under the title *My Darling Pussy*.

After working at the Beaverbrook Library, I now became increasingly known above all else as an authority on Lloyd George and Liberalism. I was able to find other important source materials elsewhere, of course; the Bodleian in Oxford had, among many other collections, the important papers of two of Lloyd George's closest associates during and after the war, Lord Milner and the historian H. A. L. Fisher, his Minister of Education and an important figure elsewhere at this time, notably in foreign policy; a major source on Coalition Unionist (Conservative) politics was the papers of Austen Chamberlain in Birmingham University Library; best of all, the National Library of Wales, had by this time acquired its own important materials on Lloyd George, notably his letters to his often harshly treated wife, Dame Margaret. Alan Taylor asked me if I would edit a volume of these for publication, to which I readily agreed. There was now building up an enormous public interest in the arguments over the downfall of Liberalism, and in Lloyd George's role in particular. Historians who had been fixated by the rise of the gentry in the sixteenth century were now becoming obsessed with the decline of the Liberal Party in the twentieth. I found myself increasingly in demand as a lecturer, reviewer and adviser on Lloyd Georgiana in general, which has continued to be the case ever since, to the degree that I have sometimes found it difficult to fight free of the Lloyd George association. In this sense, it was a breakthrough for me to write *Labour in Power* (1984), since Lloyd George had died before that particular story began. I was asked by a major publisher to write an extensive biography of Lloyd George in several volumes, but declined the offer. I didn't want Lloyd George to take over my life, as Woodrow Wilson had taken over the career of a wise American scholar I knew, Arthur Link, not to mention Winston Churchill in the case of Martin Gilbert. Poor John Grigg did so devote his life to the Lloyd George biography and, after four fine volumes getting him as far as 1917, John died and his project remained incomplete. But the dynamic role of Lloyd George in our politics, our culture and our constitutional arrangements, in peace and war, will always fascinate me, and there are constantly new avenues for investigation. Churchill's moving wartime tribute after Lloyd George's death remains a just one – that historians will always see how much of our history in the first quarter of the twentieth century was the work of this one man, 'the greatest Welshman since the age of the Tudors'.

In very recent years, two modern authors have asked me to read their major works: Roy Hattersley writing a general biography of Lloyd George, and Ffion Hague in describing Lloyd George's relations with women. The two excellent books by both these authors rekindled my enthusiasm all over again. Back in 1970, there was an exciting immediacy in writing upon these themes – we were pioneers. For the first time, I held a series of lectures in the Oxford schools on Lloyd George and British Politics, 1890–1940. The student response was astonishing. It seemed difficult to find a lecture hall big enough as students crammed into any available room, sitting in cramped conditions on the floor. It wasn't me as a person who caused such a frisson of excitement, but the Welsh wizard and the revolution in the understanding of his career that the Beaverbrook Library and Alan Taylor himself had generated. After one of my lectures, for the only time ever, I received a most courteous letter from an undergraduate at University College who disagreed with some of my conclusions, and who turned out to be Lloyd George's great-grandson, whom I duly invited round for a drink. We had a most enjoyable talk and, in later years, he was to write a good book on his famous ancestor. Another landmark of this period was a lecture that I gave for the Cymmrodorion Society at the House of Commons on 'Lloyd George and the Historians'. It was an exciting evening for me since the chairman was Roy Jenkins. He was very generous, as I always found him to be, and commented wryly on the irony of the biographer of Asquith presiding over a discussion of the merits of Lloyd George. One of the things I learned about all this, by the way, was seeing that it was useless and destructive even to think of being possessive about something in terms of its being *my* topic, from which any competitors should be repelled. Such an attitude is not only a perversion of academic values but, in any case, pointless when it comes to dealing with Lloyd George. He belongs to the world – thousands and thousands of scholars and others have studied his career, all offering their own insights. The task in hand is to make your contribution to the best of your ability – which is not to say that I have not found it irritating when some other writers, often Americans, have been guilty of the occupational hazard of unacknowledged plagiarism of my own writings.

I consolidated my work on Lloyd George with the publication of three books about his career in 1971, 1973 and 1974. The first was a general book for students and researchers, *The Age of Lloyd George* in a series for Allen and Unwin. This volume focused heavily on Lloyd George's role as a catalyst, including his linking the Old Liberalism of his Welsh youth with the New Liberalism of social reform, something which only he could have achieved. The main interest in this regard was working with my editor, Geoffrey Elton, the famous Tudor historian, whose wife had created the card index to the Lloyd George Papers until the Beaverbrook Library removed her. As a result, he was interested in Lloyd George's activities while having no admiration for Alan Taylor. At first, he covered my manuscript with all manner of queries. When I responded that I agreed with some of his comments, but not with others, he proposed dropping them all – which I resisted since some of his suggestions would certainly make the book stronger. We eventually reached a happy compromise; Elton seemed very pleased with the outcome, and we remained friendly thereafter.

My next book attracted a good deal of attention. This was my edition of Lloyd George's *Family Letters*, published jointly by Oxford and the University of Wales Press, in early 1973. In fact, with perfect timing, the very first copy I saw awaited me on the doormat of my parents' house in Aberystwyth, when my first wife Jane and I returned from our marriage at the local registry office. I could thus present it to my new bride. It consisted of edited copies, along with extended commentary, of Lloyd George's correspondence with the stoical Margaret from around 1885, before they were married, up until 1936 when their marriage had somehow staggered along for nearly fifty years. The letters started with a bang, with Lloyd George telling his fiancée, with terrifying force, of his own driving ambition, 'the wheels of my juggernaut' as he described it, and she was fiercely ticked off for being insufficiently sympathetic to his overriding need to 'get on'. After that, the letters provide much vivid description of Lloyd George's entry into parliament, his conflicts and achievements in politics down to the People's Budget and beyond, his agonies of mind in August 1914 ('I am moving through a nightmare world these days'), the crises of wartime and the peacetime coalition, and the conflicts over Liberal reunion and the challenge to appeasement in the interwar years. The letters end with a curious item of correspondence from Jamaica sympathising with Edward VIII and supporting the king's wish to marry Mrs Simpson – an instructive correspondence, often belligerent in tone, with much use of the verb 'to smash'.

There is also much of personal interest in the letters – Lloyd George's distaste for what he considered to be the puritanical superstition preached in 'a suffocating malodorous chapel', his money problems, and many predictable disclaimers (sometimes plain lies) about alleged dalliances with women. *Family Letters* remains one of the few books which contains ample first-hand material by Lloyd George himself, since he was always an uncertain correspondent (he preferred face-to-face communication). Later on, through the enterprise of my former examinee John Graham Jones, Aberystwyth acquired more invaluable Lloyd George material, the papers of his brother William and his private secretary, A. J. Sylvester. Historians can now estimate fully the Welshness of Lloyd George in a way that was impossible when I first began work on him. My book attracted much attention and I was widely interviewed on radio, television and in the press. I was particularly glad that John Grigg was pleased, because I knew he was worried at its appearance since his own first volume in the extensive biography was due out shortly. In the end, we both did well, our books being recognised as complementary, and we reviewed each other in the weeklies in good humour.

I produced a third book, for Weidenfeld and Nicolson this time, *Lloyd George* in 1974, a shortish biography with many fine illustrations. It came at a useful time, since I had just got married, and the advance allowed me to buy essentials like sheets, saucepans and even a doormat. The book provided me with an opportunity to sum up my current conclusions about Lloyd George as a radical; again, it received a large number of highly complimentary reviews, reflecting the fascination with Lloyd George and Liberalism at that period. The book has a memorable introduction by Alan Taylor, who had been critical of many aspects of Lloyd George's career and personality in the past –'He had no friends and did not deserve any', was one severe (and inaccurate) judgement. Alan tended to equate Lloyd George's bad qualities with the Welsh in general, whom he once told me in a letter that he considered generally devious and dishonest. I used to wonder if this reflected his experience of Dylan Thomas, whose relationship with Alan's first wife, Margaret, had contributed to breaking up their marriage. But in the foreword to my book, Alan is unequivocal: 'The greatest ruler of England [sic] since Oliver Cromwell' was the verdict, and it glittered in the reviews I had received.

So, my reputation as Lloyd George's *doppelgänger* was sealed. I do not really object, since so much of the criticism he had previously received, notably from former Asquithians, was so biased. Lloyd George has rightly been attacked for wrecking tactics towards his own party in the later stages of the First World War and at the 'coupon election'; harsh passages of his career have been properly condemned, notably the reprisals policy in Ireland in 1919–20 and the utterly appalling visit to Hitler at Berchtesgaden in 1936, the great disgrace of his life. Nevertheless, I am certain that the thrust of his career, from the New Liberalism of Edwardian years to the dynamic economic programmes of the 1920s and 1930s, was overwhelmingly positive. Now I think it can fairly be said that his reputation has been fundamentally revised, and his role as a kind of universal scapegoat held personally responsible for all the misfortunes that struck Britain in twentieth century has been erased. It was noticeable that when I, Alan Taylor, John Grigg, the American Bentley Gilbert and others wrote up our findings, opponents of Lloyd George, on the right and left, so vocal before, lapsed into silence. In the face of the enormous wave of new material now available, detailing his extraordinary achievements in peace and in war, detractors had little to offer. Anyway, Lloyd George's most virulent critics had always been Liberals of the Asquithian persuasion, and they had all died away by the mid-1970s. Lloyd George will always remain deeply controversial; as a Welsh Baptist outsider, a 'man of push and go', he will never enjoy the cosy patriotic aura of Winston Churchill, whom one poll found to surpass even Shakespeare in being considered the greatest Englishman of all time. But Lloyd George is the more contemporary and constructive figure of the two; he leaves his legacy not in wars or imperial dominion (though there is always Palestine and Iraq), but in the living standards and democratic practices of our people. That will be his enduring bequest and I am glad to have played some part in getting that understood and accepted. One long-term consequence of all of this was that I am now numbered among the vice-presidents of the Lloyd George Society (the only one, incidentally, who is not a Liberal Democrat), and I have addressed its members around seven or eight times, usually in Llandrindod Wells, the mid-Wales spa town where Lloyd George himself used to harangue the faithful in the Gwalia hotel. The last time I was there, my present wife Elizabeth joined in the oratory and the fun.

After these books, I then went on to focus more on Labour history, and Keir Hardie in particular, as I shall discuss in the next chapter. But I still had a major project to complete on the Lloyd George era, which was *Consensus and Disunity* (1979), a revisionist account of the peacetime Lloyd George coalition of 1918–22, and the changes in British social and economic life that resulted from it. This was, incidentally, the first of the major books that I published with Oxford University Press, at the suggestion of its history editor, Ivon Asquith (a descendant of the prime minister), who became a great personal friend. My book began from the premise that the post-war government of 1918–22, like its prime minister, had been seriously misrepresented. It had been depicted as a shabby era of deceit and corruption, a period which gave the idea of coalition a bad name – a phase from which Baldwin and MacDonald, allegedly, then saved the country. Its tarnished politics were satirised in Arnold Bennett's *Lord Raingo*, and the amoral atmosphere in parliament condemned for all time by Keynes (who got the phrase from Baldwin), 'a body of hard-faced men who looked as if they had done very well out of the war'. Despite my own prejudices as a chronicler and supporter of Labour, I did not see things that way at all.

The premise of *Consensus and Disunity* is the fundamental change that British political life had undergone during the four years of total war. The old politics, focused on such themes as free trade and Welsh disestablishment, was disappearing. The party system had been transformed and was trying to regroup to confront the challenge of Labour. More fundamentally, the language and texture of public life were being reinvented, as the achievement of women's suffrage eventually so swiftly and amply demonstrated. I analysed the achievements of the Coalition government: social reform which took the pre-war New Liberalism to a new level in such areas as housing and education; industrial relations with a genuine attempt avoid a repetition of the pre-war polarisation between capital and labour; a change of policy in Ireland; and attempts, much associated with Lloyd George himself, to redirect foreign policy to mitigate the worst effects of Versailles, which finally found the approval of the arch-critic Keynes. I then demonstrated the limitations of the various opposition groups: the indirection of the Asquithian 'wee frees' and other centrists; the obtuseness of the extreme right from the 'Anti-Waste' movement onwards; and the immaturity of the Labour Party inevitable at this very early phase of its history. As Churchill had harshly remarked, Labour was unfit to govern.

But I then tried to show how things went seriously wrong from the start of 1922. Ironically much of the Tory criticism arose from the government's most positive achievements – the eventual peace in Ireland with a settlement that still lasts, with modifications, to this day, and the rapprochement with Bolshevik Russia which Lloyd George sought to have recognised *de jure*. Most Tories hated both. There followed serious errors from the government: the collapse of much of its social policy and the savagery of the Geddes Axe; the fatal alienation of the unions after the Sankey Commission and Black Friday; Lloyd George's presidential tinkering with fundamental aspects of the constitution, including the comic uproar over his peerages; and, most fundamentally, the rise of Conservative backbench dissent. As with all coalitions, a government founded by intrigue at the political centre was undermined by party dissent at the grass-roots nationwide. Grass roots dissent in the Unionist (Conservative)

Party is now reflected in the name '1922 Committee' being applied to meetings of the Conservative backbenchers. This kind of destructive dissent happened again in the pre-election period in early 2015. The coalition, then, was a failure, but not an ignoble failure, and Lloyd George's last stand in power was not inglorious. The fact that democracy survived in Britain throughout the interwar years, in contrast to most other countries in Europe, from Portugal to Bulgaria, owes something to its efforts at consensus and moderation.

My book received very many highly complimentary reviews. I appreciated them all, even if some reviewers tried to appropriate my work as an argument for a 'government of national unity' in 1979, and linked it to Roy Jenkins's Dimbleby Lecture quoting Yeats to the effect that 'the centre cannot hold'. That was not my purpose at all. *Consensus and Disunity* is a work of history focused on the past, my last extensive study of Lloyd George's ever-changing role in our history, and my final comment on the political consequences of the peace. It is still the book of which I am most proud. It seems to me the best in terms of its intellectual ambition, its linkage of political and socio-economic change, its control over a vast array of sources, manuscript and printed, drawn from several countries. *Consensus and Disunity* represents the best of which I am capable, and I should be glad to be judged as a professional historian on that particular work. As is often the case, although it later went into paperback, it sold less well than several of my other books. But it no doubt added to my public reputation, and was probably a major reason why I was shortly afterwards elected a Fellow of the British Academy. A greater honour was that I got to know Alan Taylor much better. He dined with Jane and me in Hanborough and Queen's, and his charming (and strongly Marxist) Hungarian wife, Eva, stayed with us and was adored by our children, David and Katherine. We went round for tea to Alan and Eva's small house in Kentish Town in north London many times in the 1980s. One of the most poignant possessions in my library at home is a paperback copy of *The Origins of the Second World War*, which Alan gave me when he was in his final hospital in Finchley, when he was gravely stricken with Parkinson's disease, and the book has a spidery scrawl testifying to his unsuccessful efforts to write the names of my children. When I went to Alan's memorial service in Magdalen in 1990, it was a particularly solemn occasion for me. I reflected quietly on how much my life in the past twenty years had been shaped by this one unpredictable, extraordinary man. I still treasure the card he sent me in 1972 when I gave him an offprint of my Commons lecture on 'Lloyd George and the Historians' – on his card he wrote, 'Very good. Bethmann Hollweg has no hyphen.'

One feature period of this was that I was now asked regularly not just to write books but to review the works of others. John Gross, editor of the *Times Literary Supplement*, rang me up and asked me to review works in the wake of the decision taken to end the anonymity of contributors. In fact, I reviewed for the *Times Literary Supplement* almost weekly for the next fifteen years or so, starting with works on post-Civil War American history, before moving on to British and European themes. John Gross was an excellent editor since he would ring up to suggest possible changes, many of them simply verbal, to my reviews. This was always rewarding, since he was himself such an intellectually lively man, the epitome of his own famous book *The English Man of Letters*. At the same time, I was regularly reviewing, again almost weekly, in the *Guardian*, after I met its reviews editor W. P. Webb at dinner at Michael and Jill Foot's. The work kept me very busy, but also helped me to become more versatile as a writer, dealing with different readerships and with different demands. After all, history is for everyone, and the work gave me a chance to take this process forward.

By the later 1970s, I could look back at my time in Queen's as one of great activity and also great satisfaction. But there was more to life than simply scribbling like a lesser Gibbon. I continued to have some association with the Labour Party, though I was not at all an activist as I had been in Swansea. One interesting experience I owed to my old friend, Leslie Stone, who got me on to the editorial board of *Socialist Commentary*, a right-wing Labour monthly despite its name. I had some notable colleagues, including Margaret, the widow of G. D. H. Cole, a formidable old lady. The guiding spirit was a lovely woman, Rita Hinden, South African Jewish, deeply emotional about her politics, which was focused on colonial and Commonwealth matters. She had formed the Fabian Colonial Research Bureau with the former Colonial Secretary, Arthur Creech Jones, and was a great pioneer in an area where Labour had not had much of a policy before. I once heard Denis Healey quip that Rita was a 'Rudyard Hardie' figure. I wrote a few articles for the journal, mostly on American matters, and reviewed quite frequently. In the end, this interlude came to an end when the *Commentary* became too right-wing for my tastes, especially on matters concerning Europe but I enjoyed it while it lasted. In 1968–70, a strange thing happened. I was exasperated by some of the Wilson government's social policies and – to be frank – especially by James Callaghan, the Home Secretary, being prepared to bar entry to Britain for Kenyan Asians with British passports, probably on racial grounds. I phoned up the secretary of the Oxford Labour Party and said that I was resigning membership of the party, with a heavy heart. However, when the 1970 General Election was looming, I felt traitorous at not supporting the party in its hour of need, and phoned up the Oxford party again to say that I wished to rejoin. There was a pause, and then they said they had no record of my ever having left. Thus was the slap-happy method of recording party membership, then and later. So, officially, I was a member all along, which gladdened me, and on that chequered basis I can say that I have an unblemished record of continuous membership since I became twenty-one, a span now of sixty years. When I mentioned this episode to Jim Callaghan in the 1990s when I was writing his biography (without going into too much detail), he was wry in expression and comment –'I can imagine, I can imagine'.

By the early 1970s, my otherwise satisfactory lifestyle had one appalling void. I was in my late thirties and still unmarried. My various tentative relationships had not got very far. I had quite an intense time with a girl I had met in the university, fuelled by the liberated spirit of the so-called Swinging Sixties. As Larkin said in another context, it was between the Beatles and ITV, and perhaps a little late for me. For a time it seemed idyllic. I recall three blissful days driving with her back through beautiful Dorset – a much-neglected county in my view, with Dorchester of Hardy fame a fascinating town – from Bristol, where I had been external examiner for the BA at the city's university. But then we arranged to go together to Vienna in the summer of 1968 – I knew beforehand that it could be a disaster, and it was, with many quarrels and poor weather. I enjoyed some things – the Art Nouveau of Olbrich's *Sezession* building and the Adolf Loos Haus, and a concert in the Salzburg festival. But otherwise, my recollection is of gloomily looking at fat old women in cafes eating *Sachertorte* as the rain came down. It was all over. I have never been to Vienna since.

In Aberystwyth, however, came salvation. I was walking along the 'prom' with my old friend Ieuan Gwynedd Jones, now professor at Aberystwyth, one evening in the summer of 1971 as we often did. Suddenly, and for the only time, he suggested that we have a drink in the seafront hotel, the Belle Vue. There I met Jane Keeler, a graceful young girl from Wrexham, whose MA Ieuan had just been supervising. She had long dark hair, an enticing smile and beautiful legs. Even more than this, I liked her directness, naturalness and lack of affectation. In Aberystwyth, where my protective parents lived and everybody knew me in so small and parochial a town, I could do little to extend our relationship, though I much enjoyed having coffee with her in the National Library. A year went by during which I was on sabbatical leave, and visited Canada and South Carolina to lecture. But I heard that Jane was now working for the Board of Celtic Studies in London, mostly in the British Museum. With immense diffidence, I visited her there and finally plucked up courage to invite her to be my guest at dinner in Queen's. One momentous day in November 1972, we met for tea in Great Russell Street, opposite the British Museum, and I proposed. She accepted immediately, which led me to ask, in donnish mode, 'Are you really sure about this?' She was, and we got married in Aberystwyth registry office on 4 January 1973, a gloriously sunny day despite the date. Jane, although a member of the Church in Wales, wanted to get the formalities over and done with, and so did I. We drove off to Oxford via Ross-on-Wye where we had an idyllic three-day honeymoon, and settled down in Oxford in a rented house in Summertown. We had a proper honeymoon in late March of that year, financed in part by the advance for my biography of Lloyd George, in the Dordogne in south-west France, a place that I knew and loved. The weather was wonderful, and so was everything else. I was thirty-eight, no doubt somewhat settled in my ways, but I was happy. And in my mother's famous phrase, better late than never.

Jane had had a difficult childhood. Her father was a German that her mother had met in Berlin, and who had mysteriously disappeared. This was obviously deeply unsettling for Jane as a child. Her mother, a very charming woman, also had a complicated background since she appears to have worked in West Berlin for the Allied control authorities as a spy, ferrying people across from the east. At the time of the Berlin blockade by the Russians, this must have been highly dangerous. She had excellent German, and was adept at discretion and concealment. I never got out of her what her work actually was in Cold War Berlin, or how she got through the Russian blockade (I gathered later that she removed her activities to Dusseldorf in 1948 when the Berlin blockade was on). A close friend of hers in Berlin thought she was probably a 'sleeper', an agent working inconspicuously in enemy territory. Jane, born in Harrogate, grew up in Wrexham in a single-parent family, not met by a parent after school as all the other girls were. Her youth was thus quite difficult and penurious. However, she had guts and determination and, after doing well at Grove Park School, got to Aberystwyth where she took a fine BA and then an MA in History. Her difficult years, however, had left their mark on her, and her anxieties required patient understanding. She also, perhaps understandably, found my close relationship with my now aged parents hard to accept. However, we contrived to work things out, and I much admired how, as a young girl from rural north Wales, she settled into patrician life at Oxford, so totally different from anything she had previously known. Robert Blake kindly laid on a grand dinner-party in the Provost's lodgings in her honour when we got back to Queen's after our wedding – such eminences as Hugh Trevor-Roper and Hugh Lloyd-Jones were present, but Jane was remarkably at ease and charmed everybody. She had everything: she was a good historian with whom I later co-wrote a book; she was Welsh; she was solidly Labour; she was sexy and she was fun. Where I was quiet and donnish, she had what Jim Callaghan called 'hybrid vivacity', the passionate temperament of an operatic prima donna, which was exactly what I needed. So the great gaping void in my life was now most happily filled.

Our family life was shortly made complete. In July 1974, on American Independence Day, Jane gave birth to our son, David Keir, named with deference to my last and my latest book, namely works on David Lloyd George and Keir Hardie. From the start, he was a cheerful, physically active little boy and huge fun to be with. Then, in September 1977, we had a beautiful daughter,

Katherine Louise, named after Katherine Bruce Glasier, a woman socialist I admired. Katherine proved to be remarkably precocious and soon seemed to catch up, and play animatedly with, her three-years-older brother. I thought then, and think now, that my children are absolutely wonderful, affectionate towards each other, cheerful and, at a later time of horrible crisis, unceasingly brave. They both have a self-confidence I lacked as a child, so perhaps I can take some credit for that. Their own children are cast in their mould. I am enormously proud of David and Katherine, and I spent as much time as I could with them as a father. Jane had amazing qualities as a mother, always treating the children as intelligent younger people, not as a kind of trophy. How did this affect my work as a writer and teacher of history? I was, of course, a very busy Oxford tutor as well as an involved father. Yet the plain facts are that I wrote seven books before our first child was born, and wrote or edited twenty-seven more after that. I am certain that I neglected neither my Queen's pupils nor my beloved children. Jane and I organised every aspect of life carefully, including lovely family holidays in France, Italy and the Netherlands. The explanation for my continuing to be so productive a scholar is simple: I had acquired the essential key to life. I was happy, passionately so, as a husband and a father. It all made everything else, including the writing of more history books, seem so totally worthwhile.

Chapter Five

History-making:
A Labour Historian

IN THE LATE 1970s, my emphasis as a writing historian moved sideways into the field of Labour history. After that, some commentators would forget my earlier work on Welsh (mainly non-Labour) history and British history before and after the First World War, and categorise me as primarily a Labour historian. In so far as I did shift, it was a risky move. Labour history in the 1970s and early 1980s was a lively but perilous area of study. I found that I had moved from frying pan to fire, from the bracing debates over Lloyd Georgian Liberalism into a veritable minefield. A powerful author like the former Communist Edward Thompson, with his *Making of the English Working Class*, provoked not so much academic argument as a clash of faiths. My predecessor at Queen's, Henry Pelling, had been a major Labour historian – indeed, it was much more his special area than it was mine – but that was in the 1960s, a less intense period, while Henry's careful scholarly method was not provocative. To a degree, this passion was because professional historians were trying to relocate the social and political experience of Labour within a wider context, to get 'This Great movement of Ours' away from what Denis Brogan had called Labour historians' 'Mandate of Heaven' theory of a providential and inevitable upsurge of the working class. It appeared difficult to see Labour as a real part of history.

But the ferocity of argument owed more to current politics, the unions' winter of discontent, and rise of a hard-left militant tendency within the world of academic history as well as within the Labour Party. The new history was often strongly Marxist, which fed through the work of brilliant evangelists like Raphael Samuel into the *New Left Review*, a famous journal like *Past and Present*, the Society of Labour History and the work of a large number of younger scholars engaged in the field. Non-scholars like Tony Benn joined in. The new influence of Marxism upon Labour studies came to affect the study of history as a whole. In many ways, this was highly beneficial: it encouraged the study of the dynamics of social history rather than a narrow formal institutional view of Labour and the history of the Labour Party; it sought to place the experience of working people within a wider technical and ideogical context; it encouraged a more adventurous range of sources, 'history from below' so-called, and rescued them from what Thompson memorably called the 'condescension of poster-ity'; it brought the idea of class centre-stage in the treatment of working-class history, where I had always felt it belonged; it shed new light on the poor and dispossessed for whom the source materials were far more scrappy than those for the bourgeoisie, and made original use of popular evidence like oral history, not much used before. But the Marxist – or sometimes Trotskyist – emphasis in Labour studies was too often doctrinaire and intolerant of non-Marxist dissent – it was also too often plain wrong, distorting the evidence within a narrow doctrinaire framework. I felt it incumbent upon me to help rescue it. But this was not always fun. I recall addressing a history meeting in Cardiff (on some quite different non-labour topic) when, for the only time in my life, I was sub-jected to an incoherent series of attacks of a highly personal kind, playing the man not the ball, focusing on my accent, my being at Oxford and the suppos-edly reactionary tendencies of my empiricist colleagues. The level of argument was trivial but I found the tone unpleasant. I was not, however, prepared to take this abuse lying down. A few months, in a *Llafur* meeting at Maesteg, with some of the critics present, I sailed into them, christened them 'saloon-bar rev-olutionaries', and observed that the dominant tendency of the British Labour movement was not a militant tendency. I noted that the audience cheered me loudly. Ironically, three of the most vocal critics at Cardiff later became Labour MPs, two of them distinctly Blairite and supporters of the Iraq invasion in 2003; one of them, then a Communist, went down on record as saying that politi-cians should aim at being efficient managers not ideologues. I feel that over the years, it is their doctrine and outlook that has changed, not mine, and I feel that it is I who remains the pluralist democratic socialist I was then.

My engagement with labour history was stimulated by the contact I had with notable Labour Party figures of the time. Across the Evenlode valley from Jane and me lived the former Labour Attorney-General Sam Silkin, a charming man of much judicial learning. He told me that he had also opened the bowl-ing for Glamorgan, which must be unique among legal officers of the Crown. A little further on beyond Witney, in Minster Lovell, we got to know very well Douglas Jay and his charming wife, Mary. Douglas was a highly eccentric figure, but with the powerful intellect of the Wykehamist. He was the author of the classic statement of principle, *The Socialist Case* (1937), a fundamental text for the democratic left even if it contained the unfortunate phrase that 'the gentle-man in Whitehall knows best'. Douglas's historical memories and experiences

– of Attlee whose private secretary he had been, of Gaitskell his best friend, and of other politicians – I found quite absorbing. On economic issues, he was authoritative. Only one topic should I avoid – Europe. Douglas was passionately Eurosceptic, even Europhobic, and I felt that if I tried to argue the case it might bring our cherished friendship to a juddering halt. So I dropped it.

Someone else in the Labour world whom I now got to know and who was to play an even larger part in my life than Douglas was Michael Foot. Our first meeting arose in 1981, at a time when Michael's leadership of a demoralised Labour Party was widely derided. He was the scruffy, long-haired Worzel Gummidge, the unworldly bookish socialist who fell down steps and wore a donkey jacket at the Cenotaph on Remembrance Sunday (the Queen Mother liked the jacket, by the way). I wrote a rare sympathetic piece about him in the *Times Literary Supplement* for John Gross, and then received a very warm letter from Michael's wife Jill Craigie, inviting Jane and me to dinner in Pilgrims Lane in Hampstead, just down the road from UCS, and hinting very strongly that she would like me to write Michael's biography. It was a quite fascinating evening, with much focus on books. Jill showed Jane her remarkable archive on the suffragettes on whom she was working, a veritable shrine to feminism, while Michael introduced me to some of his own library – far more literary than political as I recall. He showed me two rare books, by William Morris and Robert Blatchford, editor of the Independent Labour Party (ILP) newspaper the *Clarion*, and then, to my astonishment, even alarm, gave them to me. He was always, I found, an exceptionally generous and civilised man. In return I sent him a copy of the famous South Wales tract of 1912 on workers' power, *The Miners' Next Step*. But nothing was said about my being his biographer, nor did the subject arise on any of the many subsequent social occasions we had with Michael and Jill in Hampstead and in Long Hanborough. In the end, Jill asked Mervyn Jones to write it; he produced, I thought, a very decent book, but Jill apparently did not like it at all. There was, for me, a quite moving sequel. In 1997, at a dinner to celebrate the centenary of Aneurin Bevan's birth, Jill came up to me. I had not seen her for some time and she looked old and ill. She said to me, with no explanation necessary, 'You know, Ken, I made the wrong decision some years ago.' I felt very touched and said something about it not being too late and I could still do it. Soon after, dear Jill died. But, in 2002, I did take up Michael's biography and published the volume, which gave me deep personal satisfaction, in 2007 when Michael was almost 94. I felt that in completing it I was fulfilling my trust to Jill, a brave and brilliant socialist and feminist.

My first real work of Labour history had already appeared. It was one of my most important books, published in 1975 with Weidenfeld and Nicolson, with the highly significant title (which annoyed some on the far left) *Keir Hardie: Radical and Socialist*. The idea was suggested to me by my friend and former

D.Phil. examiner, Pat Thompson, and I worked on it with mounting fascination for around four years. I had already written a small book for Oxford University Press on Hardie in 1967 while, as I have said, 'The Merthyr of Keir Hardie' two years earlier was one of my most memorable lecturing experiences, so I had some background. In 1966, while giving my parents a first visit to Scotland, I had actually visited Hardie's home in Cumnock in Ayrshire, and was given a memorable tour of the house by Mrs Emrys Hughes, who was in fact Hardie's daughter, Nan. She showed me some fascinating mementoes, such as a walking stick given Hardie by Gandhi and a table he received from the ILP in 1914, which I hope are now all safely preserved somewhere.

Working on Hardie entailed strenuous research on a wide array of sources, and in many lands. The grimmest location was the British newspaper library at Colindale, a dim enclave in north London stuck between two far nicer areas, Edgware and Hendon. The possibilities of food nearby were almost nil, the staff could be surly, the building was cold. I worked there with an old Indian friend, Partha Gupta, once of the Oxford Labour Club, and we agreed it was a bit like enduring an academic Passchendaele. But the Scottish and other newspapers there were wonderful, a unique source for the early Independent Labour Party. I particularly enjoyed the *Ardrossan and Saltcoats Herald*, in which Hardie himself had written a column in his youth. The most enjoyable experience in my research was visiting Edinburgh to work mainly in the National Library of Scotland, which had all the friendliness of the National Library of Wales. I met there for the first time an important friend, Chris Harvie, a brilliant Scottish historian with an immense intellectual range, then in the Open University and later to be a professor at Tübingen in Germany and elected a Scottish MSP. I also spent time in Edinburgh with an Oxford friend, Paul Addison, who was to write a marvellous work, *The Road to 1945*, before tutoring Gordon Brown, and it was a lovely visit in which I stayed in the former Commonwealth Games athletes village. In the National Library of Scotland I found some extraordinary love letters from Hardie to a young socialist girl in Oxford, the daughter of a chimney sweep. This was a recurrent theme with Hardie, including his passionate affair with his mistress, the suffragette Sylvia Pankhurst, which Jane and I found in the Socialist International Library in Amsterdam (a lovely trip, which we made our second honeymoon). Another wonderful experience was working in West Kirby, on the Wirral, in the home of an impressive ship-owner named Malcolm Bruce Glasier, on the rich papers of his father J. Bruce Glasier, who had been a pioneer socialist along with his wife, Katherine. They are now in a university library – but, as at Plas Penucha in Flintshire years before, working in someone's home added an extra dimension of intimacy with such sources.

Other important materials turned up variously in Transport House, in Oxford, in Cambridge, Cardiff and elsewhere, with some bits and pieces in New

York, in Ottawa and in Copenhagen. I had to travel almost as widely as Hardie himself, who went on a world tour in 1907; but, unlike him, I neither provoked riots, nor was I threatened with deportation. One amazing piece of evidence came from the world of spiritualism; I read a document on Hardie's turning up in a séance in July 1945, to give his (rather guarded) views on the problems confronting the new Labour government. It was difficult to know what to make of this. Of course, spiritualism was an important element for many pioneer socialists, including Hardie himself who had a profoundly mystical side. I had also had some marvellous interviews notably with the octogenarian Fenner Brockway, who had interviewed Hardie in 1906 and later was close to him in the ILP. Brockway's acute observations gave me a sense of Hardie that I found nowhere else – for instance, Hardie told Brockway at a Labour Party conference in 1911, 'Young man, that was a very good speech. But it was an ILP speech not a Labour Party speech.' There was wisdom there.

The most extraordinary aspect of the sources concerned the papers of the Independent Labour Party, a great party before 1914 but now a tiny fragment run by a few old men from a room in King's Cross. There was much dispute about their ownership, and multi-party litigation ensued, involving the Labour Party, the rump of the ILP, the family of the former secretary Jim Middleton and various others. Even Harold Wilson was somehow dragged in. More disturbingly, there was even a case of assault on the archivist of the ILP, who was seriously beaten up by a distinguished historian, perhaps during an epileptic attack. I had no idea that research could be physically dangerous. I was particularly sorry in this instance because the archivist victim had been especially good to me, bringing up materials to Oxford for me to look through (perhaps that was why he was attacked). It suggested, admittedly in rather extreme form, the legal and other problems that could underlie academic research. When I edited the Lloyd George letters in 1972, there had been serious dispute between the co-owners, the Beaverbrook Trust and the National Library of Wales, a dispute which at one time seemed likely to prevent publication at all. It made me feel that actually writing a book was the easy part.

My book came out in the spring of 1975, at a time of crisis in the industrial world which perhaps added to the interest. My conclusions were very different from those of earlier writers who had seen Hardie as just a class warrior, fighting on his own for Labour's independence. The history was different. He was a *fin de siècle* Bohemian. He had not even worn a cloth cap on entry to parliament, but rather a deerstalker like that of Sherlock Holmes. I found him a man who was not only an idealistic crusader, but a pragmatist, anxious to work with radical Liberals whose ideology he largely shared, subtle in building up the Labour alliance with the trade unions and the other socialist bodies, and supremely flexible in his political philosophy, a very generalised socialism based on a secularised Christianity rather than Marxism. 'Socialists,' he proclaimed, 'made war on a system not a class.' Caroline Benn, a charming woman, year later came to Aberystwyth to consult me. Her book is somewhat critical of me for taking so pragmatic and non-doctrinaire a view of Hardie; but I think that her half-Marxist view, though based on wide research, is simply old-fashioned and does not fit the facts.

On the other hand, I found so much to admire in Hardie's courageous devotion to principle. So many of the themes he took up were morally right and became the conventional wisdom later on: policies on unemployment and the minimum wage; devolution for Scotland and Wales ('The Red Dragon and the Red Flag'); equality for women; an end to racial discrimination, and colonial liberation. Only his dedication to the peace movement remains an unfulfilled objective: here he was close to being a total pacifist. Hardie also exemplified the early socialist ideal of being an internationalist, a citizen of the world. He had profound insights here. He was one of the very few critics to see that the much-praised Union of South Africa Bill in 1910 actually made the position of the black majority much worse, especially in Natal and the Cape Colony. His vision, like much of that of the ILP, was pluralist. His idea of a liberated, locally-based yet outward-looking social democracy, seems to me more acceptable than the centralised, nationally-focused approach of the Labour Party after 1945, just as the working-class democratic socialism of the ILP proved more visionary yet also more realistic than the middle-class intellectuals of the Fabian Society. An uneducated miner, who had worked in the Lanarkshire pits at the age of ten and taught himself Pitman's shorthand by scratching a slate with the wick of a miners' lamp, showed more long-term insight than Sidney and Beatrice Webb. Perhaps in 2015 the Labour Party is edging back uncertainly towards the more democratic socialism of Hardie and his comrades. After my working on his career, Hardie seemed to me greater than ever. He was no economist and was ill-informed on many issues, but he had uniquely the charisma and vision that any radical movement needs.

My book received again a very positive reception. Alan Taylor in the *Observer*, and Asa Briggs in the *Times Literary Supplement*, were highly enthusiastic and I was very proud to have the acclaim of these great men. Another enthusiast was Leo Abse in the *Spectator*, who hailed my book as the chronicle of a real hero – very different from the view he would take of *Rebirth of a Nation* six years later, when my alleged Welsh nationalism (news to me) annoyed him. One or two far-left reviewers were a bit grumpy, and in puritanical vein suggested that my treatment of the Hardie-Pankhurst relationship was prurient. I felt that it was fascinating to explore this intense physical relationship between Labour's founder and the famous suffragette, and that it explained a lot politically and did credit to them both. I was awarded an Arts Council prize for the book. An enjoyable part of publication was taking part in a live discussion on an independent television channel with the nonagenarian Manny Shinwell. At first, he was cross that I had not interviewed him in researching the book. But, once we were on air, he waved my book before the cameras and declared it to be 'a grrr-eat book' which everyone should buy. He was an astonishing personality, extraordinarily alert for a man of his great age and, of course, he was to become a centenarian.

All in all, the writing and the reception of my biography of Hardie were highly enjoyable. They gave me a new kind of persona as a historian of Labour. I now published in the *Journal of Labour History* and enjoyed a close association with John Saville, a staunch Marxist and ex-Communist, but also a fine scholar whom I advised on the *Dictionary of Labour Biography*. My new interests also had some little impact higher up the social scale. In 1981, to mark the 75th anniversary of the founding of the Historical Association, I was one of a number of historians dispatched to give lectures on Edwardian Britain: I went to Bristol. The finale was a glorious lecture by Alan Taylor himself in a livery hall near St Paul's in the presence of the Queen. And so, I met Her Majesty. She asked me on what I had lectured; delivered with a heavy heart, my first word to her was 'Socialism'. After a pause, she then shrewdly observed, 'They must have been highly motivated'. I was then slightly flummoxed myself, before suggesting, which I thought might strike the right note, that many of them were inspired by a belief in Christianity – a slightly sticky, though in its way memorable, exchange. I have a photograph of Jane looking terrified in the background, knowing that my views, like Hardie's, were republican. Still, to embark on my only conversation with the Queen, with 'Socialism' the first word being uttered, had its piquant side.

These years were a phase of my life which both professionally and personally seemed to be particularly fulfilling. Then everything changed, and I was plunged into a deep sadness, perhaps the saddest period of my life. On 13 May 1978, two days after his eighty-fourth birthday, my father died of pancreatic cancer in Bronglais Hospital, Aberystwyth. He had been alert and active until after his eighty-third birthday, still enjoying his visits to read in the National Library of Wales before going into a rapid decline, and the end was brief. I felt totally desolate. The great guide and inspiration of my life was no more. The fact that Jane found it difficult to respond to my sense of loss made matters worse. I wandered around Oxford in a daze, and experienced a number of psychosomatic ailments. I was an examiner in the History schools that year, and I found the often bad-tempered examiners' discussions a real strain. There was now also the worrying problem of what to do about my mother, now in her late seventies. My father's influence on me, on my ideas and way of life, had been incalculable. Right down to his eighties, he was working in the National Library for me on Welsh-language newspapers and periodicals that would help me with my planned book on modern Wales. He was the sharpest, kindest research assistant anyone could want. As a family, Jane, the children and I went on summer holiday to Normandy, but I came back feeling as low in spirits as before. Things only got better when I went back to Queen's and stayed there, starting to write *Consensus and Disunity*. The book's warm reception, I felt, was a kind of posthumous tribute to my father for all he had given me in my academic and personal life. After his death, even with a loving family, I felt lost and alone.

However, I went on to engage in a further intensive spate of writing, which diverted my mind and helped me recover my composure. It helped that we managed to find a residential home for my mother overlooking the sea and the promenade in Aberystwyth, while my cousin Anne and her husband Ivor, living nearby, were kindness itself. So, between 1975 and 1987, I published ten books, most of them big ones, in those twelve years. Another lengthy book followed on in 1990. I am not quite sure at this distance of quite how and when I managed to write them, with so many varied responsibilities – it was, I think, largely in college when I was not teaching, and of course during vacations.

After *Consensus and Disunity*, a quite different kind of project came in 1980. I wrote a book with Jane. It was based on her external doctoral thesis at the University of Leicester, for which I had effectively been the supervisor; Jane never actually went to Leicester at all. The subject of study was Christopher, Viscount Addison (1869–1951), whose papers were in the Bodleian and who had figured prominently in *Consensus and Disunity*. He was the only real radical among the Lloyd George Liberals. A distinguished anatomist, the most eminent doctor ever to enter the Commons, Addison worked hard to promote the National Insurance scheme in 1911. Lloyd George made him the first Minister of Health during the wartime coalition, and Addison started up the first programme of publicly-funded local authority housing schemes with his Housing Act of 1919. He and Lloyd George then brutally fell out. Uniquely, Addison then joined the Labour Party, becoming a minister, and led the protests in the Cabinet against MacDonald in the financial crisis of 1931. After 1945, Addison became a close friend of Attlee, Dominions Secretary and leader of the Lords, where he and Lord Salisbury worked out the Salisbury-Addison agreement to ensure that measures which carried an electoral mandate would safely pass into law. He was thus the only man to serve in both post-war governments, and he saw out all six years of Attlee's government before his death. It was a remarkable career and yet little known, since Addison was a quiet, uncharismatic man, rather like Attlee, who seldom hit the headlines. I found him fascinating. As his Cabinet colleague Harold Wilson said when we interviewed him at Westminster, Addison was 'a wise old man'.

I thought that at least we would not encounter the extra-mural problems of previous books, but I was wrong. There was acute tension between Addison's daughter from his first marriage, a woman of the radical left who demonstrated at Greenham Common, and his widow and second wife, the daughter of a Conservative election agent. Naturally, there were completely different aspects of Addison's career that they wished to have commemorated, and they controlled the copyright of the papers. Lady Addison in particular was a difficult old soul – Jane once conscripted Katherine as a beautiful little girl in a pink dress to give Lady Addison some strawberries. She enjoyed the strawberries, but remained as intransigent as before. In the end, it was a case of publish and be damned. Our book, to a degree, marks the characteristics of joint authorship – I decided afterwards that it was best not to write with someone else, even if you were married to them. Oxford University Press did not take as much care as before with the printing, and made some errors. Nevertheless, the book still got many excellent reviews, including one by my loyal supporter, Max Beloff. Many readers were struck by the kaleidoscopic nature of Addison's long career, as first a leading Liberal and then Labour. On health and housing under Lloyd George, on agricultural policy under MacDonald in 1930–1, and in managing the Lords under a Labour administration, Addison was a brilliantly constructive minister and a genuine radical pioneer. I look back fondly on researching his career with Jane. Our living room has a portrait of him that his widow consented to give us, along with a photo portrait of Addison at the 1946 Commonwealth prime ministers' conference, with Attlee, Smuts, Mackenzie King, Herbert Evatt and Walter Nash – a fine, impressive group of statesmen in Britain's last imperial phase, with Addison as a grand Edwardian survivor.

One fascinating episode in our research had been the interview with Harold Wilson. The former prime minister was exceptionally friendly. I noticed that, like most men, he particularly enjoyed talking to Jane. He preferred to spend time chatting to us rather than attending a debate in the Commons on the evasion of oil sanctions against Rhodesia which was being discussed, and his preference was understandable. I saw Harold Wilson at various times later on, and he was always most approachable. The last time was desperately sad, at a book launch in the Lords when his Alzheimer's had clearly set in. It was tragic to see that fine mind and powerful memory so broken. At least my friend Ben Pimlott's fine biography gave Wilson a worthy memorial, as did that of Philip Ziegler also.

I followed *Addison* with a little book for the University of Wales's St David's Day series, a bilingual volume on David Lloyd George with the English text on one page and the Welsh text on the facing page. I wrote it in a week, but I do not think it would have been any better had I taken a year on it. The amusing feature for me was that the Welsh text proved to be several pages longer than the English, but it was a nice thing to do and the schools seemed to like it.

Also on that St David's Day, 1 March 1981, I published a really major book which particularly meant a great deal to me, since it was in part the product of my father's research on my behalf. I dedicated the book to him, and with great feeling. For that and other reasons, it is the most personal book I have written and the one about which I feel most emotional. John Gross had told me it would be my best book because more of me would go into it, and he may have been right. The book followed the film producer D. W. Griffith, and it was called *Rebirth of a Nation*, a 450-page account of the history of Wales from 1880 to 1980, from the 1868 'great election' to the dawn of devolution, Gladstone to Gwynfor Evans. It was supposed to be the final volume in The Oxford History of Wales series edited by Glanmor Williams, but two of the authors predictably never delivered and the others took their time, so I got on with my own book as a stand-alone work, and published it six years before the next author delivered. Although written entirely in Oxford, it is a distillation of all the work I had done on modern Wales since I began my thesis in 1955, so it had a long ancestry of a quarter of a century's labour. Not only does it include a much far longer span than *Wales in British Politics*, but naturally covers a far wider thematic range. I sought to write a total history, finding a valuable example of the genre in F. S. L. Lyons's *Ireland since the Famine*, a comprehensive survey by a great Irish historian whom I later got to know quite well. In addition to political matters to which I gave high priority, I also covered in depth economic developments, social change (including religion and also some sport) and, for the first time, literary and cultural aspects covering works in both the Welsh and English languages. Welsh linguistic and literary themes were a quite new area for me, and I had valuable advice, which I greatly appreciated, from my good friend Professor Ellis Evans, formerly of Swansea and later Professor of Celtic Studies at Oxford, who died in late 2013. One generous reviewer, Professor John Vincent of Bristol, was later to write, 'If this is total history, let us have more of it.'

I used, inevitably, an immense range of source materials, dozens of manuscript collections in Aberystwyth and elsewhere, including now much from the Lloyd George Papers, fascinating government material in the Public Record Office, many official records, some interview material and, of course, a huge array of newspapers and journals, academic and literary. Here, as I have already noted, I was greatly helped by my father's devoted note-taking on my behalf from Welsh-language periodicals, material that I was quite unable to find in the Bodleian in Oxford. And, of course, the work was based also on my own relation to Wales, a land which I knew in its entirety now – my relative ignorance of Wrexham and the north-east had been remedied by the good fortune of my marriage to Jane. I felt I knew Wales through and through, its secret corners and private by-ways as well as its formal institutions; I believed I had followed G. M. Trevelyan's injunction to the social historian and pulled my boots on.

The account I provided in *Rebirth of a Nation* had three phases. Down to the outbreak of world war in 1914, it was a broad story of regeneration and progress after the almost humiliating obscurity of the mid-nineteenth-century when the notorious entry in an edition of the *Encyclopaedia Britannica* read 'For Wales – see England'. In the later-Victorian and Edwardian periods, it was a story of growing political democracy with the hegemony of the Liberals in national and local government, of an increasingly thriving economy in the valleys of south Wales, the world's dominant coal-exporting area with massive ports at Cardiff and Barry, an increasingly buoyant literature and a revival in the *eisteddfod*, and of much vitality in the nonconformist chapels especially after the short-lived impetus from the 'great revival', *Y Diwygiad Mawr*, of 1904–5. Overall, there was a pervasive sense of strong national identity, with a national museum, a national library and a national university as its vanguard. In the second phase, from 1914–45, there was an abrupt and corrosive change. The First World War was an ordeal not only for the loss of life, but for the startling collapse of economic life in south Wales and much resultant social deprivation. The war also saw the downfall of Lloyd George's Liberal Party and the concordant national revival of pre-1914. The Welsh-speaking world went into retreat, though there was powerful compensation in the proliferating Anglo-Welsh poetry and prose of Dylan Thomas and many others. The Second World War brought more upheaval, though also the birth of a revival of the south Wales economy through the stimulus provided by the Board of Trade (notably by my old friend Douglas Jay, working under Hugh Dalton).

The final phase after 1945 I saw as one of broad renewal, political resurgence under the Labour Party and unions, a marked revival of economic growth, with much great material affluence and social welfare. The final period saw a phenomenon little in evidence before 1939, a strong movement towards political nationalism, some success for Plaid Cymru and, after the Kilbrandon Commission, a major attempt to pass Welsh devolution. It was heavily rejected in the referendum of 1979, but I still felt justified in using the title *Rebirth of a Nation* if one looked at the overall course of events during that century. Two major periods I emphasised: one was the Edwardian high noon prior to 1914 which, in a Gibbonian conceit, I termed Wales's Antonine Age; and the other the period of turmoil and disillusion of 1918–22, which happened also to be Lloyd George's last major stand. I still feel these to be key periods in the historical experience of modern Wales, even with the new elements introduced by devolution after 1997 and forces in the twenty-first century including, of course, globalisation.

I felt both professionally pleased and personally reborn myself after writing *Rebirth*. It is still a book I feel proud of. It covers many themes new to me, but ones much illuminated by younger historians, some of whom had been my pupils – scholars like Dai Smith, Peter Stead, David Howell, Bill Lambert and Hywel Francis, whose subjects ranged from rugby to agriculture. The book attracted a swathe of reviews, nearly all highly favourable. One I particularly enjoyed was by an old friend, Owen Dudley Edwards, a famous Irishman, who wrote a warm and appreciative review but also suggested, I am sure correctly, that some of my remarks on Scotland were less than sound. So he wrote the marvellous phrase, 'There is no need for young Lochinvar to work overtime.' The only hostile review that I recall was the one previously noted by Leo Abse, a dogged opponent of nationalists and devolutionists of all kinds, who had decided that I was myself a nationalist after taking part with me in a radio debate on devolution. He damned me from the start, with little regard to fact; for instance, he claimed that I omitted any discussion of the National Health Service, which was certainly not the case. Almost everybody else proved very supportive; Bernard Crick declared it to be one of his books of the year, and I won a second prize from the Arts Council. Academic colleagues were very generous, including the ever loyal Max Beloff. I think *Rebirth* is one of my best books, though perhaps too patriotic-eulogistic to be completely objective. Then again, my sense of commitment I think gives it some warmth. The one area to which I gave inadequate emphasis, was the history of women in modern Wales, something of a gap in my work at that period though not, I think, later when I discussed a possible book on Labour women with my Lords colleague Pat Hollis. I have not attempted to write anything quite like *Rebirth* since. Oxford University Press has been keen for me to revise it, taking on the story to the present day; of course, the advent of devolution following on the traumas of the Thatcher years would provide a very different picture, and it has been tempting to revise the work. But, on balance, I have felt inclined to leave it as it is, a story of a particularly dramatic phase of my nation covering clearly-defined themes, and written from a particular perspective at a particular time; that of the decline of the old regime from Cymru Fydd to Old Labour, which had yielded so much. It is a story of a fairly self-contained phase of Welsh greatness, when a nation perhaps achieved maturity, and perhaps a particular phase of my achievement as well, both as a historian and a son.

From writing the history of a small nation, my next project was far wider, the history of Britain as whole from the Romans to the present day. My Oxford University Press editor, Ivon Asquith, invited me to go with him to see the first proofs emerge from the presses in Frome in Somerset, but regrettably my tutorial commitments prevented it. This was to prove easily my most successful book in commercial terms. It was the *Oxford Illustrated History of Britain*, a magnificently produced volume by Oxford University Press published in May 1984, on my birthday, with a non-illustrated version following soon afterwards. I edited this book and chose the contributors. It proved to a publishing success that dwarfed everything else I ever did – for one glorious, unique week in the summer of 1984, it topped the best sellers list, very rare for an academic work written by academics. I found myself sneaking ahead of Margaret Drabble's history of English Literature. The Oxford Broad Street throughout the summer of 1984 seemed to be full of Americans and other tourists staggering away from Blackwells with multiple copies of that bulky volume. At the present moment, it is reckoned to have sold over a million copies – some, it is true, in book club form, which yields hardly any financial reward. The book is known all over the world, and was well-known by my students since many of them had received it as a book prize at school. With the worldwide strength of OUP as a publishing house, I have seen it on the shelves of bookshops in Cape Town, Sydney, Ottawa, Kuala Lumpur, New Delhi and New York; it has been translated into Italian, French, Russian, Japanese and Korean. Of these, the Italian paperback version did especially well, and my children were excited to see it on sale in places like Lucca and Ancona. Perhaps symbolically, the beautifully printed French version sold hardly at all, and is mainly notable for the complete mess the French version made of my carefully crafted passages on cricket (Jack Hobbs regrettably became Hoobs).

The *Oxford History of Britain* has gone through many editions, the most recent being that in 2010, which meant updating it and, in effect, updating myself since I wrote the final chapter on post-1914 Britain, ending originally in 1983, and now with Gordon Brown's premiership just before his fall. When I was first asked by Ivon Asquith to edit such a book, I actually said no because, apart from having many other commitments as a tutor and a father, I was also heavily engaged in writing a big book for OUP on the Labour government of 1945–51. But Jane persuaded me, wisely, to think again. She correctly argued that I would much enjoy doing it, and perhaps thought as well that it would bring greater fame and fortune, which it did. It was one of very many areas where she showed better judgement than I did. So I agreed to be editor, and later took on myself the chapter on the twentieth century when my friend, Stephen Koss, whom I had originally invited to write it, felt he had too many other commitments to complete the chapter. So, I found myself leading from the front, albeit with the final chapter.

The *Oxford Illustrated History of Britain* apparently became the prototype for a long list of illustrated books of that type to be published by OUP. It became known in the trade simply as 'Morgan'. It is interesting to speculate precisely why it has proved so phenomenally successful, easily outstripping the total sales of every other book I have written. I can take the credit for one thing:

like the coach of a successful Welsh rugby team, I chose good players, perhaps the best. Of my nine colleagues, every one was a productive scholar of high repute, an excellent writer and totally reliable in delivery. Five of them – my Queen's colleague John Blair, Ralph Griffiths, Paul Langford, Chris Harvie and Colin Matthew – were close personal friends and had been for many years. Their scholarship was pellucid and they delivered their judgements with intellectual power, fairness and some humour. They produced powerfully written texts which met the still strongly-felt need for an authoritative one-volume survey of Britain – all components of it – its influence, its empire, its historical evolution and contribution to world civilisation. The sales spoke for themselves. There was little editorial intervention required on each of the authors' chapters, and they delivered smartly on time. They met their deadlines so well that we actually came out in May, in place of the originally scheduled publication in October. But, of course, immense credit must go to the mighty OUP, and to its history editor, my old friend Ivon Asquith, with whom I had many former and future collaborations. Never were the resources of this vast sprawling publishing house, which could sometimes seem almost to lose a work inside its vast machinery, seen to better advantage. The printing, the colour illustrations, very much the picture captions (an important part of the book), the tables, the maps, the index and, not least, the marketing were all brilliant, close to being faultless. When it all works, OUP still seems to me not just the biggest press in the world but the very best, and it has been an honour to publish with them so many times. Oxford's press famously always received massive profits from its dictionaries and its bibles – but, running very close behind them, if not overtaking them in the book's early days, was the work of a distinctly more secular author, K. O. Morgan, and his merry men.

Despite all this endeavour, I was still mainly focused in my mind at this period on labour history. I had contracted with OUP in 1980 or thereabouts a substantial monograph on Attlee's Labour government of 1945–51. The attractions of this project were many. The records were now becoming available, year by year, under the thirty-year rule, and I was one of many who would speed down the M4 to the new Public Record Office at the New Year's first opportunity to see what treasures the latest haul would yield. In fact, I found the records of the Attlee government to be excellent, much better than those of the Lloyd George government earlier on or, indeed, the Churchill government that followed. Attlee's own papers, in the PREM (Prime Minister's personal) files were of absorbing interest, while both committee papers and the full Cabinet minutes were remarkably complete. On such important matters as the debates on the American loan in December 1945; the arguments over steel nationalisation in 1947; the transfer of power in India; or the passionate disputes over the rearmament budget and consequent cuts in the Health Service in March 1951, which led to the resignation of Aneurin Bevan, the record gave the views of individual ministers by name and in full. Pivotal matters in modern British history could be examined in detail as never before. The one significant exception was the GEN 75 Cabinet committee, which met in late 1946 and the start of 1947, and whose proceedings were recorded in brief, almost in obscurity. This was the committee, dominated by an emotional Ernest Bevin, which committed Britain to producing the atomic bomb and a nuclear weapons programme. In the instance of GEN 75, the right to know did not seem to apply.

But my decision to write the book was not only the product of exciting new sources becoming available. It was partly a response also to intense public interest in the Labour Party in power during its heyday after 1945, at a time when the troubled and divided Party of the early 1980s seemed cast into perhaps irreparable decay and decline. It was also the result of my own earlier work as a historian. I was anxious to complement my previous book on the post-war government and social change in 1918–22 with the experience of another, very different post-war government after 1945. I had had some insight into these comparative features in writing my book on modern Wales and, of course, in writing with Jane on Lord Addison, the one Cabinet minister who served both with his erstwhile inspiration Lloyd George after 1918 and his great friend Attlee after 1945. Another factor that appealed in a way was that here was a book on a later historical period, which for the first time I had wholly lived through. The tensions, the austerity and the achievements of that unique time in our history was still fresh in my mind. In general I felt enthusiastic about this period of my childhood, and I was anxious to see why many other historians seemed to be so negative about it.

My book, of course, was the product of an immense range of sources, manuscript collections great and small. I found much of interest in the papers of such relatively lesser figures as the Colonial Secretary Arthur Creech Jones, and of the Euro-federalist R. W. G. Mackay; by contrast, such giants as Ernest Bevin or Aneurin Bevan appeared to have left virtually nothing. There were mountains of newspapers, and pamphlets on policy and strategy that could be weighed by the ton. I even read what Manny Shinwell claimed to be the one policy document he found in the filing cabinets of Transport House when he became Minister of Fuel and Power, bent on nationalising the coal mines – a Welsh-language pamphlet by James Griffiths titled *Glo* (Coal). But the foundations of my research were two mighty elements: the Public Records at Kew, and the papers of the Labour Party at that time held in the party offices in Walworth Road.

Kew, as I have indicated, was of course a priceless store of knowledge. I found following the various crises documented there to be almost unbearably exciting. I became particularly absorbed – as reviewers noticed – in the conflict between Hugh Gaitskell and Aneurin Bevan over the defence budget and cuts in the Health Serice in early 1951. The debates, as stated, were fully recorded. What was fascinating to me was to see how Gaitskell the economist and alleged calculating machine, and Bevan the supposed demagogic, romantic Welshman, came across. It seemed to me that it was in fact Gaitskell who was to prove the emotional romantic, with his determination to stand with the Americans (rather like Tony Blair over Iraq in 2003) whatever the social or economic consequences at home, whereas Bevan produced a cogent series of economic objections to the scale of rearmament demanded – the effect on exports, the prospects for inflation, shortages of raw material, bottlenecks in the labour market, the shortage of machine tools and other matters. Bevan argued that the scale of rearmament being called for by Gaitskell and his allies was simply more than the country could afford. When I spoke years later to Lord Bancroft, who worked on the Defence budget in the Treasury in late 1951 after Churchill had returned to office as prime minister, he was quite clear on one thing – Bevan was right and Gaitskell was wrong. Churchill himself became the ultimate Bevanite by scaling back the defence budget decisively. In addition, the right-wing diarists like Gordon Walker were quite wrong in alleging that Bevan's opposition to the rearmament programme came out of the blue. On the contrary, Bevan had argued cogently against it in two crucial Cabinet debates, on 1 August 1950 and on 2 January 1951, and nobody could be in any doubt as to where he stood on the matter. There had in fact been a campaign of disinformation by anti-Bevanite Labour ministers thereafter. One of my distinguished Oxford colleagues and friends refused to acknowledge all this even when I sent him photocopies of my notes from the Public Record Office. This was one area where reviewers noted that I had challenged the conventional wisdom from the public records; in fact, in my view, I had destroyed it, and Bevan's reputation in this area had been fully restored. In writing a careful account based on the national archive, I had also vindicated a great socialist hero.

My other great resource was the official archive of the Labour Party. It was then piled up in party offices in Walworth Road, and is now beautifully preserved in the People's History Museum in Manchester. The work I made of it was immensely assisted by the presence of Stephen Bird, its official archivist and one of those unique scholarly advisers you feel should be due for an Order of Merit, perhaps as a hero of Labour. Stephen was a modest man, so professional and skilled was his work in sorting out the Labour Party archive, who once told me he was often consulted for advice on how to do it by the Conservatives in Smith Square. I worked at Smith Square myself, and it was certainly not as efficiently organised as was the Labour archive under Stephen's unerring hand. It was an exciting time to be working in Walworth Road. My research visits often coincided with stirring meetings of the Party's National

Executive there, and in the corridor I would often pass key participants like Tony Benn or Eric Heffer. The Labour Party archives were in themselves thrilling enough. I was especially struck by the general secretary Morgan Phillips's papers, with their bulky files of critical or dissenting letters and memoranda from party members destined to be shoved under the table, if not under the carpet, at conference time. Phillips also had envelopes headed 'Lost Sheep' detailing the misdeamours of rebels of various kinds, some of them leading to disciplinary action and even expulsion in relation to some far-left deviants like John Platts-Mills, D. N. Pritt and Konni Zilliacus, but most were left to wander off unharmed like the strays of Bo Peep. A watchful eye was always kept on the free expression of opinion among the grass roots. There was much important material on the formulation of party policy, and I recall some important discussions on foreign policy, ranging from the Schuman Plan in Europe to the Middle and Far East, in which the young Denis Healey at the start of his career and not yet an MP was an important player.

The book, *Labour in Power 1945–1951*, attracted a very great number of reviews. Henry Pelling, my predecessor at Queen's, also wrote a scholarly book on the Attlee government, but it was too dour to arouse the same level of interest. A range of important scholars – Asa Briggs, Ben Pimlott (later to become a very close friend), Paul Addison, Peter Clarke – were all highly complimentary. One exception was Edward Thompson, who wrote a bad-tempered Marxist complaint that I had totally failed to see the upsurge of socialist revolution in Britain in 1945, and how a right-wing Labour government had suppressed it. This had been the refrain of an earlier doctrinaire book by a highly intelligent scholar, Ralph Miliband, *Parliamentary Socialism*.

The Attlee government had significant shortcomings, as I have noted above. When it fell from office, the economy was still in a precarious state and Britain's international commitment much over-extended by the worldwide role it felt obliged to play. Even so, at the end of my work, I felt – much as I had done as a seventeen-year-old schoolboy in 1951 – full of awe at the government's achievement, the significant reconstruction after the colossal ravages of world war, the building up of a fairer society and a durable welfare state, its international role in trying to preserve stability in key areas, and its historic decision to grant independence to India and its neighbours, and to proceed upon a path of colonial liberation. I felt, and feel now, that it genuinely tried to create a sense of national solidarity, and to do so not through cautious timidity but through bold and radical policies among which the National Health Service stands out. There has been no other Labour government remotely like it, and Attlee, despite limitations which I detail in my book, deserves his stature as one of Britain's greatest premiers. In 2013, I took part with Melvyn Bragg, Joan Bakewell and David Putnam, in a panel for the edification of the Labour peers, who were

Kenneth O. Morgan

waiting for a late vote, to discuss Ken Loach's film *The Legend of '45*. The film movingly depicts perhaps in over-romantic terms the social achievements of that democratic socialist moment in our history. Less acceptable is the latter part of the film, where Tony Benn and other well-known regular critics talk of how the outcome was class betrayal and surrender by spineless leaders, then and subsequently. Their conclusion seems to me unbalanced, both measured against the historic circumstances in which Attlee and his team found themselves mired, and against the legacy which, with all the inroads from Margaret Thatcher and others, remains as a basic component of British civilisation and an inspiration for the world down to our own times. Attlee's government was one of our greatest, and I am proud to have been its chronicler.

I had one other major contribution to make to Labour history in this period. This was a volume *Labour People* published by Oxford University Press in 1987, a study of a range of Labour figures from pioneers like Keir Hardie, Ramsay MacDonald and Arthur Henderson at the time of the party's foundation in 1906, down to such figures as Denis Healey, Roy Hattersley and Neil Kinnock in the modern period. Some were updated versions of reviews I had written in the *Times Literary Supplement* and elsewhere; one of these was my piece on Michael Foot, which had attracted the attention of Jill Craigie in 1981. The majority were written up for the book, and I rattled it off during a summer term's sabbatical leave, sometimes completing a chapter a day. As before, I felt the finished work was better for it, with momentum more important than long contemplation of individual paragraphs or even words. Some of my character sketches were based on personal knowledge, such as those of Rita Hinden and Neil Kinnock. I began with a paradox. The Labour Party, which prides itself on common endeavour rather than the cult of the individual, and whose conference claims to be a grassroots forum rather than an opportunity for the leader to address the rank and file on the saluting base, has nevertheless undoubtedly a tradition of leadership, even a cult of personality. The leaders take many different forms – professional politicians, union leaders, local government bosses, influential intellectuals – all of these types are represented in my book, where I also try to create a typology of Labour leadership and compare it with that in other parties and other countries. No-one who has written on Keir Hardie could fail to miss Labour's near-worship of dominant individuals. Having also written on Aneurin Bevan, I again find it blindingly obvious. This phenomenon reached a new level under Tony Blair, for a long while the most powerful leader that Labour had ever had. Blair made a political virtue of it, too – in 1996 he told the hapless John Major from the dispatch box ,'You follow your party, I lead mine.'As Alan Taylor would say, this was indeed one of history's'curious twists'.

My thirty or so leading figures are a mixed bag. They include not only mainstream personalities, Cabinet ministers and the like, but also some conspicuous rebels – Victor Grayson, Noah Ablett, Tony Benn. Others might have been added – Richard Crossman, Barbara Castle and Jack Jones in more recent years would have been obvious contenders. But I felt that my Labour people were sufficiently varied and in a way also sufficiently representative. I felt they showed the Labour Party in its true light – a coalition, a mosaic, a miscellany drawn from different classes and social groups, not an inward-looking body from which class outsiders would or should be excluded. Labour history was only intelligible if it was seen as part of history as a whole. The book was launched with a splendid party in the House of Commons, at which the speakers – Douglas Jay, Michael Foot and Neil Kinnock – were all in fine form. Douglas, ever a wry critic of the oratorical excesses of the Welsh, said that I combined Celtic imagination with Anglo-Saxon regard for fact. Michael made merry with the House of Lords. It was particularly good to have Neil speaking there. He looked relaxed and cheerful as he seldom did around the time of the general election of 1987, when he was being virulently attacked by the right-wing tabloid press. He felt at the OUP party that he was among friends (many of the OUP top brass were, to my knowledge, Labour) and he blossomed accordingly. He told a much-appreciated story of how he swam across the Thames, and the Murdoch press reported it as 'Kinnock fails to walk on water'. And, so I thought, my main work on Labour history was done, and I would move on new academic pastures. But I did not know that significant meetings with, first, Jim Callaghan and then Michael Foot (both of whom are given sympathetic treatment in my book) would lie not too far ahead.

This, then, was a productive, happy time of my life. I had written twelve books in sixteen years. It was probably, for me, the golden period for my writing, in my mature forties and early fifties, commonly the high point of most academic careers in terms of creative work. My work now received public recognition with probably the greatest honour a historian can receive in his professional life when, in June 1983, I was elected a Fellow of the British Academy. Apparently, I had been put up for election in 1982 and was deemed the strongest candidate; but my election was deferred then because, typically of British life, at the age of forty-eight, I was considered too young. As far as I recall, I wrote almost nothing in 1982–3, but at least in 1983, at forty-nine, I was a year older and wiser, which made all the difference. Two of my vocal supporters, it seems, were the then Thatcherite Max Beloff and the Marxist Eric Hobsbawm. I felt it to be an extraordinary honour to be in the same room as so many giants in my field in the post-1800 History section; I was also for a time in the Politics section too, but found that group a little quarrelsome and less interesting. As tended to be the way with new Academicians, I almost immediately became chairman of my History section and found it most fascinating, with important decisions to be made on research grants, appointments and similar matters.

The Academy plays a far more active public role today than it did then in defending the Humanities and Social Sciences, and has always seemed to me an ornament to our culture. Nothing in my career has given me more pride than to be elected one of its members. In 1985, there were two more very pleasant events. Dear old Swansea made me one of the two Arts Honorary Fellows that they elected in 1985 (Kingsley Amis was the other one), while I also received a Doctor of Letters degree in the Oxford Sheldonian theatre. To my joy, the degree was conferred on me by Robert Blake as a pro-Vice-Chancellor; the degree lunch, in an almost empty Queen's Hall, was graced by an extraordinary and deeply moving address to us by the Dean of Degrees, my dear friend Siegbert Prawer, expert on Goethe, Heine and Marx, a great Professor of German Literature, and a brave refugee from Nazism. Some of the few present, recent BA graduates, were only twenty-one. I was fifty, but we were all part of the academic guild, all citizens of the republic of learning, and Siegbert explained this in unforgettable words. One of the nicest things I was able to do was to introduce Siegbert to Michael Foot – it turned out that each was a great hero to the other, and they relished each other's company. The rest of us left them talking animatedly, in an empty Queen's Hall, on Byron, Heine and Stendhal.

Life beyond my study was fulfilling too. Jane and I lived in a village called Long Hanborough, where we had moved in 1976. It was about ten miles west of Oxford, beautiful country not far from the Cotswolds and very close to Blenheim Palace. It was, politically, Conservative territory. Our MP was Douglas Hurd, whom in later years I got to know in the Lords; he was followed, after a short interlude, by David Cameron; both of them were excellent constituency members and pleasant people. In Long Hanborough, we made some wonderful friends, notably our near neighbours, Paul Levy, a great character, expert on the Bloomsbury Group and also cuisine correspondent of the *Observer* and *Financial Times*, and his dear wife Penny, an art historian. Our children were healthy and happy, enjoying lovely holidays in first France, then Italy. One memorable holiday was in La Garde Freinet, in Provence, a town up on the hills a few miles off the Côte d'Azur and also, so we discovered, a home from home for British intellectuals, especially economists. At the home in Provence of Robert Skidelsky we met a number of enjoyable people including the former Treasury adviser Nicholas Kaldor and the novelist Angela Huth. We also enjoyed regular holidays in Aberystwyth where my mother, happy in her retirement beside the promenade and with her grandchildren, was doing fine.

One remarkable change in our lives was that Jane had also become an author. After co-writing *Addison* with me, she worked on a pioneering study of the police and industrial relations in Britain, 1900–39. This showed how the Home Office and police responded to the perceived threat from the trade unions; a national challenge, it was felt or argued, needed a national response.

Jane's study also graphically demonstrated how brutal the police response often was, especially in Wales, from the Penrhyn quarry strike in 1900 to the unemployed demonstrations in the 1930s. Jane's highly original and thorough piece of work was widely and well reviewed, including by Michael Foot. More remarkably still, Jane then changed disciplines, moving from social history to criminology, and obtained a position in the Oxford Institute of Criminology. I formed the impression that she was an even better criminologist than she had been a historian. Her academic interests had changed and so, to a degree, had her way of life, since she now became a magistrate and, at a young age, got on the Woodstock bench. Apart from being useful for her academic work, this had plenty of human interest. She often sat on the bench with the Duke of Marlborough and took delight, when someone was in court for shop-lifting in Tesco's, Kidlington, in explaining to his grace how the check-out system worked in a supermarket. It seemed he had never been in one. One great bonus for me from Jane's various movements in post in the 1980s was that I got to know well her one-time employer, Sir Henry Phelps Brown, the doyen of trade union studies and industrial history. As an economist who advised government, he analysed the 'hinge effect' in wage pressures, and invented the 'Phelps Brown formula' for determining wage differentials. He was a kindly, deeply wise man – he consulted me on his book on *Egalitarianism and the Generation of Inequality* (1988), which I greatly enjoyed, while he dispensed wisdom galore when reading for me *Labour in Power.* With his friendships including such eminences as Professor James Meade and Sir Oliver, Lord Franks, this ever youthful octogenarian (he had been a cross-country running blue at Oxford) was a man it was a privilege to know. Another senior Oxford economist whose company I hugely enjoyed was Sir Alec Cairncross, former head of the Economic Service in the Cabinet Office under Harold Wilson, and a scholar-civil servant of infinite wisdom. On the debates over devaluing the pound in 1964–7, he was especially fascinating.

I remained, of course, heavily engaged in Queen's and the university during the 1980s. My lectures in the schools seemed always to go well, with undergraduates becoming rather more responsive than the laid-back public school boys I had first encountered. I had a minor role in the most celebrated incident in the university in the 1980s, namely the vote in Congregation in 1984 to deny Margaret Thatcher her honorary degree at Oxford, her old university. I was active in getting signatures for a petition against it (getting quite a number in Queen's) and felt strongly that her educational policies alone argued against her being so honoured. The speeches in Congregation, which I naturally attended, reflected the same, with references to playgroups and nurseries alongside her policies towards the universities. Oxford's scientists played an especially prominent part. Thatcher behaved with much dignity afterwards, and I used to feel pity for her in the Lords later on, this confused old woman, once so famous, unable to work out what to do in the simple ceremony that marked her receiving a peerage. Another person denied his honorary degree was President Bhutto of Pakistan. I was canvassed on the issue on my way in to the Sheldonian theatre by a pleasant young woman, whom I later recognised to be his daughter, Benazir, like her father destined to come to a grim end.

I also, to a limited extent, had an external role of a different kind in the university world outside. I had made a lifelong South African friend, Bruce Murray, a professor at Witwatersrand University in Johannesburg, having been his mentor when he worked in Oxford on an excellent book on Lloyd George's People's Budget. One morning, when I was beginning a tutorial, Bruce rang me up from South Africa – it was in the mid-1980s, perhaps 1986 – saying that the authorities wanted to deport an English colleague of his, Philip Bonner, for alleged political subversion. Could I help? I asked my undergraduates for their thoughts, which was helpful. I then rang up Robert Blake, my Provost and friend, and a Conservative peer, and Anthony Kenny, then the chairman of the Cecil Rhodes Trust in Oxford, asking them both if they could write to stress the connection between Oxford and Wits; both readily agreed to do so. I then tried ringing up the South African High Commissioner in London, a fellow academic, Denis Worrall, and to my surprise got straight through to him. I stressed the damage Bonner's deportation would do to South Africa's international reputation, along with some other points. After that, there was silence for some weeks. But, to my delight – and, frankly, surprise – Bruce rang up again to say that the authorities had reversed their decision and that Bonner would stay. I cannot imagine that my advocacy carried much weight, but perhaps the great reputation of Oxford in South Africa had its effect. About ten years later, I was myself teaching in post-apartheid Wits, and met Philip Bonner for the first time. Bruce was full of humour:'Ken, you know you made the wrong decision some years ago …'

These were years of change in the university, in many ways change for the better. One such change occurred in Queen's, and I had direct responsibility. Oxford's colleges were gradually changing their statutes so that they could accept women undergraduates. When I went to Queens, there were only five women's colleges, but then a gradual reform occurred. In 1980, as I recall, my Philosophy colleague Jon Cohen and I decided to put forward a motion of a similar kind in Queen's. I did some canvassing beforehand, and felt certain that we had the required two-thirds majority. I led off the debate in general terms, saying that it was absurd that Queen's excluded half the human race. The vote was interesting, since Fellows voted in order of the date of their appointment. That meant that the professors, all senior scholars, would vote first; I had canvassed them carefully beforehand and found out that all of them would vote for my motion, since they all had daughters and/or granddaughters. We needed a two-thirds majority, and we won by 26 votes to 4, an overwhelming vote. Very surprisingly, Robert Blake was the only one who spoke against at length. I pulled his leg afterwards, saying that he had used exactly the same argument that Sir Robert Peel had used in opposing the Reform Act of 1832 – he took that in good part. Years later, his three daughters told me that they had ticked him off afterwards because they all wanted to go Queen's. So the college had been changed, the most fundamental transformation there since Robert Eglesfield founded it in 1341, and I felt delighted with the Fellows of Queen's for their enlightened views on this issue. In a conservative era for Britain, with Margaret Thatcher committing herself to the view that there was no such thing as society, my own beloved college had joined others in promoting positive social change. In later years, as a tutor, I felt the college had improved enormously. All seemed to be well in the best of all possible worlds, in Queen's and the Oxford History and Social Studies faculties. That happy outcome would keep me contentedly in Oxford with Jane and the children for the rest of my working days. Or so I fondly thought. The one certainty the historian should acknowledge is that life, for good or frequently for ill, is unpredictable.

Chapter Six

History-making:
A Contemporary Historian

IN THE LATE 1980s my focus as a historian changed yet again. I had always felt that very recent times could and should be treated historically. I had never believed that there was a point at which history could be said to have stopped, and be turned instead into a vague 'current affairs'. My own experience as a tutor in both the Modern History and PPE schools at Oxford, where I taught history in both, reinforced my view. It seemed absurd to me that for undergraduates, reading supposedly 'Modern History', the compulsory course in English history should end at 1914, twenty years before I was born: it was later amended to 1964 during my time in Oxford. I responded very positively to a new foundation launched in 1986 called the Institute of Contemporary British History, intended to stimulate research on Britain since 1945, for the education of the general public and the stimulation of students and policy-makers alike. It published a splendid new publication, *The Journal of Contemporary British History*, first entitled *Contemporary Record* and changed in 1996 to *Contemporary British History*. Apart from a wide range of excellent articles by young scholars on Britain since the Second World War, it also most valuably included reports of 'Witness Seminars' in which major decision-makers, often senior civil servants, reflected on key aspects of their careers. The journal's first editorial in 1986 began with the words, 'History is a precious commodity. Cumulatively it provides the grey cells of the nation's collective memory. If that memory is fragmentary, partial or distorted it can warp today's perception and tomorrow's decisions.' This, finely expressed, was exactly my own view. As it happened, I was myself to resume my teaching career at the age of 77 in 2011 as a Professor in the reorganised Centre for Contemporary British History, now a research institute at King's College, London, merging history with constitutional law.

So I reacted to the founding of the Institute in the 1980s by trying to turn myself into a contemporary historian as well, not a great problem since my books on the Attlee government and modern Wales had already dealt with aspects of Britain after 1945. I was no longer marooned, like some beached whale, as an Edwardian. I thus signed up with Ivon Asquith and Oxford University Press for a large book covering the broad history of Britain since the end of the Second World War, in effect my own times. I chose the title *The People's Peace*, following up the commonly used description of the war as 'A People's War'. It spanned the period 1945–90 and was published in November 1990. As it happened, this was just after another momentous event in modern British history, the resignation of Margaret Thatcher.

Working on this book in the later 1980s was a bracing experience, very different in many ways to that of my previous books. Some of the old sources were simply not available – in particular, the public records from the late 1950s were closed under the fifty-year rule, while I found that those for somewhat earlier periods, such as our policy towards Persia/Iran from 1951, were inexplicably closed by the Cabinet Office. There was now, however, governmental support, for the historian's right to know, with the information initiative commendably pursued by ministers, notably by William Waldegrave, the Minister for Open Government under John Major. The new, more contemporary material released under these initiatives was brilliantly exploited by my friend, Peter Hennessy, first as a *Times* journalist then as a Professor of Contemporary History. He was able, for instance, to expose for the first time the circumstances under which the Attlee government developed the atomic bomb after 1945, and the entire profession owes him a huge debt of gratitude. I was to notice the considerable effect of the Open Government policy when talking to civil servants later on, when writing the lives of Jim Callaghan and Michael Foot. It was a contrast to the sealed lips that I had so frequently been met with earlier. The Waldegrave Initiative was probably also a great help to me when I was writing Jim Callaghan's biography. Sir Robin (now Lord) Butler, the Cabinet Secretary, allowed me to draw freely on Jim Callaghan's Cabinet papers during his premiership, even though they obviously came under the then thirty-year rule. My biography of Callaghan no doubt owes a great deal to Sir Robin's liberal approach. A later, rather shaky, support for open government came under the Blair government with the passage of the Freedom of Information Act. Tony Blair himself astonishingly condemned his own 'imbecile' measure in his memoirs, and with gusto. The release of information was in fact hedged around by so many qualifications and I did not find my own work particularly assisted by it. It seemed mainly to be taken up by journalists, though not always with the same scholarly commitment as Peter Hennessy.

Of course, there were in addition ample printed sources to fill up most of the gaps. They served to confirm for me the wisdom of Alan Taylor's famous dictum, 'The Foreign Office has no secrets.' By contrast, I could apply myself to newer sources at the same time. One of the novel features of contemporary history was the much greater use of oral history. It was a resource to be used with much care, and had been somewhat misused by a few younger labour historians in writing 'history from below'. But, for insight into the minds of policy-makers and those whom their decisions affected, it was a precious and unique resource, and the new Institute showed how it could be used to explore such major themes as German rearmament in the 1950s or the withdrawal east of Suez a decade later. I began myself to use far more interview material – never using a recording device, partly because it could put people off (as it did in the case of Callaghan), and partly because my own technical incompetence made managing recording devices a risky proposition. There were also the audio-visual riches of the BBC and other institutions; I found much of value in radio material and also some video archives. For instance, the footage of Jim Callaghan in January 1979 returning from Guadeloupe during the winter of discontent and saying words to the effect'Crisis, what crisis?', when questioned by reporters about the industrial troubles of the time, was highly instructive. In particular, in my view, it shows that such an uncharacteristically unguarded remark was provoked partly by irritation at being questioned by a persistent young reporter.

There were obvious dangers in writing about one's own times, about experiences very near at hand, on which I often had my own strong opinions. Taking an historical approach, even if only over a limited span of years, helped to guard against undue bias, though it is ultimately the reader who will judge how successful I was in so doing. Then again, having lived through, or close to, the events I was describing gave me a kind of personal insight of much value. For instance, I well recalled leaving for America in July 1962 when the Conservative government seemed totally dominant and Macmillan appeared as 'Supermac' in Vicky's cartoons, and then returning in September 1963, by which time the mood had totally changed – Macmillan was being lampooned as a doddering old Edwardian in satirical media such as the new *Private Eye*, 'That Was the Week That Was' on television and 'Beyond the Fringe' on stage. Everything suddenly seemed fragile and evanescent. There had been Profumo and other scandals, a 1960s-style irreverence had taken hold, and the Tories suddenly seemed on the way out. In the end, the Labour majority in 1964 was only 4 – after all, Macmillan had been a very effective prime minister whom I had met over lunch at Oxford and greatly admired – but personal insight gave an added dimension to what the printed and other records told me. There were people who advised me that writing about the times through which one was living would inevitably make my book prejudiced and unhistorical, but I tended to discount this. Historians of any period can be equally *parti pris*; I had read as an undergraduate highly partisan books either for or against William the

Conqueror or the Reformation – the important thing was to try to behave as a scholar, without fear or favour.

My book is divided, like Gaul, into three parts. There is what I called 'The Era of Advance' of 1945–61, launched by the new social consensus of the Attlee years, establishing the Welfare State, running the economy successfully on broadly Keynesian lines, and moving towards ending the age of empire through colonial liberation in India and elsewhere. Although associated with post-war Labour, this approach was continued with much effect by One Nation Tories after 1951, especially by Macmillan, and there was nothing like the retrograde class approach after 1922. The next phase of 1961–79, I called 'The Years of Retreat', in which the social consensus gradually fell apart. This was especially so in the 1970s, when the economy ran into repeated crises over the balance of payments and the parity of sterling; there were new challenges over race, gender, youth and the Celtic nations; and a final denouement of sharp industrial and political conflict which, in 1979, with the election of Margaret. Thatcher, seemed to mark the end of a post-war *ancien régime*, the collapse of what Paul Addison had called 'Attlee's consensus', with Thatcher as a kind of incipient Robespierre. A third section, shorter than the other two, I called 'Storm and Stress', dealing with the challenges and conflicts of the Thatcher era. Every book needs a pivot, when the argument is pulled together and then regains momentum to take it strongly to the finish. In *Wales in British Politics* it was the Liberal governments of 1892–5; in *Rebirth of a Nation* it was the account of Wales just before and just after the First World War; in *The People's Peace* it was the later period of Conservative rule, 1959–64, years of new economic difficulties, the failure to enter Europe, Skybolt, Profumo, and premonitions of national decline. It is a large, ambitious book of almost six hundred pages. I would naturally want to amend various facts and judgements now, but I felt and still feel happy with the work as it stands. It was like no other book at that time. It covered, within a clearly political framework, social, economic and cultural developments. Pat Thane's review congratulated me for bringing women centrally into the picture – not often a feature of my earlier works. I felt the book had coherence, despite the vast range of source material I had used, not to mention personal demands involved with heavy tutorial work at Queen's, followed by a change of scene and a change of job. It was a new work for me and, I think, one of my best.

The reviews, which might have been scathing given the highly controversial issues dealt with, were generally excellent. I had very warm commendation from fellow-scholars Ben Pimlott, Paul Addison, Peter Hennessy, John Grigg, Noel Annan and Pat Thane, and surprisingly few brickbats. Friends like Neil Kinnock and Douglas Jay were privately kind. Anthony Howard, often a sharp critic of erring academics, was serene and complimentary in his review, and congratulated me (undeservedly) for my foresight in anticipating the fall of Margaret Thatcher. The most hostile review, by Ferdinand Mount, one of Thatcher's special advisers, was one I particularly enjoyed; apparently, Mount had a second home in west Wales near Aberystwyth (not targeted by the Sons of Glyndŵr, I gathered) and he wrote satirically, though not at all unkindly, on my treatment of Wales. He wrote (in the *Sunday Telegraph*) about my nation much in terms that right-leaning newspapers used in writing about India at the time of the Amritsar massacre, and it made me glad of my background. His headline was, 'O blessed land that breeds not a single windbag.' In a sentence that I particularly treasure, he wrote, 'Seldom since Geoffrey of Monmouth can there have been a Welsher history of Britain and never a Welshman more reluctant to speak ill of his fellow-countrymen.' He was not intending to be complimentary, but I would be glad to have that as my epitaph. Mount cited my favourable comments on Cledwyn Hughes, George Thomas, Jennie Lee and others – he could have added another on Mandy Rice-Davies, a product of my old stomping-ground of Pontyates. Mount's view would have been confirmed had he been able to read a highly eulogistic review of my book in the Welsh-language weekly *Golwg*.

All in all, I felt gratified to have written this book, which I felt had taken my reputation forward into a new area. The book continues to sell well, twenty-five years on. It has been my second-best seller after the *Illustrated History*, and has become a standard text in French universities teaching English Studies (*sic*), and two subsequent editions have enabled me to take the story on into the Labour years as far as the general election of 2001 – so it has all been very satisfactory.

At this period, I was not only writing on recent and current politics but, in a modest way, taking part in them. Like many other leftish academics, I felt in a very despondent state of mind in the Thatcher years and anxious to try to bring them to an end. I had a number of dealings with major Labour figures at that this time, including Neil Kinnock, whose gallant efforts I admired in confronting Thatcherism and making the Labour Party again electable, after the disasters of Bennery, Militant and undisciplined trade unionism. I had canvassed with Alastair Parker in the 1983 election in Oxford East (a totally safe Labour seat, which we lost) and found out how working-class voters were disillusioned with what they saw as the extremism of the Labour left, and Tony Benn in particular. Losing Oxford East to the Tories was like losing the Rhondda. Neil Kinnock then made the electoral triumphs of New Labour possible. I came across him again totally unexpectedly during a delightful family holiday in Tuscany in 1988. Walking down the Via di Citta in Siena, I heard a very familiar voice booming 'Ken Morgan!' with a force that would have been heard in Umbria. It was Neil with Glenys, who were staying in San Gimignano, and we went on to have a very jolly lunch with them in the Campo where the famous horse race, the Palio, takes place. My son David particularly enjoyed talking to Neil about rugby, which he played enthusiastically himself. The following year we were all again in the area, in Umbria this time, and we arranged another lunch in Siena, again most enjoyable.

When the 1992 election approached, Neil asked me, as he would have asked other academics, for papers on various topics, educational and other. In particular, I wrote him a paper on the prospects for Labour in a hung parliament, focusing on the events of 1924 and 1929, the first two, both minority, Labour governments. My paper apparently impressed, and the Labour Party through Charles Clarke put me up in London to be in party headquarters on election night so that I could tell the (presumably) interested viewers what had happened under Ramsay MacDonald sixty years earlier. I had a jolly and optimistic meal with Patricia Hewitt, later to be Health Secretary, beforehand. But it became obvious from an early declared result, Basildon, a Conservative gain, that Labour was not going to win. I stayed on a while to hear of Glenda Jackson winning Hampstead, before leaving to collect my razor and pyjamas from my room in the hotel I never used, and took the first train out of Paddington. I arrived home around six in the morning to drown my sorrows with much coffee. I felt the whole occasion was a deeply saddening event. The Conservatives got home because John Major was not Margaret Thatcher and by tarring Neil Kinnock as unfit to be prime minister. I also felt Kinnock was pilloried for being a Welshman, and in particularly a working-class south Wales Welshman in accent and body language, in a way that Lloyd George or even the suave Nye Bevan were not. Kinnock would have been a very good prime minister, though maybe it was fortunate for him that he missed out as he would have had to devalue the pound in the ERM crisis that following September – an episode that destroyed John Major in the longer term. Kinnock would have joined MacDonald, Attlee and Wilson as devaluing Labour premiers; he went on, in the meantime, to become an excellent commissioner in Brussels, and is now a cheerful and greatly respected colleague in the Lords. As a minor compensation, I secured Neil an honorary degree from the University of Wales, of which institution he was of course a graduate. I have often wondered whether, had Labour won in 1992, Neil might have given me a job of some kind, perhaps in higher education. Jane, who much liked Glenys and was herself staunchly Labour, would probably have given me encouragement. But in that respect alone, the Labour defeat was fortunate. I think I am a decent historian and I would have been at best a middling, over-sensitive politician.

By this period, I had long ceased to be in Oxford. In the spring of 1988, I had been interviewed for the principalship of the University College of Wales, Aberystwyth, and had been appointed there. I took up my new post on All

Fools Day (as friends liked to point out), 1 April 1989, and remained in post in Aberystwyth until the end of September 1995. Even at this distance of time, I am still somewhat surprised that I made this move, after twenty-three wonderful years with my friends in Oxford, and with Jane and the children respectively settled in a job and good schools in Oxford, and the decision to stay in Aberystwyth was a hard one to make. I suppose I was beginning to get mildly restless in Oxford. I enormously enjoyed my work, but college tutoring can be repetitive; I sometimes felt that if I read another essay on Lloyd George and the decline of the Liberal Party I would go mad. I also felt that I had qualities within me that my position at Queen's did not altogether call upon – for instance, as a communicator. So, in 1987, I went up for interview at beleaguered, near-broke Cardiff University, which was proposing to appoint a new principal, to run both it and the University of Wales Institute of Science and Technology (UWIST), the ex-polytechnic across the way in Cathays Park. The Park was an academic no man's land; I immediately discovered mutual and extreme ill will between the proposed academic partners on each side of the Park, and would never have taken the job in a million years. As it happened, Cardiff appointed no-one at that time, but later chose Sir Aubrey Trotman-Dickinson, the head of UWIST, by far the best appointment for a post that would involve some blood-letting. I returned to Queen's loving it more than ever. But this did, perhaps, indicate some feeling that as I entered middle age I might try to do something else some time.

In 1988, I was written to by my old friend Gwyn Alf Williams, saying that Aberystwyth, which I knew so well as a town, was also looking for a new college principal. This seemed more plausible for me than Cardiff. At interview, I apparently spoke confidently, on the basis of no knowledge, on the problems of university management. I was also quizzed on my knowledge of Welsh, where I did rather better. After an interlude, I was offered the job. I consulted Jane, who was at first very doubtful (after strongly encouraging me to go for interview) and then David and Katherine (who were both surprisingly enthusiastic, and thought it would elevate my status in life). I asked not to take the job until Easter 1989, because of Jane's work commitments, which meant I then had a year to ponder the decision I had taken. It was not the happiest of times. There was some extraordinary uproar before my arrival about the large sum of money allegedly being spent on our home in Plas Penglais, and the dreadful local newspaper, the *Cambrian News*, whipped it up. I was rung up at Queen's during a tutorial by a *Sun* journalist, who asked me in crude terms how I could justify living in the lap of luxury while students were starving in the gutters. This was in fact quite absurd; the sum of around £50,000 spent on the Plas by the authorities was basically to pay for a new boiler and rewiring which, apparently, were sorely needed. All Jane and I got for ourselves were new curtains from Laura Ashley, who Jane persuaded to give them to us for free. So there was an unpleasant air before I even got there.

More seriously, I got the strong impression that my predecessor had been pushed around during the Thatcherite cuts, and the officials in Aberystwyth wanted me to commit to a policy of compulsory redundancy. As a university teacher, I could never accept this. It would be destructive of morale; one lecturer in Hull had already won a court case against the university for firing him in not dissimilar circumstances. I wondered whether to go to Aberystwyth at all, especially as I was so happy at Oxford, the best university in the land. In the end, I went down to attend an early meeting of the Planning and Resources Committee, and stated my view on compulsory redundancy with firmness and clarity. It was accepted at once, and I felt my authority was unquestioned. Without this albatross around my neck, things felt fine when I began work at Aberystwyth, initially without Jane who was finishing off her work on child victims. Life in Aberystwyth was amazingly different from what had gone before, and took some getting used to even though I had spent so much in the area since my earliest childhood. The town was an odd place, with some vocal criticism from Plaid Cymru elements on the university council and the capricious local newspaper, and little help from the local councils which spread some near-libellous comments about me when I inquired about buying a house in the town. People would stop me in the street with complaints about things like multi-occupied housing. Sometimes I wondered whether these scattered dissidents wanted Aberystwyth not to have a world-renownd university at all, and to lapse into being a small ex-seaport like Aberdyfi.

The prosperity of the town depended almost entirely on the university, with around two thousand out of eleven thousand inhabitants employed there, quite apart from the further business given to building firms, banks, shops, cafes and pubs. I took pleasure in giving the employment statistics I obtained from the local job centre when I addressed our court and council. With a national unemployment rate of around 8 per cent, in Dyfed it was 5 per cent and in Aberystwyth, thanks to the university, not much more than 2 per cent. But it was sometimes hard for these facts to sink in. Also, there was a ridiculous uproar when I suggested we got a university car to bring visitors to our distant institution, and also to carry me to university meetings along the by-ways of Wales. The local newspaper appeared to suggest that Jane wanted to use this for her shopping, and printed an unpleasant cartoon of my totally blameless wife astride a horse. I saw the rat-faced editor in his office, and have never been closer to using violence on another human being; fortunately, I resisted.

But the university itself was fine, with many distinguished scholars desperate for leadership and morale-boosting from the top after recent serious cuts. There was much emphasis on the Council upon Welshness and the use of the Welsh language. I discovered this in my first two weeks when there was a threat of industrial action (in the form of a refusal to mark examination papers) by members of staff who had a (well-merited) grievance over the levels of their pay. We produced what I thought was a statesmanlike and moderate letter about a possible working timetable to be sent to all our staff. But when I stated my assumption that everyone would have it the next day, I was surprised to be told that would not be the case. When I asked why, I was informed that the document had to be translated into Welsh. An industrial dispute would be put on hold while every lecturer, including our German, Indian and Japanese colleagues, had a Welsh-language letter prepared as custom required. I reflected that this was expensive and time-consuming, but it was also important to many people and was, anyway, better than bombs. The letter went out, and strike action was averted. Relations with the Association of University Teachers, of which I myself had been a member for twenty-one years, were excellent throughout my time in Aberystwyth. I believe the association felt I was on their side. For myself, I was very comfortable with the fact that my stipend was a grade above that of the best-paid professors and that I did not receive the over-remuneration of which vice-chancellors nowadays are the fortunate beneficiaries, whatever their success or failure in post.

The Welsh emphasis was no obstacle to Aberystwyth's progress; indeed, in some ways it enhanced it. The college offered an attractive range of departments, no applied science or medicine, but good science in Physics, Pure and Applied Maths, Biological Sciences, Agricultural Science, and Computer Science (strengthened by the recent acquisition of the College of Librarianship); a brilliant Department of International Politics launched by Sir Alfred Zimmern as Woodrow Wilson Professor in 1919; the famous teaching Law department of Llywelfryn Davies; the celebrated Geography department of Emrys Bowen; and much strength in the humanities with History, English and Welsh and Celtic Studies. The staff, for so small an institution, included an unusually large number of Fellows of the British Academy and the Royal Society. As a university teacher myself, I had great fellow-feeling for them all. I was greatly moved, after seeing the English department, when one of its more elderly lecturers came and knocked on my office door: 'I just wanted to say, Principal', he said, 'that this is the first time in twenty years someone had told me I was doing a good job.'

The college had been rocked by the abolition of two departments before I arrived. They were Chemistry (and there was nothing I could do about that) and Music. The latter was of course a huge blow, in Wales of all places, and I put in much effort to encouraging music on the campus, chairing the college Music Club and appointing a Director of Music to encourage music to return under the new teaching modules in 1994. There was also a small Visual Art department, which at first viewed me with suspicion, even hostility, but soon realised that in me they had a strong and reliable friend. The department more than doubled in size during my time, and they even named a lecture theatre after me in their new facilities. When I went to Aberystwyth, people were gloomy and talked of the Art department as being next on the list for closure. I was insistent that there was no list and there would be no closures, and so it proved.

When I went to Aberystwyth, the university college had just over three thousand students, a tiny number with many departments so small as to be scarcely viable. Some gloomy observers greeted my arrival with the view that the institution might even have to close – a prospect which some seemed even to relish. When I left in the autumn of 1995, there were getting on for seven thousand students; there had been no possibility of any closures, and we had been in the black every year. I was enormously assisted by the staff, which had strong morale and the sense of solidarity natural to a small institution beside the sea, some fifty miles away from any other town of any size. The staff also included some fine scholars; three were FRS and three FBA, a remarkable number. My vice-principals and deans were all excellent and deeply loyal; two successive vice-principals were Alun Morris, Professor of Mathematics, and Mike Tedd, Professor of Computer Science, joined later by Noel Lloyd, another Professor of Mathematics. My great weakness as principal was my inadequacy in mathematics, and they could do the adding up for me. Somewhat to my surprise, after virtually no experience of university administration, I found that I quite enjoyed it; I thought it less intellectually taxing than writing a page of a history book. In addition, my new job enabled me to use some talents I had in areas I was unable to find at Oxford. Among these was the handling of labour relations, where I felt I had success in restoring people's morale after the near-despair of the Thatcher years with all the cuts. This applied to all the workforce, skilled and unskilled; and I could also exploit the prospects for public relations, where my long background in journalism and broadcasting could be deployed to provide good publicity and coverage for the university's benefit.

The Council, while it had a small minority of tiresome critics, had some simply wonderful people who were devoted to Aberystwyth as a local institution, in which the community and the county of Ceredigion felt justifiably proud. They put in long hours on college committees or in making appointments with neither reward, nor public acclaim, for their toils. I remember among them a wonderfully loyal group – Alun Creunant Davies, Richard Morgan, Gwerfyl Pierce Jones and Meurig Rees – none of them spring chickens. Aberystwyth and Wales should be proud of them. My president was a delightful man of great ability who gave me steadfast encouragement in tough times, Sir Melvyn Rosser, a distinguished accountant. The treasurer was Alun Davies, an industrialist, an endearing man who gave me much support, partly because his wife was an Aberdyfi girl; he was, however, perhaps a shade prone to saying politically incorrect things of the kind 'They ought to be strung up!' when excited. My eventual registrar was Daniel Gruffydd Jones, a former senior civil servant who had been private secretary to Michael Heseltine and so might have found working for me rather dull. He was a charming, civilised classics graduate from Bangor, and a man of admirable judgement; we enjoyed exchanging Latin tags to each other, perhaps to the irritation of some colleagues. I felt with all of them that they would give me generous encouragement to pursue my historical work as well as act as principal. Aberystwyth was always helpful to senior staff with serious research interests and commitments, and as an institution no doubt felt it would be an asset to the college if its chief executive could produce books like *The People's Peace.* The National Library nearby was a marvellous resource for my work, and indeed a major reason why I had gone to Aberystwyth in the first place. So I had opportunities to do some academic work, excellent people to work with, the beautiful pre-Georgian Plas Penglais of 1696 in which to live, a thriving arts centre nearby with a theatre, concert hall and art gallery (and eventually a bookshop), alongside the mighty National Library to which I was devoted. I lived right by the sea, breathing its clean, refreshing air every day (Trawsfynydd power station to the north and the aftermath of the fall-out at Chernobyl permitting). And I had even acquired the title of professor, one of various titles in my life for which I did not have to compete.

There were distant views of dear Aberdyfi, and I often felt sentimentally that I was renewing links with my grandparents and that they would be proud of me. My beloved mother, at the age of eighty-seven, died soon after I arrived, which grieved me sorely. She had been a colossal, self-effacing but also selfless support throughout my life. In her old age, I had loved doing things like taking her, via Aberdyfi, to Talyllyn lake for a pot of tea while we contemplated the distant outline of Cader Idris. I felt she died happy knowing that her son Ken was in Aberystwyth and head of its famous 'Coll'.

My office was in an astonishing Gothic building of the 1860s, a former hotel taken over by the fledgling college when a mid-Wales railway line project collapsed. Sometimes, when there was a strong wind and a high tide, I had to evacuate my offices as spray came in through the window frame. On the opposite side from the seafront and the rusty Victorian pier was Laura Place, a delightful Georgian terrace built by John Nash, and beyond it the former students' union, a glorious Regency creation by Nash again, where free lunchtime concerts by brilliant musicians were put on and which I regularly attended; in addition, the students were generally friendly. One president of the students' union was a young labour enthusiast, Gareth Thomas, now a Labour MP for Harrow; another was a delightful young woman from Swaziland. The student body was highly cosmopolitan, not least because Aberystwyth as a small, physically safe town with no racism of any kind (except occasionally directed against the English) was highly attractive to overseas students, especially women. Malaysia was much the largest group, with the students mostly studying Law, Business Studies or Agriculture; the USA was a distant second. We had some delightful social occasions, such as Malaysian Night and parties organised by the British Council, whose many overseas students at Aberystwyth were looked after by the lovely Mair Williams, the wife of one of our Economics professors, my old friend John Williams.

In general, I felt the university college in Aberystwyth was much improved by the involvement of citizens of the town, and also the students in its affairs: it was something totally unknown in Oxford, where colleges were self-contained affairs in which the people of Oxford city played no part, other than as servants or shop-keepers. In democratic Aberystwyth, letting the community help in decision-making greatly improved the quality of our management, as well as making for happy relations between town and gown. The university seemed to thrive as well. The Thatcher government's policy on higher education, so often criticised (including by me), was in fact exceptionally helpful. We were encouraged to enhance our income by taking on many more students, even if below the unit of resource. This was exactly what a small place like Aberystwyth needed to remain viable. Government policy enabled us to be more adventurous in raising funds, and so we were able to secure long-term loans with the banks to enable us to build the student hostels we needed to house our larger numbers.

So after very few months, I felt totally at ease in Aberystwyth, more so when Jane joined me in the Plas and Katherine went to the quite excellent local comprehensive school at Penglais, the best she ever went to, where her academic record was outstanding. David, meanwhile, stayed on as a boarder at Magdalen College School in Oxford, not a perfect arrangement but one which enabled him to remain with his friends while he did his A levels. Jane also liked being back in Aberystwyth where she had been a student, and was active in the Music Club and in the Old Students body, of which she became vice-president. She also lectured (for no payment) on Criminology in the Aberystwyth Law department, and also very successfully in the Bangor Law department, while keeping up her attendance on the Woodstock bench every other Tuesday. She was an amazing, very attractive, hostess and her stamina seemed extraordinary. We gave several drinks parties for the staff in the beautiful Plas, apparently a great novelty, though they would be normal in Oxford. They were all very successful, not least because they gave members of the staff in different departments a chance to know each other. With Jane in command, people later spoke of it as Aberystwyth's Camelot era – not that it stopped one or two puritanical critics from grumbling in the local newspaper about the cost (which we bore) and the undesirable presence of the demon drink in respectable Aberystwyth. 'They were drinking like fishes', was one local comment. Jane and I also had lovely trips together, nice holidays with the children in Italy, Amsterdam and Paris, a visit to New Delhi to attend the Commonwealth Universities Conference (the first time Jane had ever taken a long-haul flight) and, finally, in January 1992 to Malaysia where we looked at universities in Kuala Lumpur and Terengganu in eastern Malaysia, and were royally attended by Tan Sri Arshad, a great friend, and by the strong branch of Old Students in Kuala Lumpur, the largest branch in the entire association worldwide. We came back that January serene and happy, in the best of all possible worlds.

Then catastrophe struck. In the space of a month, my world was to be tragically turned upside down. I was playing tennis with Jane on the courts beside our house, when I noticed she seemed to be moving very sluggishly; when I asked her whether she was all right, she replied that she had not been feeling great since we got back from Malaysia. She went to se our doctor, who told her she had severe anaemia (a blood count of seven, not the normal twelve), but that a strong course of iron pills would probably do the trick. He did, however, add quietly, 'I should tell you, Ken, that there is a remote possibility that she could have a tumour.' Jane took her pills, and by March the blood count was normal and she appeared to be fully recovered, as physically active and gloriously beautiful as ever. Even as late as mid-May in Carmarthen, on a beautifully sunny day, I watched with pride as Jane, a commanding and striking figure, launched a new Dyfed Victims Support scheme in the town with a fine speech in English and also, a rare thing for her, a little Welsh. But then, on the last day of May, there was an awful development. After hosting a dinner party for our friends Douglas and Mary Jay in our home at Long Hanborough, Jane told me that she had not enjoyed the evening much, which was most unusual for her. The next morning she told me that she had been awake during the night with back pains; she saw our doctor again and he, sadly, confirmed that she did indeed have a tumour of the liver, as he had originally feared: she would do well to live for a year. The next two months were a nightmare. I took Jane down to the Royal Marsden Hospital in Surrey for radium treatment on two occasions, but it did not have the desired result. Jane was losing weight, and her memory was also affected by the strong drugs she was taking. David and Katherine were astonishingly resilient for teenagers; Jane remained extraordinarily brave and lacking in self-pity of any kind. Then, on 7 August, the children and I watched with horror as Jane had a final violent spasm in Bronglais Hospital; she died, beautiful to the last. I had not seen anyone die before. It was quite tragic, and impossible to believe. Jane had been so active – a horse-rider, a tennis player, an all-action woman. Now she was gone. Fourteen years younger than me, my deepest love, my partner, best friend and life's joy was taken from me. I was a widower and felt utterly bereft. When Jane left me, my world seemed to die too.

I dimly recall that we had a large funeral in Llanbadarn church in Aberystwyth. All our friends seemed to turn up to console us in our grief, as did Jim and Audrey Callaghan. Then we had a committal service in Church Hanborough, with Oxford friends present, where Jane, a Christian and member of the Church of Wales, was laid in the earth. That is where her grave is, alongside the beautiful thirteenth-century parish church. And that is all I can say about the next twelve months of my life. It remains a complete blank in my memory. I suppose a doctor or perhaps a psychiatrist could explain it; it was presumably the product of an appalling shock to my system and my psyche. I began to feel various pains myself, especially physical stiffness as though I had extreme arthritis. In time, and after much painful attempt at walking, the stiffness went. I had been terrified for a time that my poor children, having lost their mother so completely unexpectedly, would end up having no parents at all. I am told that I was active, even aggressive, as vice-chancellor in Aberystwyth, but I recall nothing of it nor of the issues involved. I was acutely aware of the need to protect and comfort David and Katherine. David was beginning his studies at Warwick University; it was a bleak start indeed, and he made friends with another boy – later his best man – who had also just lost his mother. Katherine, only fourteen, I felt suffered even more, internalising her grief. She buckled to at Penglais school amazingly well, and actually got an A grade in every subject at GCSE level, a tribute to the school as well as to her; she then won a scholarship to Cheltenham, formerly an all boys' school, for which she had applied before Jane died. Katherine did not want to go, but I could not think of any other way of having her looked after. In the event, she did not greatly enjoy Cheltenham, and I could see why when I went to its speech day – it was still essentially a boys' school, which took girls in the sixth form. The headmaster dwelt lovingly on such male activities as the rugby team and the Officer Training Corps, but said nothing about the school play, in which Katherine had taken a major part; the institution was simply an exhibition of chauvinism.

It was an awful time, which I would not wish to inflict on my worst enemy, if there were such a person. Usually on the weekends, I would drive to Cheltenham, via Hanborough, or else via Cardiff through the heavy traffic if I were presiding over the University Council, to pick up Katherine and share the weekend with her. Then I would drop her off at Cheltenham, as late as possible, around nine on the Sunday evening, before driving over the hills through the darkness back to Aberystwyth. Fortunately, the weather was always good. I would get back to the empty Plas at around one in the morning, and pick up the latest pile of brown foolscap envelopes containing university business. Then I would just sit down at the kitchen table and cry.

My memory returns in September 1993. I seemed then to get back hesitantly to normal life – I say hesitantly, because Jane's death seemed to deprive me of my self-confidence. Jane had been so sparkling socially, often covering up for my awkwardness, and I used to wonder whether on my own anyone would find me in the least interesting as a person. I should add, however, that Aberystwyth, with its warm and close-knit atmosphere, was a good place in which to be bereaved. I received immense kindness from many people there, some of whom I did not really know; especially brilliant, loving friends at that sad time were Denis and Sue Balsom, respectively a prominent university political scientist and a leading member of Welsh and British public bodies, including OFCOM. They had both been good friends of Jane as students, and we all remain close now. Neil and Glenys Kinnock, busy as they were, also went out of their way to comfort me. Anyhow, I had to go back to doing my best for Aberystwyth as I had done before my period of darkness, and commit to a wider range of public duties. The first public event I recall after my return was a very heart-warming occasion among people that I loved in the beautiful upper Swansea valley at Banwen. My good friend Hywel Francis, an ex-student, now become head of Continuous Education at Swansea, would be a future Labour MP, and he invited me to open a new University of the Valleys for part-time students, which I did with some emotion. What went down particularly well was my first word – 'Comrades'. I have the pictorial record that Hywel presented me with hanging above my bed.

More important still, I had now acquired an exciting and important new role, Vice-Chancellor of the University of Wales (or rather Senior Vice-Chancellor, since I could not be vice-chancellor of two places at once). It was Aberystwyth's turn for its principal to be head of the federal national university of Wales; I was steeped in its history as one of the glorious achievements of the late-nineteenth century national movement in Wales, and the institution figures prominently in my writings. I was to be Senior Vice-Chancellor in the University of Wales's centenary year, which made me much the most appropriate person to preside over it. I had resisted two suggestions that I become the head of an Oxford college because I felt that leading one of Wales's most historic and prestigious institutions was more of a job. I also knew that my mother and Jane had been looking forward to my undertaking the role.

My term began with a curious episode. I had not imagined that, whatever hazards might confront me in my new post, the Italian Mafia would be one of them. During my first two days in post, after my returning from a most enjoyable academic trip with David to Malaysia and Singapore, I was told that there was a potential scandal with an institution in Italy franchised by Cardiff to teach students for the University of Wales degree. The university registrar had been to Italy and reported that it appeared not to be a real educational establishment at all, and perhaps even had criminal connections. We cut ties promptly, but it was an interesting example of the variety of the Vice-Chancellor's life. After that,

I got on with my work as the University's head for the next two years, naturally remaining a very active head of Aberystwyth as well. There was always much argument. There were frequent difficulties with the Welsh Funding Council and over attempts to centralise unduly the University of Wales, which all the college vice-chancellors, including me, resisted. There were also arguments between ourselves. Cardiff, the largest of the colleges, always wanted to break away and set up on its own. The other five institutions (Bangor, Aberystwyth, Swansea, Lampeter and the College of Medicine) did not take the same view at the time, though Swansea was inclined to follow Cardiff's lead. I did not favour secession because I believed strongly in the national university; I could not see any way in which the individual institutions suffered from the arrangement: we all made separate approaches to the Funding Council and ran our own affairs without any external interference at all.

I did feel, though, that the University of Wales added an extra ingredient. In addition to specialist institutions like the conference centre at Gregynog, the University of Wales Press, the Board of Celtic Studies, and the Centre for Advanced Welsh and Celtic Studies at Aberystwyth, it offered a framework for inter-collegiate collaboration which benefited all of us. There were joint lecture programmes (in 1981, I had myself given the O'Donnell history lectures in all five of the colleges). There could also be teaching collaboration via video conferencing; for instance, Bangor, Aberystwyth and Cardiff taught different varieties of Physics, so the federal university connection could build up all our strength (in practice, the video system was only used for committee meetings). As in other spheres of life, union could only mean strength. In addition, I felt the historic tie of the university connection in a way that some of the other five vice-chancellors perhaps did not. I had the feeling, when I presided over the University Council, that we were the nearest thing that Wales had to a parliament. In fact, we continued together – and, as I discuss in what follows, when I left my post the University of Wales was stronger still, with eight colleges now within it.

But the University had many positive features and many pleasures. We all collaborated on the university level without difficulty, and I travelled to preside over meetings in the different locations, which was a joy. It was a particular pleasure in Swansea to have a meeting in a lecture room where, thirty years earlier, I had myself lectured on The Modern World. There were also meetings in Gregynog, the beautiful hall with its superb grounds near Newtown in Montgomeryshire left to the university in the bequest of the famous Davies sisters, patrons of music and the arts, as a university conference centre. The University Council was always interesting, with two marvellous successive pro-chancellors presiding, Lord Cledwyn and Gareth, later Lord, Williams, both good friends with great gifts of chairmanship. On one occasion, I was very struck as a historian at how a debate on Welsh issues arose when the two sides mirrored the failure of the Cymru Fydd (Welsh home rule) movement at Newport in 1896 – Welsh-speaking local councillors from north and mid-Wales vs Cardiff and Swansea businessmen. To make the comparison more striking, Lloyd George had led the nationalist side in 1896; in 1993, it was led by W. R. P. George, the great man's nephew.

There were four positive aspects of my time as Senior Vice-Cancellor that I recall with especial delight. The first was that, partly through judicious use of the video conferencing system, I was able to bring two new institutions into the University – Newport College, and the City College of Cardiff, both former teachers' training colleges – after clearing up problems of any confusion of nomenclature with the long-established University College. We were now eight. The second aspect was the celebration of the University of Wales's centenary in Cardiff in November 1993. After a degree ceremony in the afternoon, we had a great dinner in the City Hall (later to be unsuccessfully promoted as the building for the Welsh Assembly following devolution). The chief guests on that occasion were Prince Charles, the University's Chancellor, the Aga Khan and Mary Robinson, the President of Ireland, whom I had the great privilege of showing round the Cardiff Law School that morning. There was a bit of delay in laying the high table at the dinner, and I found myself alone with Prince Charles in quite a small room for perhaps five minutes. At first he was a little embarrassed, but I began a conversation and we got on fine – so fine, in fact, that the Prince seemed a little irritated when we were told the table was now ready. I felt that, behind the diffident and stiff facade, here was a decent, intelligent man whose human qualities were not always allowed to blossom. In 1994, he came to Aberystwyth to conduct a degree ceremony, and again I was impressed, especially at his ease in talking to African and Asian parents. At the Cardiff dinner, he spoke, perhaps in a rather off-the-cuff way, as did I and Mary Robinson – the latter brilliantly so. I recall thinking that if a small nation like Ireland could find as its president so totally charming and deeply intelligent a person, why could not a Republican Britain? My own speech was, I think, one of the best I ever gave, since I focused not on academic details but on the history of the University and the values it conveyed. One passage that went down well with the students present was when I spoke of the University promoting sexual equality, and added, 'And, I hope, equality of sexual preference as well.' This was an indirect reference to the presence as an honorand of Lord Jakobovits, the Chief Rabbi. A strong Thatcherite, Lord Jakobovits was an outspoken opponent of homosexuality and had made the extraordinary suggestion that genetic engineering should be adopted to avoid the birth of homosexual children, which had led to Cardiff students demonstrating outside the building in protest. At the dinner, I sat between two great men, Jim Callaghan, who was very warm about my speech, and Nick Robinson, a highly intelligent historian with his special interest in creating an Irish architectural archive, deeply loyal to his famous wife Mary, but also leading a life and an important career of his own. All in all, this was a night to remember.

The third positive aspect during my time as Senior Vice-Chancellor was heading a University of Wales deputation, representing all the institutions to Brussels, to promote the University. I stayed in Brussels, for the second time, with two delightful people; Sir John Gray, the Ambassador to Brussels, a native of Burry Port and supporter of the Llanelli rugby team, and his charming Greek wife, Anthoula. It was a joy to stay in the embassy on two occasions (I had been there before as Aberystwyth's vice-chancellor). One interesting event was a dinner that John had arranged in my honour in the embassy, so that I could meet leading figures in Belglum's university life. I recall speaking with two very pleasant people; one male, one female. One was Rector of the University of Louvain; the other was Rector of the University of Leuven, both the same and not very large town. They spoke cordially to me but uttered not a word to each other, a symbol of the gulf between the Flemish-speaking and Francophone Walloon peoples. I mentioned this afterwards to John who said that that was simply how it was, and that his job was like being ambassador to two separate countries. In our final University gathering with the EU people, I spoke at some length to Bruce Millen, a very nice Scotsman who had been in Jim Callaghan's Cabinet before becoming an EU commissioner. He told me how he had effectively to act as Secretary of State for Wales because, he said, the strongly Eurosceptic Secretary of State John Redwood (famous for his music-hall failure to keep pace with the Welsh national anthem) would not distribute Objective One funding for environmental programmes in Wales. The Brussels visit was enjoyable in every way, since it made us all feel we were a real team. I was gratified to hear from one of the Belgians present that he was glad there was a University of Wales, since the university name was properly attached to a territory rather than merely to a town.

The fourth positive aspect was a big battle which I won. Early in my term as vice-chancellor, two English scientists prominent within the institution proposed that the University of Wales Press, which was losing money at the time, should be scrapped. One of them declared that his staff never had anything to do with the Press, which led me to ask whether there were any arts or social science people on his campus. I was appalled that it should even be suggested that such important a cultural institution in Welsh life should be brought to an end, quite apart from my own strong links with the University of Wales Press as an author. I decided to fight to save it, not through the University Council (which could be unpredictable), but through a recently-created body, the Central Services Committee. Its personnel were, for some reason, largely local government councillors from Dyfed and Gwynedd, virtually all Welsh-speaking, some of them Plaid Cymru. I was careful to conduct our meetings in Welsh, always worth several votes. In the end, we eventually got our proposal through the Council quite easily that the Press should be given a subvention of £500,000 to help it through its crisis. As it happened, the Press deficit was even greater in 1994, so I mumbled something about turning ocean liners around. In 1995, we were making real progress, the Press was saved and a sterling institution was preserved, without which many publications on Welsh matters or in the Welsh language would never have seen the light of day. I thought the whole episode demonstrated how non-academic, good-hearted local councillors, some of them working men, showed a far deeper understanding of the local and national importance of an academic press for the culture of their nation than university scientists who could pursue their subject anywhere. Single-handedly, I had steered the saving of the University of Wales Press, one of the best things I ever did – though no doubt, as they say in parliament, I should have declared an interest.

I retired from the Senior Vice-Chancellorship of the University of Wales at the end of the summer of 1995. I was approached to serve for a further three years, taking me to 1998, but I had a better idea – I was going to retire. It had been a privilege and joy to follow all those eminent Welsh people who had directed this central symbol of our nationhood in the past. I could not foresee that, in the next twenty years, the forces of secession would grow overwhelmingly strong and that all the colleges save for Lampeter would go their own way. At the time of writing, there are only three quite small institutions left to preserve the historic identity, though at least the University of Wales Press remains. There was one last instructive little occasion in July 1995, when I led a deputation of academics before the Welsh Select Committee in the House of Commons to present evidence on the University's links with the European Union. I was asked precisely what sum the University institutions obtained every year from Europe; I had taken care to find out the total amount from the various vice-chancellors and finance officers. It was significantly more than twenty million pounds; the Committee had been advised by the Welsh Office that it was around two million pounds. Thus far could Euroscepticism take you in disinformation.

While I was head of the University of Wales, Aberystwyth was pleasant and tranquil. Our honorary fellowships were spectacular affairs. In 1994 we gave one to the world champion hurdler Colin Jackson, a Cardiff man. He arrived by helicopter with an unnamed friend, who turned out to be the Olympic 100-metre gold medallist Linford Christie. Jackson was a quiet, charming man, who helped us greatly later in Aberystwyth by writing to support our successful bid to various sports bodies for funding for a new all-weather sports pitch. By contrast, there were two events that were personally painful, both relating to Jane. Glanmor Williams and Ieuan Gwynedd Jones had devoted much effort to putting together a book in Jane's memory, *Social Policy, Crime and Punishment*, a powerful book in its own right to which many of Jane's friends freely contributed. Additionally, Aberystwyth generously named a huge new student village of 800 houses after Jane – Pentre (Village) Jane Morgan – immediately visible as you drive down the hill into the town. Both instances were typical of the deep warmth and humanity of Aberystwyth and its people, and a permanent legacy to Jane and her immense commitment to the university.

Now, however, I had decided to retire, four years earlier than per contract. The University of Wales, Aberystwyth, as it had now been renamed, was a stronger collaborative, viable unit than it had been in 1989, and in reasonable financial health. I felt content that it was in good heart and good shape. Its departments, notably International Politics, were mostly doing well and put up higher ratings in the 1996 Research Academic Exercise. Science had been boosted that summer by the merger of our Agricultural Sciences department with the local Agriculture College, with the likelihood of increased research income especially in Europe. Our merger of the former College of Librarianship with the Computer Science department had also been a great success, giving Aberystwyth much strength in information science, a subject that could be pursued whatever the geographical location of the institution. Health informatics was one specific area we developed; we had also made good use of the European link, created through the Motor Scheme via the good offices of Peter Walker, an excellent Secretary of State for Wales of Keynesian persuasion, and whom Jane and I had welcomed to lunch at Plas Penglais. The link with Catalonia, Lombardy, Rhône-Alpes and Baden-Württemberg was a valuable one, and flourished especially in Baden-Württemberg which I visited with the other Welsh vice-chancellors.

I felt that Europe was unambiguously a splendid thing for both town and gown in Aberystwyth. The European social fund helped the town with the repair of the Victorian promenade, and with our Arts Centre theatre, which was correctly seen as a resource for the community and for mid-Wales as a whole, not just for the University. We in the University benefited from EU funding for our new all-weather sports pitch (the old grass pitch, invariably rain-sodden, dated from 1938!), a Monnet Professorship in Politics, and a lectureship in Welsh from the Minority Languages Committee. Of course, there were also more conventional benefits such as the Erasmus student exchange scheme (devised, as it happened, by a distinguished Aberystwyth graduate Hywel Ceri Jones, who worked with Jacques Delors in Brussels). Our Art department, the only one in the University of Wales and now much revived, had moved into a splendid disused Edwardian baroque Chemistry building, and was now my warmest supporter. There was a farewell dinner for me in a university hall of residence, and I felt genuinely sad to be leaving. It had been a wonderful experience to lead Aberystwyth, and then to do so alongside the University of Wales, and I felt privileged to have had the opportunity to do it.

There was one somewhat characteristic final event for me. I had decided in my last year to mark my farewell from the University of Wales, with which I had been linked in one way or another since 1958, with a book. This would be a kind of *festschrift* to myself, a compendium of some of my articles on Welsh history, many of them among the best things I ever wrote, but published for the most part in relatively little-known local journals. They were handsomely published by the University of Wales Press at the start of October 1995 under the title *Modern Wales: Politics, Places and People,* and consisted of twenty-six articles. The book received universal praise from the reviewers; one, Huw Richards in the *Times Higher Educational Supplement* used his review to reflect in most cordial fashion on my career as a whole, comparing me with my brilliant old comrade Gwyn Alf Williams, who had recently died, to my sorrow. One unexpected bouquet in the *Sunday Telegraph,* where Ferdinand Mount had once derided me, came from John Redwood in a sensitive, beautifully-written piece, perhaps reflecting the positive side of his time in the Welsh Office; I suppose he might really have enjoyed the book too. So, I had a tangible memento of these crucial decades when I discovered myself and my vocation. I noted that there was a slightly elegiac note to some reviews which commented on how good it was that I was still capable of producing a book at the great age of sixty-one. It will be interesting to see what the reaction is when I publish another book twenty years on!

I left my post at Aberystwyth for two reasons – one negative, one positive. The negative reason, of course, was the constant desolation of my lonely life since losing Jane. However kind people would be in Aberystwyth – indeed, as in Long Hanborough when I went back there – it was a bleak life living in a large, if gracious, house on my own. The weekends, if I was there and not meeting Katherine in Cheltenham, were particularly bleak, while I was incapable of cooking a proper meal and would sometimes walk across the road to a student hostel for a cooked lunch, hoping that no-one would approach me. There was a relatively limited social life for me without Jane, and it was already a bit awkward being the spare man at a dinner party, perhaps encouraged to make some approach to a spare woman also there. It seemed best just to keep working. I was alone and felt I would be most reconciled to this change of life in my own home in Hanborough, surrounded by possessions and neighbours I knew best. There would always be Queen's for social contact, since the college had done me the great honour of making me an Honorary Fellow in 1992, which meant I could use the college for virtually anything without having to do any work there. But there was a more positive side to life too. I had, as I shall explain in the next chapter, got going on a major new book, a very important one. I had no hope whatsoever of writing it if I stayed as a university vice-chancellor, a most demanding seven-day a week job. I would have to concentrate on my writing and nothing else. As I retired, my health seemed to be good. I had retired at sixty-one, a better age to start a new life than at sixty-seven, and I was eager to get going with the writing. I had the huge solace of my children, who effectively had kept me alive by not allowing me to slump too much into negative depression. David had now completed his degree in History at Warwick, and was looking towards his new job; Katherine was about to begin reading History at University College London. Both were progressing well in spite of the trauma they had undergone. Jane's aged mother in Wrexham was within reach by car. So, I could focus more on myself.

On the last day of September, I left Plas Penglais for the final time, my car stuffed with the remnants of my belongings which had been left behind by the removals men. I left my office in the old college, where my dear and deeply loyal secretary Nan seemed close to tears. I then drove to Botley in west Oxford, where I saw my accountant to complete arrangements for my superannuation, which seemed adequate though not lavish. Then back to my dear home in Hanborough. The next day I drove to Brighton for the Labour Party conference, where I spoke to a fringe meeting on Aneurin Bevan and the National Health Service, staying the night with Jim and Audrey Callaghan near Lewes. It was a good topic for me, and I spoke with some bravura. As before, I would not allow myself to brood unduly on the fortunes and misfortunes of life at a time of personal change of direction. It would be back to work, back to history and the academic world, where I really belonged.

Chapter Seven

History-making:
A Biographer

IN A BERKSHIRE HOTEL in January 1989, I met James, later Lord, Callaghan, for the first time in many years. I was there as principal-elect at Aberystwyth: he was there as president of University College Swansea. The subject, one to which we were to return to on many dreary occasions in coming years was the future of the University of Wales. Jim did not appear to find the subject especially riveting, any more than I did, and in the first coffee break he came up to me and said he would like to ask me a personal question. I could not imagine what this might be, but he then explained that he was intending to have his biography written and he wanted my advice about a possible author. I replied that, if the worst came to the worst, he could always have me; he replied that he was sure I would be too busy in Aberystwyth. I told him that perhaps we could see how things went, and I would write to him later on with my thoughts. In the meantime, he consulted a number of other people, including his daughter Margaret, whom I had never met, and in the margin she jotted the words, 'Too Welsh?' After I was properly installed in Aberystwyth, I did outline a synopsis for his biography. We met for lunch in the Atheneum during the summer; Jim was happy with my synopsis, and a book contract was signed. At my suggestion, the contract was with good old Oxford University Press; Jim, who frankly did not know much about publishing, had proposed Collins, the publisher of his own autobiography *Time and Chance* in 1987, but Oxford was much the bigger press with worldwide renown. It was a momentous event for me, something that was to shape my career over the next eight years, and indeed well beyond, since I was later to enter the Lords and keep in very close touch with Jim for the rest of his life. When he died in 2005, just short of his ninety-third birthday, my daughter Katherine observed that it was a defining event for all of us as a family, since for the prior fifteen years Jim had been a central figure, determining the pattern of all our lives.

My main source for the book was of course Jim himself, whom I got to know extremely well and for whom I developed a huge amount of respect and affection. I had meetings with him as often as my work, far away in Aberystwyth, would allow. We usually met at his flat in West Square, quite near Westminster, where Audrey was always kind and exceptionally hospitable; I also went down to his beautiful farm in Ringmer, on the Sussex Downs near Lewes, many times too. One strange occasion there was when I found the farm surrounded by police. A list of names had been found during some IRA terrorist atrocity, and Jim's name was on it, no doubt as a former Prime Minister and Home Secretary. So, the police knocked on the door about every thirty minutes or so, to make sure that Jim was safe and well in my company. Afterwards, Jim (who was still using a car at that time) drove me to Lewes station where we waited some time for a train, practically alone on the platform and highly conspicuous. The police protection had ended when we drove away from Jim's farm, and the IRA could have mown us down many times over had they wished to do so. Jim and I also had many meetings of a less formal kind elsewhere, including in Aberystwyth; Jim was always carefully prepared for our meetings, with notes at hand, which I much appreciated. He was unfailingly very sharp and bright in his comments, offering disagreement if he did not agree with or understand my line of questioning; I could well appreciate Bernard Donoughue's comment in his diary that he found Jim, supposedly not an intellectual, to be a more demanding interrogator than Harold Wilson.

He also had strong cultural interests, especially reading works of history. Foremost among these were naval histories, and indeed his and his father's naval background was very evident in his farm, with prints of old schooners on the wall and a rope ladder to take you up to the loft. His interest in the history of the Labour movement appeared stronger than that of Michael Foot, who was seemingly more interested in radicals of the eighteenth century than the twentieth. Our meetings were invariably very pleasant and Jim friendly, unpompous and good-humoured. At times, he liked to relax and chat about lesser topics, such as the Welsh rugby team – I noticed that, although an Englishman through and through, he always used the word 'we' when talking about Welsh rugby; his long tenure in his Cardiff constituency had made him very attached to Wales and the Welsh. On no more than very few occasions did he demonstrate the famous bad temper of which I had been warned by journalists that 'Sunny Jim' was capable, and which had once in Belfast reduced even the formidable Ian Paisley to white-faced incoherence. I noticed that (perhaps a sign of a chip on the shoulder through not having a university degree) he would very occasionally call me 'Professor Morgan'; I knew then that I had to watch out and that storm cones were being hoisted. He was always an utterly stimulating and frank person to talk to, but you had to be ready not to knuckle under.

The only problem I had at all was that he could be sometimes too pre-pared, and give somewhat over-organised set-piece replies. Like other auto-biographers I had interviewed, his own memoirs were too fresh in his mind. So I sometimes tried calculatedly to get him off the rails and challenge his recollection, which was a very dangerous thing to do. The old sailor did not like being forced off course, and preferred the 'steady as she goes' approach as in his 1967 Budget speech. Yet our meetings were enormously enjoyable, and our relationship became ever closer – this was particularly the case after Jane died, when Jim was almost paternal in his concern for me and sympathetic that I was keeping the biography going at a painful time of my life. What he thought of me beyond that, I am not quite sure. I caught sight in his papers, after his death, of a reference he had written about me to some Oxford college again approaching me about a possible headship there, where he spoke warmly of my work at Aberystwyth but described me as 'not a commanding personality' – which I believe to be true, or at least it was then. I have always been a some-what retiring academic, though not averse to taking tough decisions in the face of opposition, as I have perhaps demonstrated in this book. In the Lords, I find it difficult to shout down extrovert ex-MPs at question time. But I believe Jim's judgement of me became stronger after the biography was published, and all the favourable publicity it (and he) received.

Jim had many private things to say, which I found fascinating. I recall his account of the time when, as shadow Colonial Secretary in the 1950s, he met all the great future African nationalist leaders – Nyerere, Kaunda and the oth-ers. Another highlight was his role as a bridge between the Europeans and the Americans in the debates over disarmament and the SALT (Strategic Arms Limitation Talks) meetings of the 1970s. Yet another was the intrusion of MI5 into Downing Street in the 1970s, which ended with Jim sacking its boss, and yet another was his account of the covert aid he had sent to assist the revolution in Portugal in 1975 – after the end of the Salazar regime (against the wishes of the Americans, who thought they were all Communists in Portugal). Most illumi-nating was Jim's attitude to *In Place of Strife*, Barbara Castle's attempt to reform the unions in 1969, which Jim scuppered. At a colloquium in honour of Sir Alec Cairncross's birthday in Glasgow in 1991, Jim had observed, 'I would now like to recant but not wholly.' I asked him about that, and he responded describing how in fact he thought his view of 1969 was the correct one, and that collective bargaining should still basically be on a voluntary basis as recommended in the 1968 Donovan Report – there should not be legal sanctions imposed on free trade unions, the bedrock of the labour movement. Interestingly, Jim seems to have told my friend Geoffrey Goodman, a labour journalist of much distinction, the exact opposite. In summary, I believe the truth is that Geoffrey and I are both right in our recollections, and that Jim said different things to us both, since he was still uncertain on the question after his own disastrous experience with the unions in the winter of discontent in 1978–9. Deep down, though, I believe Jim was always a voluntarist who felt that using the force of law to reform collective bargaining struck at the trade unions' central role as pillars of a free society. He was always a union man.

On balance, I felt Jim was a great man, a great social democrat with wise, humane judgement on great issues, combined of course with much tactical shrewdness in making and getting his way. I could see why intellectual Oxford products like Evan Durbin were friends, or why brilliant thinkers like Douglas Jay, Tony Crosland and John Strachey backed this plain-spoken trade-unionist non-graduate for future leadership of the party. A brief conversation I once had with John Kenneth Galbraith about him confirmed the point. The best part of writing Jim's biography was the insight it gave me into Jim, a central force in the social and political transformation of our time. I could not agree with the kindly suggestion made to me by Roy Jenkins that it was an error to write about someone I knew because of how it might distort my judgements; I felt that I remained an objective historian, writing my own scholarly book as I wished without interference or censorship. The opportunity to talk to my subject at length in intimate detail was a priceless asset. How I would have loved talking to Lloyd George or Keir Hardie.

Apart from Jim himself, his papers were also a wonderful resource. They consisted of fifty-five boxes of miscellaneous papers put together by his devoted secretary, Ruth Sharpe. Thirty-eight were originally in Jim's farm, and were transferred to the House of Lords Record Office, which allowed me to take them away, around eight boxes at a time (I could not manage such physical labour now). There were also seventeen other boxes in the London School of Economics, which have now been placed together with the other collection in the Bodleian Library in Oxford. They were an important archive, ranging from Jim's years as a young trade unionist official in the early 1930s down to his premiership and beyond. In many respects I found them more revealing than material in the Public Record Office, since they were fuller on matters of party policy or constituency detail, areas which Jim's somewhat Olympian Cabinet-focused autobiography tended to skirt around. I also found that the frequent comment that the telephone has eliminated large swathes of material from the historian's gaze was not really true here, since for episodes or conversations of any significance a full written record was normally preserved. This included full telexed conversations between Callaghan and other world leaders such as Jimmy Carter, Helmut Schmidt and Giscard d'Estaing, or a variety of African nationalist figures, and the aides-memoire prepared for him or perhaps that he wrote himself with a view to his own place in future histories. For instance, I found his conversations with Carter over the Camp David Agreement between

Egypt and Israel in 1978 to be enormously revealing, in that they demonstrated that the agreement was to a surprising degree Callaghan's own work. Fortunately, his career pre-dated the use of emails which makes life much more difficult for the modern historian.

There were other marvellous sources available. One of the more remarkable was the papers of Lyndon B. Johnson in Austin, which I used when lecturing at the University of Texas in 1994. These brought to light much material, for instance, on the ruthless financial pressure the Americans employed in 1966–7 to try to get Britain to send troops to Vietnam. It was one of the triumphs of Wilson's premiership that he skilfully declined to do so. And in addition, of course, there were dozens of important interviews I had with Jim's contemporaries at home and abroad. I discussed him with many of his Labour colleagues, who ranged from being exceptionally favourable – Denis Healey, David Owen and Merlyn Rees – to fierce critics like Barbara Castle (whom Jim had frustrated over trade union reform in 1969, and then sacked from his government seven years later). Perhaps the most remarkable of them all was Douglas Houghton, the general secretary of the Inland Revenue Staff Federation in the mid-1930s who had young Jim as his assistant secretary and projected successor. Jim, however, overtook him and entered parliament. In 1969, Callaghan, as Home Secretary, and Houghton, an ageing trade unionist who was now chairman of the Parliamentary Labour Party, cooperated in the defeat of Barbara Castle's Industrial Relations Bill. Lord Houghton was over ninety when I saw him; I thought it prudent to see him first of all, and he was excellent value. I also had splendid interviews with such key civil servants as Lord Hunt and Kenneth Stowe, all of them apparently liberated by the campaign for freedom of information and able to talk remarkably freely.

Other kinds of materials, obtained after I put a letter in the *Portsmouth Evening News*, came from some elderly ladies who knew Jim as a young man and had once rather fancied their chances. Evidence of a different and most enjoyable kind resulted from my driving down to the Copnor area of Portsmouth where Jim came from – the house where he was born, his local school, the Baptist chapel his family attended, and the local parish church which recorded that, among the children once christened there, was none less than Charles Dickens. I found Portsmouth a pleasant city, which offered important clues to Jim's outlook as shaped by his maritime background.

There were three interviewees who were particularly memorable for me. Henry Kissinger, whom I found very friendly but, perhaps predictably, too evasive, notably over areas of Anglo-American relations – like Cyprus in 1974, where it was well documented that he and Jim were at odds. I talked to Lee Kuan Yew in Singapore when I went there to lecture at the National University – an extraordinary experience, at which I was accompanied by my son David because I thought he would find it interesting. We met in the Istana Negara, the grand former governor's residence in central Singapore; Lee Kuan Yew was no longer prime minister, but still in the government, with an office across the corridor from the prime minister's where he could keep a watchful eye on all that went on. He had some perceptive comments on Jim, whom he said had a clearer understanding of Africa than of Asia, but he combined this with rather scathing remarks on British politics as a whole; he also addressed a nice question to David, who asked me later about the merits of his reply (I said that he had got his bat to the ball, even if it went off the edge, and that is what counted). Lee Kuan Yew began by expressing surprise that I was writing a biography at all – in Singapore, he said, they did not go in for biographies, but preferred general cultural analysis. Afterwards, I went with David down Orchard Road and looked in several bookshops there and noticed that, in the politics sections, a large proportion of the books were in fact about Lee Kuan Yew himself! His death in March 2015 saddened me. By far my most interesting interviewee, however, and indeed the most fascinating person with whom I have ever had a discussion, was Helmut Schmidt, the former Chancellor of Germany, and a great friend of his fellow Social Democrat Jim. A Hamburg man, Schmidt shared Jim's love of the sea. I gathered that Frau Loki Schmidt, a botanist, was also a great friend of Audrey Callaghan who had a great interest in gardens. We talked in the Atheneum after I had driven down from Aberystwyth, and I soon forgot my fatigue. Schmidt was very acute but also most sympathetic to talk to – he would ask me whether he had answered my question satisfactorily and whether I would like more detail. The sharpest part of his replies that I recall were his comments on Jimmy Carter, whom he said had repeatedly let him down: 'I respect him neither as a president nor as a man' he declared, in remarks that he allowed me to use in the book. Our talk ended most cordially with Schmidt telling me a joke about a Polish Pope, all very German. I later had a letter from a young German woman whom Jim had allowed to interview him about Schmidt in return for my having the same privilege. The old union man had arranged the deal.

I worked steadily and determinedly on my biography through and beyond my time in Aberystwyth – it helped to preserve my sanity after Jane died. I began writing the book as soon as I retired in September 1995, even though there was still more research to do. I had a delightful late talk with (Lord) Ian Bancroft, a lovely man, who sadly died of cancer shortly after – I had no idea that he was at all ill. I handed the book in to Oxford University Press at the end of the summer in 1996; it ran to 800-pages at a word count of 320,000, much my longest book. Before I did complete it, though, there was the unexpected exercise of having Jim read it beforehand. His comments were relatively brief and helpful, but one or two passages caused minor explosions. He took exception to two sections, one covering his controversial relationship with the wealthy

Cardiff financier Julian Hodge, and another his connection with the BCCI bank in his retirement to get money for Commonwealth scholarships. He pressed me to remove both passages, but I courteously refused. I could not accept censorship, which was nowhere part of our contract. In any case, as I showed, both passages actually defended Jim against calumny. My book demonstrated that, contrary to *Private Eye*, his connection with Hodge was scandal free and that he neither altered his 1967 budget to assist Hodge's business activities, nor received money from him to buy his Sussex farm in Ringmer (the mortgage details were in Jim's papers); additionally, the BCCI dealings were altruistic and resulted from the best of motives to set up scholarships to British universities for such smaller Commonwealth countries as Swaziland. So, the book went ahead as written.

Callaghan: a Life was published on 19 September 1997. That was a momentous day for me, but it could have been very much worse. I spent the previous night in Cardiff Castle with Jon Snow commenting on television about the results of the Welsh referendum on devolution; I forecast, more accurately than ever I had done before in my life, the final result – a 0.3 per cent majority *for* devolution, to my great personal joy. It seemed to me obvious that, with Welsh-speaking Cardiganshire and Carmarthenshire to come, that the Yes vote would win – but apparently I was the only so-called 'expert' on any channel to get it right, as Channel Four joyfully announced. So much for 'expertise'. Then it was back, by car, to Hanborough and on to London for the *Callaghan* launch in the Commons that evening – and it was highly fortunate that I did go by car and not by train as originally planned, because the train from Swansea on which I would have travelled had a horrendous crash in Southall, west London, which killed seven poor people and injured nearly a hundred and fifty. I rang up our young Channel Four producer who had been on the train, and he said that the experience had been terrifying, with the doors automatically locked and fumes in the carriage threatening him with asphyxiation. Had I been on that train, the day of my book launch could have been my last day on earth.

In the Commons, the launch was wonderful. Jim, for some odd reason, had been reluctant to come but he had been persuaded otherwise by dear Audrey – 'She's a nicer person than I am, Ken.' The reviews – by academics, journalists and fellow politicians – were all marvellous, with the exception of an acidulous piece by Gerald Kaufman, and I was hugely gratified. As a result, when we had a second launch a week later in Cardiff City Hall, Jim was full of congratulation and beaming with delight. The reviews had not only been very nice about me, but also very warm about Jim, saying that he emerged from my pages as far more interesting and able, both as a man and as a prime minister, than had previously been thought. I was so glad about this because I felt that Jim had been unfairly traduced over his premiership generally, especially over 'Crisis? What Crisis?', the debacle of the winter of discontent which had made him so deeply depressed ('I let the country down'), and the way the party after his time plunged into internal acrimony and electoral decline. He had held all the four main offices of state – uniquely in our history – and had left his mark on every one of them, even at the Treasury where he had been so criticised over devaluation of the pound in November 1967. I felt he was far more considerable a figure than this, truly 'a Big Man' as Tom McNally had told me. Denis Healey, at his memorial service in Westminster Abbey in 2005, called him (in the presence of both Margaret Thatcher and Tony Blair) 'our greatest prime minister since Attlee', and I share Healey's judgement. I myself gave the address at another memorial service for Jim in Llandaff Cathedral, which I found an emotional experience.

I kept in close touch with Jim for the remainder of his life. I did not see him as much as I would have liked to because he gave himself selflessly to Audrey in his final years, looking after her in a hospice as she lapsed into Alzheimer's and other illnesses. Before he died in March 2005, he had asked to be moved into the same hospice where Audrey had died a few weeks earlier, so that they could share the same final resting place. I drove down to the farm in Ringmer on several occasions, and always loved our conversations and his stimulating company. I told him, in the autumn of 2004, that if he lived on until St Valentine's Day on 14 February, then he would be our longest living prime minister (Macmillan was the current holder of that title). I knew that Jim's determination would ensure that he made it. A day or two after St Valentine's Day, Margaret Jay arranged a small lunch party for Jim to mark the event. Present were Denis and Edna Healey, Merlyn and Coleen Rees, Margaret Jay and her husband Michael Adler, Michael Callaghan and me. I felt deeply privileged to be there at all. After the meal, Denis took up a glass of wine and proposed a toast to 'the last Labour prime minister – and the best'. Jim was silent, before adding, with characteristic loyalty, 'Let's not forget Michael Foot', his own deputy as prime minister in the trials of the later 1970s. I found the occasion deeply moving. Jim died himself just over a month later; I felt as if an important part of my life had disappeared. Speaking in the memorial debate in the Lords, I could barely contain my tears. For fifteen years, Jim had been my world, and I felt honoured to have been able to write his biography. I think it may rival *Consensus and Disunity* as the best book I have ever written; neither of them got a book prize, though others did.

I had written the book in Long Hanborough after my retirement on 30 September 1995. At first, my retirement had seemed flat and empty, with a long void of loneliness opening up before me. I recall a morning wandering around the small shops of Woodstock, with nothing much to do. It was, however, much alleviated by an invitation from the History department at the University of East Anglia, inviting me to take part with them in a colloquium in an old university,

Alcala de Henares, near Madrid, which I accepted and enjoyed; I had never been to Spain before. Then David, who had a temporary job in a menswear store in Newport Beach, California, before taking up a job in London, invited me to join him on the west coast, which was lovely, a relaxing stay by the seaside. We took in visits to San Diego and to Pasadena to see the Huntington Library, where the variegated gardens were especially fascinating. It all gave me a chance to move more calmly into my new world as a retired man.

I continued to be hard at work as an academic, however, and apart from writing my book on Jim Callaghan. In Oxford, to my joy, Regius Professor John Elliot had invited me to rejoin the Modern History faculty which I had left six years earlier, to lecture on the history of Britain since the Second World War. I did this for the next five years, and enormously enjoyed it. I felt calm and assured in my retirement in a way that I had not done before. There was clearly a need for the course that I taught, given by a historian and not a political scientist or a constitutional lawyer, and I had extremely large and enthusiastic classes in the examination schools. I was even given a loud round of applause on occasion, a new experience for me standing before a normally laid-back Oxford audience that included Greg Neale, who later founded the *BBC History Magazine*, whose editorial board I joined. I also resumed examining doctoral theses, in Oxford and in Cambridge as well. They were all very good, especially the last one – a thesis on Labour's policy on economic planning post-1940, by Richard Toye, a young scholar who has since written several excellent books, including a marvellous comparative study of Lloyd George and Churchill. I also lectured in various other British universities – inevitably in Aberystwyth and Swansea, and also East Anglia where I had a lovely dinner in Norwich with Robert Blake, who lived in the area, a memorable final occasion with a dear friend and loyal supporter. Soon after, poor Robert sadly lost a leg and subsequently died. For the first time ever, I gave a memorial address in the cathedral at Christ Church, Robert's former college, in 2003. In the front row sat Margaret Thatcher, who looked at me sharply as I quoted the famous remark about Gladstone being 'the hope of the stern unbending Tories'. I thanked her for coming in the Lords afterwards, the only brief conversation I ever had with her. Later on, I wrote the entry on Robert in the *Dictionary of National Biography*.

These activities, along with many invited articles and chapters on aspects of British, Welsh and Anglo-American history, kept me fully occupied as the Millennium approached its end. I also shared with John Rowett (whose thesis I had examined), and an American friend, Fred Leventhal, joint editorship of an exciting new journal published by OUP, *Twentieth-Century British History*, which I found stimulating. Since I continued to edit the *Welsh History Review* with Ralph Griffiths, as I had done since time immemorial, I kept my eye in as an editor most actively. I also held a brief short-term lectureship in Bristol

University early in 2000, where I spoke on aspects of Labour history – a pleasant experience only slightly marred by the onset of a hip operation, almost the first medical treatment I had ever received. I was soon mobile again. In addition to these narrowly academic activities, the debate about Welsh devolution in the 1990s led to my being in demand for lectures and broadcasts, including some television in my own home. An interesting occasion was a British Academy lecture in Cardiff in 1998, one year after the referendum, on the past and future of Welsh devolution, and which was later included in a book emanating from Nuffield College, Oxford.

But my resumption of work as an almost full-time scholar was far from confined to Britain alone. I gave a talk in Bologna, in a marvellous medieval hall covered with coats of arms, and I also travelled to more far-flung places to give academic lectures. Among the most memorable was the University of Texas at Austin in 1994. My old friend, William Roger Louis, a distinguished historian of international affairs who had been supervised by Alan Taylor in Oxford in the 1960s, invited me to lecture at the Harry Ransom Center of British Studies, which had attached to it an amazing archive of eminent British writers from Shakespeare to Dylan Thomas. David and Katherine came with me, the first time they had been to America; the topic I was given was Welsh Nationalism, oddly enough the first time I had lectured on that subject. I thought I could relax in such a non-Welsh a setting, but over lunch before my lecture, a formidable elderly lady came up to me, told me she was a Welsh-American, and that she would listen to my talk with extreme care. She was Elspeth Davies Rostow, the widow of the eminent economic historian and foreign affairs adviser of Lyndon B. Johnson, W. W. Rostow; in the event she was fine, and the seminar went extremely well. In 1999, I went to Austin on my own, lecturing on the way at the University of Kansas at Lawrence, famous for being Judy Garland's home base in *The Wizard of Oz*. I lectured in Austin on British critics of the Boer War this time, reflecting my recent work on the topic. I was to go there three more times – in 2007, 2010 and 2014 – and always found it most stimulating, an artistic, lively city set in beautiful countryside.

In 1997, I went even further afield. My dear friend Bruce Murray got me invited to lecture in South Africa – first a lecture in the University of Cape Town, then to do a full lecture course in his own Witwatersrand, on Edwardian Britain, and it proved a marvellous experience. We then did much historical travelling, seeing the main sites of the 1879 Zulu War, including Isandhlwana, where the British army was totally wiped out and, nearby, Rorke's Drift, a legendary defensive victory by the British, mainly Welsh, soldiers later celebrated in the famous film *Zulu* by Stanley Baker. It was astonishing to see how tiny the entire battle site was. I went again to South Africa in 1998, once more at Bruce's invitation, and again gave lectures in the university at Cape Town, and at East London,

Rhodes University in Grahamstown and, most fascinatingly in the famous training establishment of the old ANC leaders, Fort Hare, on the border of the Transkei. My subject this time was Blair's Britain, and I had a shrewd question from a Londoner in the audience. I saw him afterwards, and he turned out to be the university electrician, who to my delight had just happened to drop in out of interest. My main reason for going to South Africa on this occasion was to lecture in a big conference at the University of South Africa (UNISA), the mainly black university in Pretoria on the centenary of the Boer War. I found the conference most stimulating as it concentrated on non-military aspects of the war, including medical and gender matters. The conference delegates were taken to see what had been a Kitchener concentration camp in 1901 and, to my horror, I noticed that most of those commemorated in plaques on the wall were below the age of five. As Campbell-Bannerman said at the time, it was indeed 'methods of barbarism', virtual genocide by the British authorities; a quarter of Boer mothers died.

In the autumn of 2000, I went again to Wits, after first visiting Niagara Falls with Bruce, and gave a full lecture course again, this time on American history from the Civil War to the New Deal. This was, if anything, even more fascinating an experience than my previous visit. With the ending of apartheid, black African students now formed a majority and listened intently as I spoke of the racial difficulties in the United States from Reconstruction after 1865 down to the civil rights movements after 1945. I also extended my research on the Boer War and wrote several major articles on its critics and the media coverage of it. Emily Hobhouse, the brave journalist who exposed the concentration camps, became my historical heroine, along with Sylvia Pankhurst. I noticed in the museum in Bloemfontein that Emily painted watercolours of the Transvaal hills; there is also a self-portrait there. Strangely enough, she was not included in the *Dictionary of National Biography*, and I got Colin Matthew to put that right. South Africa was a remarkable country to experience at this precise time – apartheid had come to an end, generating in the universities big debates on how to attract and finance black students. At the same time, there appeared a palpable release of energy now that a hated brutal regime had been overturned, through the immortal courage of Nelson Mandela and his ANC comrades. One felt an historic mood of regeneration. A fascinating man that I met over lunch at Wits was its president, Judge Bam, who had been on Robben Island with Mandela, whom he had got to know for the odd reason that they shared he same birthday. Men like Judge Bam were bringing a potentially great nation back into the civilised world, and it was inspiring to see them do it.

I had no specific book on hand after *Callaghan*. I meditated about doing a book on the public memory in modern Britain, on the lines of Pierre Nora's brilliant work on *Lieux de Mémoire* (sites of memory) in France, but it made slow progress even though I got couple of articles out of it in France itself. Then, in early 2002, I was approached by my Labour colleague Baroness Kay Andrews – a good friend and distinguished graduate of Aberystwyth as well as being a native of Ebbw Vale – who passed on a request from Michael Foot, now not far short of ninety, that I might write his biography as I had written that of Jim Callaghan, which Michael, it seemed, much admired. This was at once an attractive proposition. I had, as mentioned above, been indirectly approached about writing Foot's life by Jill Craigie back in 1981, but nothing had happened then. I knew Michael quite well – he and Jill had stayed at our house, with their little terrier Dizzy (after Disraeli) a great hit with David and Katherine. Michael was not exactly from the same place in the Labour Party as me – I was more of the centre-left and had never joined the Campaign for Nuclear Disarmament, which I thought too emotional and optimistic even if marvellously idealistic. But Michael was a tremendous charismatic orator and communicator, whom I had admired years ago for his rousing assaults on the Tories at the end of May Day demos in Cardiff.

Foot was a deeply humane rebel, a backbench critic for most of his political career, who entered government in 1974 at the age of sixty and who had shown exemplary loyalty to Jim Callaghan throughout the troubles of the 1970s. Michael's biography would also have a different emphasis to my book on Jim; the latter was always on the party right, a pragmatic trade unionist. Michael, in the meantime, was on the left, especially in foreign and defence matters. Both men were patriots and enthusiasts for Britain's naval glories, however, in Jim's case centred on Portsmouth and in Michael's on Plymouth. It was the Pompey chimes versus Drake's Drum. A fundamental difference was that whereas Jim wrote little, Michael was a great *littérateur* – indeed, his library at home in Pilgrims Lane seemed almost more like that of an English literature critic than of a politician. Michael cherished an idiosyncratic family tree of authors – Michel de Montaigne, the sceptic from Bordeaux, Dean Swift, William Hazlitt, Lord Byron, Heine and H. G. Wells – and his writings referred to them with great, perhaps excessive, frequency. His library books were stuffed with pages and notes containing literary allusions, while he wrote (apart from famous pamphlets like *Guilty Men*) at least two major works, one on Dean Swift's role in the downfall of the Duke of Marlborough in Queen Anne's reign, and another his remarkable two-volume tribute to his socialist hero, Aneurin Bevan. There were also lesser works on Byron and Wells. My agent, Bruce Hunter, a good friend, concluded a contract with HarperCollins this time, not with OUP, and for the next four years Michael Foot dominated my mind and my life.

My main source, much more than was the case with Jim, was Michael in person. His papers, now housed in the People's History Museum in Manchester, were patchy but included some fascinating files on the period when he edited *Tribune.* There were some bits and bobs in private hands, and Michael at home had almost nothing. So, for several years, I made the familiar journey down the hill from Hampstead tube station to Pilgrims Lane. I was hugely helped in personal arrangements by Jenny Stringer, a friend of Jill's, who had in effect become Michael's carer. Interviewing Michael at his home was fun in many ways, despite his great age. There were books everywhere and a general sense of ordered chaos – it had been apparently even worse in the 1980s when Michael's top-floor lodger was the even more unconventional and scruffy Donald Dewar. We usually talked downstairs, a slow descent for Michael who walked with great difficulty, apart from having poor eyesight (indeed, he had lost the sight in one eye altogether). There was a Welsh-speaking housekeeper from Aberystwyth, who looked after him and made us nice lunches. We ate them in the kitchen, which was described cheerfully as a present from Rupert Murdoch, after Michael successfully sued the *Sunday Times* in 1995 for publishing an absurd article alleging that he was a Communist spy in league with the Russians, and for which he received a significant sum of damages – much of it went to help *Tribune*. I noticed that one of the suspicious aspects of Michael's behaviour was said to be that he lunched at the well-known lefty restaurant, the *Gay Hussar*, in which case I could well have come under suspicion myself. We usually spoke for about a couple of hours before Michael got tired. If the problem with Jim was trying to get him off the rails, the problem with Michael was getting him on them, as he tended to ramble inconsequentially – on one occasion, I came prepared to talk about crises in the Parliamentary Labour Party, only for Michael to talk at length about his friendship with Ernest Hemingway. In the end, I decided the wisest course was for Michael to talk about what he wanted. I would learn far more if he went on about Hemingway rather than forcing him to talk about topics that did not at that moment interest him. *Gulliver's Travels* was another favourite topic, on which I loved hearing him speak.

He had strong views – or rather prejudices – which it was best to accept, however dogmatic they were. But if his views were strong, his manner was diffident. One of the things that struck me was that this famous demagogue and tribune of the people was really quite a shy and modest man, who had to force himself into becoming the scourge of tyranny and injustice that he so majestically became. But I did dissent in our interview with Jim Naughtie on the *Today* programme, following publication of the book in March 2007, when Michael seemed to claim that the great Nye Bevan was a supporter of both CND and of Welsh devolution. I had to say that both points were quite incorrect, and that if Nye had been with us he would be agreeing with me and not with Michael. After all, Nye had famously spoken of Britain going 'naked into the conference chamber'. As always, Michael reacted with charm and good humour. Jane had observed long ago, contrasting him with some other more boorish Labour politician, that 'Michael is a gentleman'. In her judgements of people, she was invariably right. She also noticed that he was particularly courteous to women, a view apparently noted by both the Queen and the Queen Mother, with whom Michael liked to discuss ships and dogs. Roy Hattersley told me that Michael had once strongly backed up the Queen at the Privy Council when she protested at the Spanish government's attempt to prevent Charles and Diana calling in at Gibraltar on the royal yacht during their honeymoon – 'After all, it's my son, my yacht and my shipyard.' Michael responded 'Your Majesty, Queen Elizabeth, I could not have put it better.' At my seventieth birthday party at my home in 2004, Michael spent much time with my daughter, Katherine, urging her to become a Labour Party candidate, and the sooner the better! The shade of Jill would be urging him on.

Writing Michael's biography was not only a scholarly project but a way of life. It impacted on my day-to-day affairs in numerous ways, all of them fun. Michael was a lifelong supporter, and former director of Plymouth Argyle Football Club, of which I knew nothing; I had to follow its latest results, usually disappointing, as a prelude to my next meeting with Michael. He was fond of football. There was a famous story of how he was asked by a steward at Selhurst Park football ground whether he was carrying an offensive weapon – he replied that he was, and pulled out a copy of Milton's *Areopagitica*, a famous tract of the 1640s vindicating a free press (the steward let him in). His favourite holiday destination was Dubrovnik, which he visited when waging a passionate crusade for international assistance when Croatia was attacked by Serbia and Montenegro. So, in 2005, Katherine and I took our summer holiday in this enchanting coastal walled city on the Adriatic, with its magical streets, restaurants and monasteries, and beautiful islands beyond. That was a huge bonus for my research, as was meeting Michael's two dear Croatian friends, the beautiful Vesna Gamulin and her sea-faring husband Jadran. They have remained close to us and my present wife Elizabeth and I much enjoyed meeting them again in 2011. It was people like Vesna who helped to convert Michael from the dogmatic Euroscepticism of the 1970s to the humane Eurocentrism of his latter years, a valuable service indeed.

The most consistent bonus of writing about Michael was closer to hand, the famous left-wing Hungarian restaurant in Greek Street, the *Gay Hussar*, now sadly no longer with us. We met every month with a staunch group of friends: Ian Gilmour (once a Cabinet minister under Thatcher), a man of much charm and learning; Ian Aitken, a shrewd ex-*Tribune* journalist; William Keegan, the economics correspondent of the *Observer*; Jenny Stringer, and me. It was all great fun, once the waiters had hauled poor old Michael up the stairs to our private dining room, even if I came to feel that I had had enough goulash to last a lifetime. Michael would often be silent, and I would wonder if he could really hear what was being said. Then you mentioned some particular name, perhaps Burke or Byron, and he would hold forth brilliantly for ten minutes without pausing for breath. Living with Michael was an acquired taste, no doubt, but his literary interests were largely mine, too, while his passion for books I found totally compelling. At my launch party for the book in the House in March 2007, I saw Michael talking to my old school chum Roy Humphrey. I would have loved to have overheard the conversation between the two greatest bibliophiles I ever met. Michael also had conversation there with William Hague, who had just written a fine life of Pitt the Younger. I asked Michael what topic they had discussed, and he replied that it was the career of Charles James Fox, on whom Michael had in his younger days considered writing a biography, something which William Hague managed to do for Pitt quite triumphantly.

There were plenty of eager witnesses of Michael's career for me to approach. Indeed, I found much of my best evidence over tea or coffee in the Lords. A whole range of former Labour colleagues presented themselves, from Neil Kinnock to Shirley Williams and David Owen, another son of Plymouth. Tony Benn, with whom I discussed Michael over an Arthur Scargill mug of tea in his house in Holland Park, was far less positive and saw Foot as having sold out to the Right. There were sympathetic Liberals like David Steel who had negotiated the Lib-Lab pact of 1977 with Michael, and many Conservatives who loved him personally and had enjoyed some marvellous knockabout speeches of his in the Commons – Geoffrey Howe, James Prior and Nigel Lawson were among these, and even Norman Tebbit, whom Michael had once called a 'semi-house trained polecat' and who in consequence had included a polecat in his Lords coat of arms, a tribute to his sense of humour. Another Conservative, Sir Patrick (later Lord) Cormack kindly showed me the portrait of Michael in Portcullis House, clad in his donkey jacket on the bleak mountains of Gwent. I also had excellent talks with leading trade union figures like Jack Jones, a giant of a man, Len Murray, and the distinguished journalist Geoffrey Goodman. There was also much insight gained from the professional observations of Michael's private secretary Roger Dawe, who greatly admired him as a minister, and a lawyer like Lord Wedderburn who praised his legislative achievement on behalf of the unions. But much key material was derived from newspapers and journals, with *Tribune* a particular resource of value. I was able to work in the newspaper stacks of the New Bodleian with one vital technical aid – a tea trolley which was down there, for some reason, and enabled me to wheel huge files of newspapers around with ease. I could not do that now, because the system has totally changed and the New Bodleian has been closed down for renovation. So I was fortunate in my timing.

Working on Michael's biography was a jolly experience from start to finish, and the book flowed along. There was far less recourse to the Public Records than had been the case with Jim, but more literary and historical research – including into the politics of Queen Anne's reign for which had inspired Michael's study, *The Pen and the Sword*, in 1957, something that had largely escaped me when an undergraduate. My 550-page book finally appeared in 2007 to a lovely array of enthusiastic reviews, notably from Tony Blair's adviser Andrew Adonis in *Prospect*, David Marquand in the *New Statesman* and Philip Ziegler in the *Spectator*. Dominic Sandbrook in the *Sunday Telegraph* contrasted the attitudes of Foot and Benn in tems of party loyalty. I figured for the only time ever in a *Guardian* leading article (possibly by my friend Martin Kettle?), 'In Praise of Michael Foot'. One or two reviewers, however, thought I ought to have been harsher with regard to Foot's undoubted failures as party leader, and I am inclined to agree with them. As my friend Michael White wrote in the *Times Literary Supplement*, like many others, I had fallen under Michael's spell. There were also very many television and radio interviews, including one with James Naughtie on the *Today* programme mentioned previously. I am pleased with my book on Michael, especially because of its emphasis and balance. I point out that Michael was no economist and that he made little contribution to Labour's ideas; his gifts lay elsewhere, as a charismatic evangelist for the democratic socialist middle way through the medium of his books, pamphlets and public oratory. He naturally inclined towards the soap box and the demo, and he created socialists like hardly anyone else of his day.

As a writer, Michael was incomparable at his best, the greatest radical pamphleteer since the days of John Wilkes two centuries earlier. Partisan and unfair though it is, *Guilty Men* demolished the appeasers for all time, and also crucially linked Labour for once to the cause of patriotism and national defence. Indeed, while he was a surprisingly effective minister under Wilson and Callaghan in the 1970s, the key to Michael's career and personality can really be found in books. Even the young Tony Blair was captivated back in 1981 reading Michael's glittering essays *Debts of Honour*. A letter from Blair, which I quote in the book, I found rather charming and felt that the derision from some reviewers of what they saw as Blair's sycophancy was unfair. Michael and Blair had a surprisingly strong personal bond, ever since Michael helped the young Tony to become Labour candidate for Sedgefield in 1982. In July 2003, I attended a remarkable gathering in the garden of 10 Downing Street to celebrate Michael's ninetieth birthday; all manner of unlikely rebels and mavericks were there that sunny evening, as the prime minister of New Labour paid fulsome tribute to the life-work of this old-time unregenerate socialist, peacemonger and scribe. The printed word was always his most influential medium; he was a deeply civilised man, an heir to the Edwardian men of letters. Culture was central to his politics, especially historical and literary culture, and in his own matchless words, 'Men of power have no time to read, yet the men who do not read are unfit for power.' Hazlitt could not have put it better.

In extreme old age, he was now treasured as a great survivor from a legendary past. The great interest my book aroused showed the enduring hold that he and his values had over our public life. His memorial service in Golders Green crematorium in 2010, following his death at the age of ninety-six, was a moving event with tributes variously from Neil Kinnock, Monsignor Bruce Kent of CND, and the prime minister Gordon Brown. The large congregation conveyed a grieving message that we would not see his like again.

These books on Callaghan and Foot gave me a new public persona, that of the biographer. Although I had written books on Lloyd George, Keir Hardie and Addison in the past, I did not think of myself as primarily a biographer at all. I could not follow some other eminent historians, like John Campbell, whose writings consisted solely of biographies. This seemed too narrow for me. I enjoyed writing about leading individuals like Jim Callaghan, but my books were really life and times works, rather like the biographies of the great Victorians, say Moneypenny and Buckle's life of Disraeli. I hugely enjoyed writing on Jim and Michael as two remarkable, if contrasting, personalities, and trying to explore their inner mysteries. But biography was nevertheless a somewhat limiting experience for me, which involved an obsession with one individual to the detriment perhaps of considering the wider context, which was what really gripped me as a historian. It was a huge privilege to be asked to write the Callaghan and Foot books, and I was enormously gratified by the public enthusiasm for this new direction of my work, but I am not minded to write a biography again.

While writing on Jim and Michael, I was now returning to a balanced, calmer existence after the trauma of Jane's death. Around the time I went to the Lords in the year 2000, I felt in myself that even as a widower I should try to move on and to shake off the legacy of constant grief and depression which was undermining me. In this process, there were many caring friends who entertained me, especially Ben Pimlott and Jean Seaton at their home in Islington. I always felt close to them, and found it devastating when Ben, at the peak of his career, died young with leukemia. I found Ben's death the most shattering experience I had since Jane passed away, and felt deeply distressed as I wrote his obituary in the *Independent*. But, of course, my children David and Katherine were the greatest solace of all; they gave me something to live for, to offer hope for what remained of my life. They both spent much time with me, especially on overseas travel. They came with me to Texas in 1994, when we went on to Baton Rouge and New Orleans, and again came to New York City in 1997. David and I had holidays together in 1998 when we went to Goa, and in 1999 when we visited Gambia. I thought the latter particularly delightful, especially a boat trip around the southern coastline of Senegal. Back home, after a happy and profitable time at Warwick University, where he played for the university rugby team and met his wife Liz, David has worked successfully in various jobs, including for some time the controversial security firm G4S, and is now the director of a large building firm. He and I also had some bracing visits to watch the Wales rugby team play, usually unsuccessfully until the end of the 1990s, and since then doing much better. We had seat debentures for the new Millennium Stadium in Cardiff, of which we took full advantage. In Wembley in 1999, we saw Wales score a thrilling 32–31 victory over England with a dramatic try by Scott Gibbs near the end of the match, converted by Neil Jenkins to secure victory. David had never seen Wales beat England before. As we hugged each other in joy, I heard amidst the uproar some voices singing my name – they turned out to be old Aberystwyth students singing the miners' hymn to Arthur Scargill – 'Does dim ond un K. O. Morgan' (There's only one K. O. Morgan') – which I found very touching. Subsequently, I had the joy of seeing key matches in Cardiff in 2005, 2008 and 2012, in each of which Wales won the championship and the coveted Grand Slam in the Six Nations tournament. A later time I saw Wales play was in triumph over France with a French wife!

But my main fellow intrepid explorer was Katherine. She had now earned two good degrees, in History from University College London, and in International Relations at the London School of Economics. She also spent an enjoyable six months in Brussels as a *stagiaire*, where I visited her twice, and she would shortly then join the staff of the Treasury, triumphing in the extremely tough fast-stream examination. There, she worked close to Gordon Brown and acted as private secretary to the Paymaster-General, Dawn Primarolo, with great success, working also with Ed Miliband, Stuart Wood and other luminaries of the left. While Katherine would take trips with student friends to places like Peru and Ethiopia, she would also increasingly take more comfortable and relaxing trips with her father. We began in Europe, a visit to Prague in 1996, and a glorious stay in Paris in 1998, where we heard two magical chamber recitals in Sainte-Chapelle. Lisbon followed, a much less attractive place I thought, and then Marrakech, which was simply a delight. In the spring of 2001, we went together to Rome, where in successive days we saw the Vatican museum and Sistine chapel and Wales beating Italy at rugby in the Stadio Flaminio, a match in which the spectators seemed to be almost entirely Welsh – it was like a home game. Both events were inspiring. Later, in 2001, I took Katherine to Australia (where we walked around Ayers Rock, and I satisfied my Don Bradman obsession with a visit to my hero's boyhood home in Bowral. We also had a lovely dinner with Douglas Newton, an Australian academic friend whose thesis I had got published with OUP, on the quayside at Sydney. In 2003, we went to beautiful Sri Lanka and then to St Lucia for the wedding of one of Katherine's Brussels friends. The ceremony, beside the pool in a hotel, began with a man in a white suit intoning the sacred words, 'On behalf of the St Lucia Tourist Board'. In 2005, we went to Granada to see the Alhambra, part of my recovery from my only serious car accident in which a manic Portuguese, so it seemed, tried to kill me. It must have been drink or drugs. Financially, it cost him dearly, but I still have the limp.

A spate of really energetic travel with Katherine followed in 2006–8, first to China (Beijing, Xian, the Three Gorges dam, Shanghai and Hong Kong), which was exhilarating and terrifying at the same time; then to the magic of Angkor Wat in Cambodia after my fourth visit to Malaysia; then to the island of Zanzibar, safe at that time; and finally a really glorious visit to Jordan in 2008. In the course of the latter, I not only marvelled at the majesty of Petra, but floated in the Dead Sea, following my father who had done the same while serving in the Field Artillery during the First World War. Every one of these tours was unforgettable. Katherine was a great person to travel with, solicitous of my welfare, but also anxious to get about and see things, and always great fun. I was able to visit parts of the world that I had only known of in my forays in my stamp albums as a small boy in Aberdyfi. I was so fortunate to have her, and David too, as companions and comrades to console me during widowerhood. Katherine also organised a splendid seventieth birthday celebration for me on a brilliantly sunny day in 2004 – Michael Foot came along, and things ended with him, my old Aberdyfi friend Ann Clwyd MP and myself singing the 'Red Flag' – not a song commonly heard in west Oxfordshire.

But there was one other country I saw much of in these years, and it proved to be the most influential of all in shaping my destiny. It was France, a country I already knew and loved as a frequent tourist, but which I now visited regularly as a guest lecturer in academic conferences. It began with a visit to Bordeaux in 1999, where my host was a Bordeaux politics teacher, Anne-Marie Motard, who later spent two years in Oxford in St Antony's college and became a close and cherished friend. Then I went to Rouen, where I was looked after by another good friend, Antoine Capet, who made me titular head of the research school. In subsequent years, I went on many other visits to conferences, mostly English language conferences, which French academics now appeared to conduct with ease, putting the Brits to shame, although I myself was a reasonable francophone. The conferences were all held in beautiful places – Bordeaux and Rouen again, several times, Lille (twice), Paris (frequently, at the Sorbonne Nouvelle), Poitiers (twice), Tours, Limoges, Pau (twice), Montpellier (three times) and the enchanting Aix-en-Provence, home of Cézanne (twice). Lyons and Nantes followed in 2015. All were stimulating in the particular French style, with wonderful food and drink, exciting conversation, and intelligent and attractive men and women.

Then in Bordeaux, in February 2003, just before the Iraq invasion which was on everyone's minds, at a conference on the so-called Anglo-American 'special relationship', I was approached at lunchtime by a fair-haired young woman called Elizabeth Gibson. She was doing research on the British House of Lords, and wondered whether I could help her. Amusingly, I heard afterwards that she had been told there was a peer present and assumed he must be a tall upstanding Englishman. Instead, she found herself confronting a Welshman of fairly diminutive stature – average height for Wales, as Dylan Thomas said. We had an enjoyable chat, and I readily agreed that she could call on me in Hanborough in the summer to take our academic discussions further. Then I thought no more about it, although I did notice that she had beautiful blue eyes.

The subsequent story, I think, does credit to us both. She called on me annually at Hanborough in August, and discussed the British constitution with me. I noticed that whenever I was about to utter some comment, she took out her notebook. I also acted as external examiner for her doctoral thesis in the Bordeaux Law School – which was just as well, because the home examiners were fairly poisonous. I learned that Elizabeth's father was Scottish (hence Gibson) and that her mother French Swiss from near Lausanne, and that she was of the small French Protestant minority and cherished the Huguenot tradition (a very positive factor for me). Then, in the summer of 2007, things took a different turn. She told me that her relationship with the Englishman who drove her to Hanborough had ended. We then both spoke at a conference on Devolution in Poitiers in February 2008, where Elizabeth introduced my talk with a warmth that startled me. We had a long talk that evening in the hotel courtyard; I felt we were much closer now. She invited Katherine and me to her fortieth birthday party in Bordeaux; I invited her to stay with me in Hanborough that summer. By good fortune, there was a summer gaudy (feast) to be held at Queen's, where fine Bordeaux claret was served. The weather was finally sunny, and we walked by the ruins in Minster Lovell, where I had once walked with Jane before we were married. After Elizabeth's stay with me in Hanborough, we both knew that our relationship had fundamentally changed, even though I was over thirty years her senior. The feeling was stronger still when I stayed in Bordeaux for her party (Katherine had been unable to come) and we had a prolonged romantic lunch in a fine restaurant, Le Noailles, in the centre of Bordeaux, opposite the *Grand Théâtre*. She came to Hanborough again a few weeks later. We walked along the valley of the Windrush, and I asked her to marry me. To my surprise and joy, she accepted immediately. We were married on 25 April 2009, in a Protestant church as Elizabeth wished, St Mary Undercroft, the chapel of parliament just under the great expanse and medieval hammer beams of Westminster Hall, and celebrated afterwards on the Lords terrace. Many friends were there from France, Wales and elsewhere.

My beloved cousins, led by Anne and her dear husband Ivor, serenaded us with 'Sosban Fach', the battle hymn of Llanelli rugby club, as we left. David was my best man, and spoke splendidly. We had an idyllic honeymoon in Bellagio beside Lake Como, in warm sunshine. The following spring, we had a second honeymoon, in India this time, a country that Elizabeth had never previously visited. We gazed upon the Taj Mahal and relaxed in Jaipur and Simla; after seventeen years of miserable solitude, I was happy.

I had not really thought of remarrying before this. In large measure, it was through the abiding memory of Jane, but also partly because I never seemed to find anyone appropriate. As I moved through my late sixties and early seventies, I assumed that my life would follow the predictable downhill course of other elderly widowers. There had been one charming widow who clearly wanted to marry me but, much though I liked and admired her, I felt quite unable to reciprocate her feelings, and came to realise from her reaction that disappointment in love is painful at any age. With Elizabeth, it was different. She was beautiful, slim and graceful, more placid than Jane, and a wonderfully active partner and companion. She still taught a good deal in France, in the universities of Bordeaux and Tours, but in time she moved more to Britain, which she told me she preferred as she felt freer and less constrained by French bourgeois formality. Elizabeth has now obtained a teaching and research position in King's College, London, while gaining professorial qualification in France; she also teaches in the Oxford summer school and is connected to Kellogg College, Oxford, for external or part-time students. She is writing an important book for the University of Wales Press on constitutional reform in Britain and France. Elizabeth and I had some lovely visits to local Oxfordshire properties run by the National Trust, whose president was Simon Jenkins, the *Guardian* writer (and who now lives in Aberdyfi in a house on the seafront which, in my boyhood days, was the Church Hall where I once performed in a show about Robin Hood with the Wolf Cubs). Elizabeth also showed a deep enjoyment of Wales, including very much Aberdyfi, where she loves her early morning runs around the harbour and feels quite at home with its friendly citizens and its beautiful language. She has come with me twice to the national *eisteddfod*, of which I am now a bard, and found it fun (I think) – so my nationality is no problem. Her home in Bordeaux is a lovely place for me to stay, near a beautiful municipal park. And thus, totally unexpectedly and to the joy of my children, I married again and have never felt it to be anything other than idyllic for all the difference in our ages. Other delights followed. David married Liz Yonge in 2003, a lovely Kent girl he met at Warwick and a counsellor, and has two beautiful children, Joseph and Clara. Katherine married the admirable Tim Spillane in 2010, a solicitor working on labour law, half Welsh and an Oxford history graduate, with Thomas and Samuel as their dear little boys. After the bleak winter solstice of Jane's death and its seemingly unending aftermath, life was there to be enjoyed to the full once more.

My work as a historian would now proceed quite as well as before. Elizabeth was a very knowledgeable constitutional lawyer, with powerful expertise both on the British and French constitutions. We would often speak at the same conferences in France and in Britain. Her interests helped to push mine in new directions. In 2014, after speaking at a conference in Paris, I found myself producing a learned publication on 'Pre-trial detention and civil liberties in Britain since 2000' – not a topic I would ever have dreamed of writing about in earlier years. I produced another talk on the same theme to lawyers in Dublin in April 2015. I felt that being with Elizabeth, and observing her own research and writing, added a new dimension to my own interests. I published several academic articles each year. In early 2011, I produced a volume of collected articles on the liberal and labour left with I. B. Tauris, *Ages of Reform*, a kind of tribute to my connection with Richard Hofstadter long ago in Columbia. In 2013, I edited a volume to mark the 150th anniversary of Lloyd George's birth, as my first book had marked his centenary in 1963. Then, in 2014, I published a lengthy volume *Revolution to Devolution*, mainly historical themes on which I had lectured, but also reflecting the achievement of governmental devolution in Wales since 1999. To my joy, it was published by the University of Wales Press, which I had managed to save as Vice-Chancellor of our national university back in 1993. The main point was that I remained academically active and mentally alert because I was happy again. I had, miraculously and by chance, found another amazing wife, someone to share life with, someone to cherish and inspire me, someone to love. As my eightieth birthday came and went, with a great lunch party in our garden in warm sunshine in Long Hanborough, I felt a sense of renewal and reawakening. After a long dark age, life was good, a new future was dawning and there was still all to play for.

Chapter Eight

Experiences:
The House of Lords

I HAD SELDOM GIVEN much thought to the House of Lords. Like most people on the left, I saw it as an undemocratic anachronism, consisting almost entirely of people who were there because of the deeds, or commonly the misdeeds, of their ancestors. I well recalled Lloyd George's denunciation of them as 'five hundred men chosen at random from amongst the unemployed'. Even with a growing minority of life peers (and the admission of women), they hardly seemed to be a living part of the constitution. I had noted that Lord Addison, leader in the Lords for six years, had favoured an elected House. Then, around the end of October 1999, when I was contemplating how to celebrate the Millennium, I had a phone call out of the blue. It was from Jonathan Powell, Tony Blair's chief of staff at 10 Downing Street, asking me if I would agree to go to the Lords as a working Labour peer. I was a little stunned, and said that I would think about it and call him back. Then I called David and Katherine to see what they thought; both strongly encouraged me to take it. I would find it interesting and it would give me something significant to do in my retirement; also, it would get me to meet people in London, rather than simply stay at home writing books. I was surprised by their view but, as I began to collect my thoughts, I saw their point. The Lords, whatever I thought about it, was a legislating part of the constitution, which did significant work. The Labour government had just reformed it substantially by getting rid of the hereditary element altogether, save for a small rump of ninety-two chosen from within. I would undoubtedly find the work of interest and, crucially, it could add an important dimension to my history writing. Two days later I went down to the House and talked to the Labour chief whip, a pleasant man called Denis Carter, to enquire about what I was expected to do as a peer. He replied that the party hoped I would be able to attend around 70 per cent of the divisions in the House – which I said I could promise to do, provided it was understood that

I would not necessarily vote with the Labour Party and would preserve my independence of judgement. Denis agreed to this with a smile, and so I agreed to enter the unelected House of Lords.

I had plenty of time to think about it, since I was due for a hip replacement early in the New Year. Also, Katherine wanted to attend my introduction, and she would not be clear of her M.Sc. examinations at the London School of Economics until July. The list was eventually announced in March, when I was actually in hospital – my hip had just been done, and I was interviewed by BBC Wales from my hospital bed as the only new Welsh peer. My colleagues on the list seemed to me a distinguished lot – they included people like Bhikhu Parekh, an esteemed Indian political scientist who became a great friend; Julian Hunt, former head of the Met Office; Matthew Evans, chairman of Faber & Faber; Dan Brennan, a Queen's Counsel and a Crown Court recorder; and Janet Cohen, a prominent woman on the Stock Exchange. It was certainly no problem to be bracketed in their company; indeed, it felt like an honour. The Tory press could discover no clapped-out superannuated politician among us, nor anyone who had forked out lavishly to party funds. They were reduced to calling this list of eminent professional people 'colourless'. The *Guardian* welcomed me individually, while my journalist friend and fellow-Welshman, Alan Watkins, implied in the *Independent* that the government might watch out because I was a potential troublemaker! Eventually, on 12 July 2000, I was introduced in the Lords as Lord Morgan of Aberdyfi (after a brisk debate with Garter King of Arms about Aberdyfi's importance as a town). I enjoyed a lunch beforehand with old friends – Jim and Audrey Callaghan, Alastair and Julie Parker, Sir John Gray and his wife Anthoula, Ben Pimlott and Jean Seaton, Nicholas Baldwin of Wroxton College – and David and Katherine, now both 'Honourable'. My sponsors were two celebrated Welshmen; Gareth Williams, the Attorney-General, and Merlyn Rees, a former Northern Ireland Secretary who noted sardonically that the day was Orangemen's Day, when the people of Northern Ireland went head to head while commemorating the 1690 Battle of the Boyne. I was almost the first peer to take the oath in Welsh, after Lord Elis-Thomas had told me I could. The only problem was finding out which words I should actually say, and I read the final oath from an old piece of carbon-copy typing paper. Some Conservative peers laughed at the tongue-twisting oath, Jim Callaghan beamed benignly – he had probably been the reason for my elevation, anyhow, though I never asked. So the deed was done, and my status changed for ever. The only sadness was that dear Jane was not there to enjoy a day she would have loved.

The Lords had a bigger impact on me than I had expected. Its major attraction was the people in it. They ranged from celebrated politicians to distinguished professional figures to plain, almost inevitably fairly elderly and mostly male, oddballs. There were few current Cabinet ministers present, although Peter Mandelson and Andrew Adonis, both influential personalities, were with us in the later years of the Brown government. The successive leaders of the House – Baronesses Jay, Amos, Ashton and Royle, along with Gareth Williams on the Labour side and Lord Strathclyde for the Conservatives – were at least members of the Cabinet, until it happened that David Cameron excluded the likeable Baroness Stowell from Cabinet membership in 2014 in a gesture of contempt towards their Lordships' House. A rising number of peers, up to near a third in our ranks, are women (a very good thing), while we have significantly more disabled and ethnic minority members than the House of Commons: it was said that Gujarati was the second strongest language among the peers (Welsh being third, with about fifteen speakers). It could also be argued that the Lords had more working-class members than did the Commons, with our array of former trade union officials on the Labour benches. There were individuals of great distinction on all sides, including the cross-benchers, among them eminent lawyers, academics and civil servants. These usually raised the quality of our debates immensely, higher than in the Commons and, since one would not be heckled or much interrupted, it was always worthwhile trying to prepare a decent speech for a House that would at least listen courteously even if it disagreed. There were also a few genuine eccentrics, all extremely popular. In my very first lunch in the peers' dining room, I found myself sitting next to the remarkable Lord Longford; much of his lunch found its way on to his tie. Prominent on the Conservative side were the Earl of Onslow, a passionate autodidact libertarian who sported bright red socks, and the inimitable Baroness Jean Trumpington, always a great personality in the House. I had a special bond with her for two reasons: first, I had met her in Aberystwyth at the Plant Breeding Station when she was a minister in the 1990s when she told me had been a land girl for Lloyd George; second, her late husband Alan Barker, an American historian, had been headmaster of UCS and I had met him when lecturing there to the History sixth form. As a fascinating Lady Bracknell figure, Jean was unique.

For one with my academic interests, the greatest fascination was being able to meet and talk to important political figures in what was a very small and intimate place. The atmosphere was always very friendly and non-partisan; everybody felt great about being there, and treated everyone else as a privileged member of a closed guild. So one could have lunch with Geoffrey Howe, Nigel Lawson or Norman Tebbit among the Conservatives and be regaled with their fascinating memories, or David Steel among the Liberal Democrats. It was like a permanent witness seminar. On the Labour side, there were also great personalities from the past. None was more remarkable than Barbara Castle, whom I had known previously only as an interviewee. She was ninety and nearly blind, but still took a vigorous part in debates, notably on pensions and welfare issues. I had one extraordinary evening with her, when I came up after a late dinner with a Welsh Conservative peer, Brian Griffiths from Fforestfach near Swansea. Debates had ended and the House was empty when, coming towards us, was Barbara on the arm of Norman Tebbit, who asked me if I would look after Barbara until her driver arrived. I readily agreed to do so. She was in great form, full of stories of how half the politicians of the world had made a pass at her (Pandit Nehru was one name, I recall). But time went on and on. The House was totally deserted, without a policeman or telephone operator on duty. When it turned well past eleven, I was getting quite anxious about how to look after this very old and frail woman. Barbara couldn't read her diary and didn't know which telephone number belonged to the friend due to pick her up. In the end, I started to work my way methodically through the list and, to my huge relief, number seven or thereabouts was the right one. The lady driver was at Hyde Park on her way to the Palace of Westminster. When she arrived, the excitement wasn't over, because Barbara insisted that they drive me back to the Reform Club – but on the back seat sat a large dog and another woman. I eventually made it back to the Club by no means unpleasurably, sitting on the lap of this second (young) woman; it was a memorable evening in its way. Barbara was a dauntless personality, and I could well see why Michael Foot had as a young man been so in love with the beautiful, red-haired Barbara Betts.

I particularly enjoyed being among the Labour peers – I took issue with one or two other academics who chose to be cross-benchers because that was how their temperament dictated. I had clear political views. The Lords, for all its consensual, courteous atmosphere, was a partisan place, designed to back up or challenge the government of the day, not just to discuss the eternal verities. The cross-benchers, I felt, were over-rated by outside commentators; some of them turned up only to discuss their particular speciality, and a few did not turn up at all. Presumably, they just liked being called lord or baroness. Latterly, however, there have been some superbly effective cross-benchers, notably the lawyer David Pannick. Anyway, I was by instinct a team player who liked being among colleagues or, as some of us still said in the Labour Party, comrades. Our ranks included some figures of great distinction – the gynaecological scientist Robert Winston, the crime novelist Ruth Rendell, the human rights barrister Helena Kennedy, the film producer David Puttnam, the historian Patricia Hollis, the broadcasters Melvyn Bragg and Joan Bakewell, all of them scintillating people and an adornment to the House whose work they took very seriously. In my early days, we also included other wonderful people like Richard Attenborough and Richard Rogers, architect of the Pompidou Centre in Paris and the Senedd building in Cardiff. I also loved chatting over tea at the Bishops' Bar with some of my rank and file colleagues, who included fascinating former MPs and trade union officials. Labour was by far the party group most representative of the nation: we had many genuine working-class members, whereas the Liberal Democrats and, of course, the Tories, were irredeemably bourgeois. I heard many fascinating reminiscences at the Bishops' Bar: it was always helpful to have some knowledge of football on these occasions, and I was well equipped in this respect, as an Arsenal supporter like John Tomlinson and some of the others. One great event in 2005 was when Tony Clarke, an ex-postal workers' official and Arsenal fan, brought the FA Cup (which Arsenal had just won) to the Lords, and I could hold it aloft like another Tony Adams! To my great pleasure, the Labour ranks in time would include two of my former university students, Roger Liddle from Queen's and Donald Anderson, who would have had the misfortune of hearing my very first lecture at Swansea in 1958. There were also several of my pupils in the Commons, including Martin Horwood (Liberal Democrat), James Clappison (Conservative) and my dear friend Hywel Francis on the Labour benches. Our membership in the Lords also included several Welsh men and women – John Morris, Elystan Morgan (cross-bench but always Labour voting), our former leader Ivor Richard, Leslie Griffiths the Methodist leader, the steel-worker Keith Brookman (to whose daughter I had awarded a degree at Aberystwyth), the USDAW leader Garfield Davies, and women colleagues like Kay Andrews, Anita Gale, Delyth Morgan and Eluned Morgan, and my office-mate, Lyn (*née* Llinos) Golding. We were also duly joined in time by Neil and Glenys Kinnock, both of whom predict-ably made a strong impact. With Welsh-speakers among Labour and Liberal Democrat peers as well, I found ample opportunity to improve my Welsh in their lordships' house. One former Oxford colleague whom also I saw a great deal of when I first went to the Lords was Lord Dacre, Hugh Trevor-Roper, very frail and almost blind, who seemed to be ignored by his fellow Conservatives. But he recognised my voice, if not my face, and cheered up mightily when I asked him for his recollections of Cambridge, which he had despised. Twice I went with him on the tube to Paddington, where he wanted to take the train to Didcot. It was as well that I was with him, as he could see neither the infor-mation on trains, nor where his own train actually was. I wondered how on earth he managed when he was on his own.

The meetings of Labour peers were enjoyable, though tending to give undue priority to former Labour MPs and Millbank apparatchiks, especially ex-Blairites, of whom I was not one. It did, however, strengthen even more our access to ministers while Labour was in government down to May 2010, which was a great bonus. A particular privilege was that peers were allowed to attend the Parliamentary Labour Party meetings which, as a historian, I found fascinating under the Blair and Brown premierships. I marvelled at Tony Blair's easy command over these once tense gatherings, and also his shrewdness. On one occasion, a Labour MP questioned him over health and safety legislation.

I was sitting very close to him and I could see he had no idea; he then asked John Prescott, who could seemingly offer little help either. I wondered how Blair would reply but he came out confidently with the bold statement that everybody knew of Labour's fine record on health and safety matters, and he was proud of it. Everybody broke out into applause; it was a lesson for Vice-Chancellors down the ages. Gordon Brown, a more thoughtful politician, did not have that easy rapport and meetings with him were far more tense, especially as his government began to run into the sands in 2009–10, though it was still of much interest to me and I much admired him.

My great day came in January 2006 when my old friend Ann Clwyd, at that time chair of the PLP, asked me to give the PLP a talk on the founding of the party back in 1906. I found this most enjoyable and my talk was well received. The other speaker was meant to have been Tony Blair, and I would have been fascinated to hear the response of someone not obviously involved with Labour's past (that was Old Labour, after all). But, unfortunately, his plane was delayed at Johannesburg and John Prescott deputised, quite inadequately. However, I had an interesting chat afterwards with Gordon Brown, a trained historian, who had been taught by my old friend Paul Addison at Edinburgh, and whose first book in 1986 on Jimmy Maxton of the ILP, I had reviewed in the *Times Literary Supplement*. I had given him a strong review there and felt presumptuous enough, in the heady emotion after my talk, to tell Brown that I had been responsible for his subsequent success! One joy was that Katherine, who worked for Brown, was also present as the private secretary of Dawn Primarolo, then Paymaster-General in the Treasury, later to be made Deputy Speaker.

I made some wonderful new friends in the House, and reinforced old friendships. On the Labour side, I established a strong friendship with Bhikhu Parekh, a great Indian political scientist who had written variously on Bentham, Marx and Gandhi, and also on issues of human rights and national identity; he also produced a pioneering report on multi-culturalism, and he was a great intellectual force in our debates. There were other distinguished academics on the cross-benches – notably three fine historians, Robert Skidelsky, Peter Hennessy and Hugh Thomas. A particular pleasure was to be associated again with my old Columbia friend Robert Maclennan, now a Liberal Democrat peer and a fount of wisdom on constitutional matters especially. Over the decades, I have found him an especially loyal and affectionate friend. A most remarkable personality whom I had briefly met when we were both vice-chancellors was Trevor Smith, Lord Smith of Clifton, a man of pungent wit and great insight, a fierce critic of his own Liberal Democrat party, and a caustic savant who held forth in the Smoking Room (so-called) of the Reform Club, of which we were both members (as later was Elizabeth). Trevor had been Vice-Chancellor of the University of Ulster, and was Liberal Democrat front-bench spokesman on

Northern Ireland. All in all, I felt that it was a privilege to be in the Lords with all these talented and stimulating people, whose contribution to public affairs was often immense. I also feel that, since 2010, with the Lords much expanded by some fairly mediocre ex-MPs and right-wing financiers appointed to some degree as recognition of their contribution to party funds, that the new membership is rather less interesting and does not have the same intellectual mettle.

Life in the Lords was busy for a working peer; I felt we earned the stipend we didn't receive. It was exceptionally busy in my first twelve months, which was a tense period politically just before the 2001 General Election. The Conservatives tried many ambushes at late hours after dinner, when most elderly peers would have gone home. Of course, the Labour Party was in a minority in the Lords, and always liable to defeat. At one time, there was a very late vote indeed at around half past one in the morning. I felt a bit fed up with having to face this endurance test in my retirement years – but then I saw Barbara Castle next to me in the lobby, brave, blind, indomitable and ninety, and I felt quite ashamed of myself. If the venerable Barbara could put up with it, then so could I. I had no bed in London that night, so I waited for the Oxford Tube coach at the Marble Arch stop, around half past two in the morning alongside Hyde Park, where all sorts of strange and indistinguishable figures shuffled around in the darkness. I wonder who they were. Later on, our rules were changed making no votes possible after ten in the evening, though we did indulge in a spot of late-night prevarication on our side over the Constituencies Bill in 2011. Tit should always follow tat.

Our most public business in the Lords was, of course, the debates. As I have said, they were always worthwhile because one would get a fair hearing before a courteous, but critical and formidably intelligent, audience. I made my maiden speech in November 2000, speaking in the debate on the address on higher education. It was a strange experience, not exactly nerve-racking (my nerves had been racked often enough in the past), but curious to see myself holding forth with people like Shirley Williams and Roy Jenkins listening to me on the other side of the House. I managed to get in favourable references to two of my cherished subjects – devolution, and the links with Europe – and it was apparently well received, though I found it impossible to judge. I have spoken regularly over the years since then, especially on constitutional and legal issues (of which there have been many), education, Welsh affairs, children's and other social issues, and European and international affairs – notably Iraq, as I shall mention later. I tried to choose topics on which I felt I had some expertise, rather than speak on everything as some others tried to do. The debates were usually placid, many of them fairly formal second and third readings of bills that had gone through the Commons. We were always aware of being the lesser, non-elected House, and invariably deferred in the 'ping-pong' at the end.

But there were passionate encounters too, when the Lords would show their teeth. Some, as I shall mention shortly, were on civil liberties issues, such as the counter-terrorism bills, where I was fiercely opposed to Labour policy. We once had an all-night session in 2005, on the proposal to have a pre-trial detention period of up to forty-two days, and marginally won our point in the end. There was only one issue on which the Lords simply rejected a government measure, which had to be passed again a year later to become law under the terms of the 1911 Parliament Act; this was the bill to ban hunting with dogs, to which the Lords, with its many farmers and landowners, strongly objected. I hated fox-hunting, which seemed to me barbarous and utterly cruel, and I was in a consistently small minority of around seventy, mainly Labour and Liberal Democrat, who voted for it. There were high passions, huge Countryside Alliance demonstrations in Parliament Square being confronted by smaller groups of angry and potentially violent opponents of cruel sports, and I had to walk to my office through serried ranks of partisans from both sides. Both sides, it seemed, even my fellow critics of hunting, were shouting at me, sometimes obscenely. I felt some of the pro-hunting speeches were simply absurd, as well lacking in morality – they seemed to argue simultaneously that hunting both maintained and reduced the fox population, and also to suggest that the entire economy of the countryside would collapse if hunting disappeared. No doubt sales of some Christmas cards would also suffer. I was glad that in the end it reached the statute book, even if subsequent enforcement of the legislation has proved difficult

On the whole, however, the viewpoint of the Lords was liberal, far more so than in Lloyd George's day when they were just a Tory assembly. We seemed more enlightened than the Commons, whoever was in power. At attempt to introduce a bill for a European Referendum in early 2014 was thrown out by a huge majority, an amendment by the former Cabinet Secretary, Robert Armstrong, being carried easily. More striking still was the approach to moral issues, notably homosexuality. In 2013, the Gay Marriage Bill went through the Lords by an enormous majority in a full house, assisted by very sympathetic guidance from the government minster, Baroness Stowell. There was an overwhelming belief that tolerance and the force of equality demanded this measure, and that the human implications of the legal recognition of homosexuality, decriminalised long ago, should be accepted. There was resistance from some churchmen. Elizabeth was fascinated to see the demonstrators for either side campaigning outside my study window in Old Palace Yard across the road. The Christians sang rather mournful hymns; the Gay rights people (some of whom, like Ben Summerskill, I had met), loudly played 'Get Me to the Church on Time'. It was a song I knew from taking my parents to see *My Fair Lady* back in 1958, but which tended to pall slightly when I heard it for the eightieth time. Elizabeth joined in the dancing at one point, a cheerful spectacle. Although a

Christian, she absolutely shared my tolerant view. The debate in the Lords was very one-sided. The Archbishop of Canterbury, a liberal man, seemed embarrassed in giving a formal, negative view on behalf of his church. I think that the greater tolerance and humanity towards sexual and other minorities is one of the best features of Britain as a society in my time. I noted that when gay marriage was proposed in Elizabeth's France, a Catholic country, there was far more resistance and riots on the Champs Élysées.

The great bulk of our legislative debates, of course, were on measures that had already gone through the Commons. Occasionally there were bills that, for tactical reasons, the government might introduce first in the Lords. One such was the Royal Mail Bill in 2008. The Lords offered a less confrontational atmosphere, but also gave an opportunity for potential opposition to build up. In that spirit, I myself introduced an amendment opposing privatisation. This failed, but in fact the government decided not to privatise the Royal Mail after all; unfortunately the Conservative-led coalition has since followed this policy, and Vince Cable made a botched job in selling off cheaply a great public asset which dated from the reign of Charles I. The Academies Bill was another such venture that began with us.

The more important aspect of the business of the Lords, however, lay not in formal debates, but in the much more detailed, less spectacular work as a revising and amending house, scrutinising the clauses of a government's proposed legislation with intense care. Here, the Lords was at its very best with often expert, highly intelligent peers making forensic cases against aspects of a bill. Often we would win our point. Political scientists have shown that the bulk of recent amendments carried in the Lords have been accepted subsequently, demonstrating that the upper house is far more influential than is commonly stated. One limiting factor, however, has been the partisan use made of the Financial Privilege section of the 1911 Parliament Act to rule out amendments that might incur or involve expenditure, since that is the domain of the Commons alone. If that were rigidly applied, it would make the Lords totally powerless, since almost everything costs money. I criticised Lord Strathclyde, the Tory leader, for what I saw as a serious historical misreading of the Parliament Act, which was contrary to what Asquith had said in 1911. Several humane amendments, passed by Labour and cross-bench votes, to the Welfare Reform Act, whose harsh terms had been meekly supported by the Liberal Democrats, fell by the wayside on this erroneous technicality.

On one occasion, the Committee stage became unusually fraught. This was over the Constituencies Bill in 2011, a hybrid measure to redraw constituency boundaries, but also including a referendum on electoral reform (that is, proportional representation), to appease the Liberal Democrats. We on the Labour benches were incensed that this bill, which we considered to be electoral gerry-mandering and which would cost Labour probably around forty seats at the next election, had scarcely been discussed at all in the Commons through ruthless use of the guillotine. We were, therefore, encouraged by our whips to speak late, and at length, on our amendments. I myself made my longest speech in the Lords, about forty minutes or so around eleven in the evening, on the proposals on Wales, which would have cut down the number of Welsh seats by a quarter, from forty to thirty. The change had not been discussed in the Commons, a grave and almost unconstitutional step, and would have greatly diminished Wales's political influence. I did not think that we were filibustering at all, as the Tories alleged. In my case, I was giving clear historical and constitutional reasons for opposing an important measure affecting my own nation, reasons which had not even been considered in the Commons. Our amendments were all lost, but there was a remarkable sequence. When the Lords Reform Bill failed in the Commons, the Liberal Democrats spuriously claimed that it was linked to the constituency changes and, in retaliation, all of them in the Lords, even government ministers, voted against the constituency boundary changes coming into effect. The result of this capricious behaviour was that the 2015 General Election was fought on the old boundaries, to Labour's advantage. The prospects of a Conservative victory next time were theoretically reduced.

Another role of the Lords is to hold the government to account at Question Time. This is a somewhat miscellaneous affair, but still far more orderly than question time in the Commons, especially the pantomime of Prime Minister's questions. As the size of the Lords became ever greater after 2010, it was more and more difficult to get in; with my quiet academic style, I tended to be shouted down by aggressive ex-MPs, as did other academics and most women. Bhikhu Parekh, with his soft voice, never even tried. However, in time, I became better at shouting – a new exercise for me – and I found question time an interesting, even enjoyable, period, which sometimes got one on to the parliamentary programme on the radio at the end of the day.

The Lords also had a notable legal role. The Law Lords, formerly a committee of the House, were removed in 2005 with the creation in Parliament Square of the new Supreme Court. This was surely rightly so, as it was an important aspect of the separation of powers laid down in the Act of Settlement in 1701, and the Lord Chancellor had already been stopped from exercising a role in the legislature, the executive and the judiciary at one and the same time. However, the Lords became ever more active in the legal and constitutional sphere as the Labour government introduced a series of measures which many of us felt were damaging to civil liberties. Here, the Lords were far more effective than the Commons, owing to the many fine lawyers we had among us, notably Lord Lestor, Lord Goodhart and Lord Thomas of Gresford among the Liberal Democrats, and Helena Kennedy on

the Labour benches. I myself took an active part in debates on such matters as ID cards, restricting the power of trial by jury, and reforming the role
of the Lord Chancellor. Most ominous of all were the new powers given to
government over immigration and asylum-seekers, and above all the counter-terrorism measures introduced after 9/11. In this instance, suspects or
alleged suspects, who had committed no crime, were treated far worse than
criminals who had. They could be detained without charge or trial from
14 to 28, and then 42, days (Tony Blair suggested 90) with no clear knowledge
of what the charges might be against them, with no proper recourse to legal
representation and no information as to how long they would be detained.
In fact, the great bulk of detainees were released with no charge, but only
after an unpleasant and perhaps frightening experience. Far from making the
country more secure, it would have the effect of antagonising the numerous
ethnic and religious groups subjected to such controls. Such state imposition
could nurture sympathy for terrorism, making it of little surprise when some
British Muslims travelled to Syria or Iraq to join jihadists or other terrorist
groups. Overall, the Act embodied the very bad principle of key judicial decisions being taken not by judges but by the executive. The Home Secretary was
being elevated above the judicial process; it was a move away from the rule of
law towards *raison d'etat.*

I spoke and voted resolutely against all these bills. There were twenty-four
of us Labour dissidents: we included the former Lord Chancellor, the admirable
Derry Irvine, which added to the attention placed upon us and gave us more
publicity. I thought all these proposals were quite at variance with the libertarian
and humane traditions of the Labour Party, and were indeed in conflict with the
Human Rights Act that the government itself had passed. The original Council
for Civil Liberties, when it was formed in 1934, included on its executive Labour
figures like Clement Attlee, Stafford Cripps, Edith Summerskill and H. G. Wells.
It was particularly ironic in a country that would in 2015 celebrate the 800th anniversary of Magna Carta, with its emphasis on open justice and freedom from
arrest. I was dubbed 'a rebel peer' in the press; in this case I was proud to be so. In
fact, in this area, the Coalition after 2010 proved to be a big improvement, reduc-
ing the pre-trial detention period from 28 days to 14 (still too many), and abol-
ishing the new ID cards and the storage of many kinds of personal data, digital
and otherwise. However, they rather soiled their record by introducing the kind
of secret courts that had been condemned by the great Lord Atkin of Aberdovey,
my near-neighbour as a child, as an issue on which justice should not be silent
and the rule of law should prevail. We could do with him still.

Another important aspect of work in the Lords is the committee system.
There are many important committees in the Lords, including highly expert personnel in many cases, such as those dealing with European matters and human

rights questions. I was placed on the Constitution Committee in 2001, a new body which drew up its own reports on constitutional matters, much in the public eye after the Blair government's reforms, and which also monitored the constitutional correctness of government legislation across the board. We had a brilliant chairman in Professor Philip Norton, a celebrated political scientist still in post as a professor at Hull University, and I found this committee, which included ex-ministers like Ian Lang, most stimulating. Our most significant achievement was a report on devolution, which involved travelling to Edinburgh, Cardiff and Belfast. We produced an excellent report, I believe, which inter alia proposed the abolition of the secretaries of state for Scotland and Wales and the reform of the Barnett Formula, a necessary change to my mind.

I also served on a Joint Select Committee on Gordon Brown's Constitutional Reform Bill of 2008, a wide-ranging measure which pointed the way towards a written constitution, which I have always supported on democratic as well as academic grounds. I noted here that the members of the Lords rather dominated proceedings, partly perhaps because we were abler, partly because some of the MPs hardly ever turned up. We had a vote on whether the act of going to war or engaging in military action abroad should be governed by statute rather than covered by the clandestine operations of the royal prerogative. I had always thought this was vital, bearing in mind what had happened in August 1914; in any case, I thought the royal prerogative, linking the Queen with all manner of horrendous activities overseas, was unfair on her. We lost by one vote, though parliamentary sanction for overseas treaties at least went through. I was much engaged in all of these matters, especially after Elizabeth and I were put on a group at King's London in 2012 to draw up a scheme for a written constitution. I much wanted to be placed on the Lords Constitution Committee again, where I felt I could make a real contribution, and I was delighted when the Labour whips had me reappointed in the spring of 2015.

The final area in which the Lords never failed to be stimulating was in the role of peers engaged necessarily as legislators in public debate. We were thus much pressed by all manner of bodies to endorse their causes. On such controversial matters as fox-hunting, stem-cell research, gay marriage or dignity in dying, we were much lobbied by all sides. I myself was involved with a number of such matters, some concerned with higher education or Welsh affairs. One was the cause of child welfare in which, as a father, I had a keen concern. I joined a body called the Children are Unbeatable Alliance, to prevent children being physically assaulted by their parents. I was partly influenced here by Jane's writings on child victims, which talked of how children could be upset by being indirect victims – not as those being assaulted, but as witnesses to their siblings being attacked by physically stronger adults. I was horrified when Tony Blair talked casually of 'giving children a little smack'. It was disappointing when our amendment to the Children's Bill failed very narrowly in commit-tee in the Lords, because I had been told by Julie Morgan (Rhodri's wife, who was leading on the bill in the Commons) that if we had won the Commons would probably have followed our lead. But I think, nevertheless, that the role of members of the Lords in handling lobbies, charities or public interest bod-ies is a responsible one, and one which makes being there worthwhile. Good causes in this sad world need all the help they can get.

I was most of the time very loyal to my party and voted in the great major-ity of important votes. The whips took my dissent over civil liberties issues in good part – there was none of the often malign pressure exerted on MPs in the Commons. However, there was one issue in this period where I took a strong public line against the Labour government. This was the invasion of Iraq in March 2003. I thought, and think, that this was a shocking affair, illegal and marked by serial lying as serious as that in Suez back in my student days. It was an attack on another country which was in no way threatening us, against international law, not to mention historical and religious precepts of a 'just' war. It was not endorsed by the United Nations, was based on mendacious and pla-giarised claims of Saddam Hussein having weapons of mass destruction, was given spurious sanction by the so-called Law Officers of the Crown, was dam-aging to our own reputation in Europe and the Commonwealth, and met with mass opposition at home. In the end, hundreds of thousands of lives were lost, and Iraq has been plunged into virtual terror and turmoil ever since. Since 2014, ongoing IS attacks have shown vividly how profound was the disintegration and demoralisation in this hybrid country since the invasion of 2003. It was particu-larly appalling to be doing all this as partners of George W. Bush, and as a result of clandestine agreements (denied at the time) made in Crawford, Texas, a year earlier by Tony Blair. Since some materials presented to the Chilcot Inquiry have come out, it looks even worse than was thought at the time, with evidence of the attempts made to influence documents on security and strategic matters, and the private links between Number 10, Alastair Campbell in particular, and the security branch of the civil service. Iraq is an example not only of what the Butler Report called 'sofa government', but of the ignorance of history and the law by a 'New' Labour government that had little understanding of the old ways of justice. Since then, the justifications offered for the Iraq venture have been shredded by almost every international lawyer of note around the world. I hope that when the long-running saga of the Chilcot Report, wilfully delayed by the relevant civil servants, finally sees the light of day, those responsible will be held to legal account. As Michael Foot wrote in 1940, quoting the French revolution-aries, bring forward the guilty men for judgement.

I was, therefore, very active in the protests against the Iraq invasion. Despite my arthritic hip, I marched with hundreds of thousands of others, including Katherine and one of her friends, from Parliament Square to Hyde Park, the largest ever demonstration in British history. It was a dignified and orderly affair, with many elderly people and many children, and none of the aggressive Marxists or Muslims that the press claimed to see on such occasions. I took part in radio debates, including a very angry exchange with the Labour MP Chris Bryant, who supported the attack on Iraq. A friend in the Reform Club said that he had never heard me in such combative mood. There was another interesting experience. I was invited by the Charlbury United Nations Association effectively to debate Iraq with our local MP, who was David Cameron. He was extremely pleasant, but simply repeated the Blair government's line. I was puzzled that a leading Conservative MP, naturally sceptical of government pronouncements on everything else, could be so totally uncritical on this supreme issue. Cameron said he was surprised that a Labour Party peer could criticise his own leader, whereas he, a Conservative, should back him. I responded that I was not in the least surprised. He was a fluent and persuasive speaker, but the United Nations Association was clearly on my side and I was happy to feel that I had carried the day.

I also wrote a strong piece in the *Guardian* (placed there by Katherine on my behalf), which made a big impact nationwide and globally. At home in Long Hanborough, as I cycled the next day to the local post office with the latest *Welsh History Review* corrected proofs (a distance of about half a mile), I was stopped by at least twenty people, many of whom I did not know, thanking me and saying that they would take part in a demo for the first time in their lives. The decent citizens of Hanborough had many international counterparts. My *Guardian* piece provoked scores of emails from all over the world, dispatched during the night before the *Guardian* had even been published in this country: it had already appeared beforehand on the Internet in the United States. Large numbers of people, therefore, wrote to me from North America, many of them women terrified for their children. I was deeply moved and thought how tragic it was that I, a totally unimportant politician in an unelected house thousands of miles across the sea, should somehow be a voice for what they believed. In the end, I had received well over 600 emails, all of which I tried to answer, and nearly all of which supported me. Of the ten or so that did not, no more than one or two were abusive. One American correspondent wrote 'You lefty Limey pukes can all bugger off.' I replied that I could not complain of being called a lefty, and I may have been a puke, but I objected very strongly to being called a 'Limey'. On the other hand, I had hundreds of very moving supportive messages, some from academic colleagues who favourably surprised me, and many, many others from ordinary people in virtually every country in the world, from Japan to Brazil. For fifteen minutes, as Andy Warhol said, I was famous. It was brief but precious, and I felt a sense of pride as did my children.

My best known intervention which led to my greatest prominence was the speech I made in the Lords on Iraq around the end of February. I consider it the best speech I have ever made, anywhere and on any topic. For once in my life, reason and passion were perfectly intertwined as I drew on my historical knowledge to denounce what was an appalling policy blunder, quite apart from the moral overtones. I think my fellow peers looked upon me differently after that, and I was associated thereafter with my radical views on Iraq. Some in the Labour Party took sharp issue with me at the time. As further evidence has come out, many of them have changed their minds, and all praise to them for that. Peter Hain is one I have in mind, and Harriet Harman appears to be another.

In the end, I came close to doing something that would have given me extreme pain, and caused pain to others, including Jim Callaghan; I nearly left the Labour Party. I was simply shocked at my party's duplicity and dishonour. I had already, with Bhikhu Parekh, whose views were identical to mine, sent a message to the Labour whips detailing our objections to the invasion and telling them that they could no longer rely on our votes in the Lords. Then I attended a dreadful briefing meeting by Jack Straw before the invasion, with peers and MPs present, which was simply an exercise in Franco-phobia. Straw spent the entire meeting pouring scorn on the French, as hypocrites of poor judgement, after the powerful (and entirely accurate) attacks directed at Britain by President Chirac and, at the UN, by Dominique de Villepin. I felt the French had been far more in touch with the judgement and moral sense of the world than Britain had, and I felt disgusted. I was accurately quoted in a Sunday newspaper for having said the day that bombs landed on Baghdad would be the day I left the Labour Party. I had talks with such Liberal Democrat friends as Trevor Smith, whose party had been the only one to condemn the invasion, while Charles Kennedy had been splendid throughout. I then had a private talk with Shirley Williams, the Liberal Democrat leader in the Lords at the time and someone I knew quite well. Rather to my surprise, Shirley, I think wisely, counselled me against doing anything too extreme. While the Liberal Democrats would have been pleased to have me, it would have been hard for me as a well-known historian and political commentator. I guess she may have thought that I might regret suddenly losing a large number of friends, especially at my age.

At any rate, out of prudence or caution, I did not leave the party or lose my friends. I hated the policy on Iraq and civil liberties, but my instincts were all strongly Labour on everything else. It was hard to disavow the beliefs and loyalties of a lifetime. As time went on, especially after I saw how the Liberal Democrats behaved so spinelessly in supporting the coalition after the 2010 General Election with all the illberalism and cuts in the welfare state, I felt relieved to be where I was. But I still feel that the record of the Labour Party was deeply damaged by the Iraq affair – indeed, our majority went down by about a hundred seats at the 2005 General Election, which foreshadowed our later defeat in 2010 – and that our honour was stained by it for ever more. A major factor in my supporting Ed Miliband as leader in 2010, and working on his behalf, was his honesty and courage in disavowing our terrible blunder and crime in Iraq.

After a decade and a half there, what do I feel about the unelected, half-reformed House of Lords of which I am a member? It is easy to criticise, and has often so been. The *Guardian* never refers fairly or accurately to the Lords – its articles inevitably are sprinkled with references to ermine, which in fact you wear briefly, once, in five years. The press delights in foolish cameos such as Norman St John Stevas asking about the design of our Christmas cards. Clearly, under present rules, the Lords are far too numerous and old. It is difficult to be a working peer if you still have a full-time job, though some excellent young peers like Martha Lane-Fox and Tanni Grey-Thompson have more latterly joined us. We are also too white, though new entrants like Doreen Lawrence are a welcome improvement. A handful of peers on all benches have disgracefully abused the expenses system, though it has been less marked than in the Commons. Our debates could be improved; there is much repetition and irrelevance. The Lords is wedded to self-regulation, but I would prefer the elected Lord Speaker to be more interventionist as in the Commons. The quality of what we do can be overrated. We are called a house of experts; to a degree, we are a house of ex-experts, since so many of us are necessarily retired and one's professional knowledge can soon become out of date; as a former Vice-Chancellor, I know mine is. Some people pour scorn on the formalities of debate – 'the noble lord', 'the noble and learned (or gallant) lord', the right reverend prelate' and so forth – though I actually welcome this as ensuring that we talk to other in a civilised manner and without getting personal.

But I also feel the Lords has done sterling work in my time, and greatly improved public understanding – at least if only the press would condescend to report it. I do not think that a unicameral parliament would improve our government. Many a time have I seen government legislation come to us accompanied by perhaps three hundred amendments – then I realise that over half them are government amendments, which reflect the fact that the Commons, with its guillotining of time and its partisan atmosphere, has not been able to give them adequate attention (or perhaps lacks the ability to do so). The scrutinising of measures by the Lords, especially as it is pre-legislative scrutiny, adds to the quality of our laws and thereby to the quality of our daily lives. Our membership does enable a body of highly intelligent people to apply their collective judgement to the merits of legislation, in an atmosphere of greater consensus and reasonableness than in the Commons. To that degree, the party influence and the role of the whips, while properly there, have a lesser impact on the minds and consciences of individual members of the house. It is instructive to see formerly partisan ex-MPs go native. Always we are mindful that it is the elected House of Commons which will eventually determine what is done, and it is important to retain the ascendancy of the Commons, so strenuously preserved against the Crown in the seventeenth century and then against the Lords in 1911, as the central principle of parliamentary life.

The Lords has been pilloried often enough, and usually deservedly so. There was the scorn of Bagehot towards a 'dignified' house of limited intelligence and the satire of 'Iolanthe', seeing it as 'doing nothing in particular and doing it very well'. In its hereditary past, it was a reactionary place, opposing Lloyd George's Budget and Irish Home Rule, and supporting capital punishment. But to me now, it is a serious institution which does valuable, professional work. I opposed the House of Lords Reform Bill in 2012 because I thought it would both diminish the quality of the Lords' work and produce inevitable conflict between two elected houses. For that reason, Lloyd George opposed an elected upper house in 1911; he could foresee a day when a Liberal-led Commons would be faced with the implacable opposition of an elected Lords dominated by diehard Tories. Today, the Commons has been much enhanced after the committee reforms of Tony Wright's report – and perhaps also by Speaker Bercow, who has given a much stronger role to backbenchers. The partnership of the two houses has worked well enough. At times I have surmised that, contrary to Bagehot, it is perhaps the Commons that may be the dignified part of parliament and the Lords that is efficient. Certainly, it seems to be more active a body than the much-criticised, even though elected, French Senate. No serious critic has seriously thought of having a unicameral legislature. In being a working member of the Lords for fifteen years, I think I have given good and useful public service.

But the Lords clearly cannot be left as it is. The selection process is clearly quite inadequate. Its open-ended membership is far too large and gives rise to near-corruption, while the influence of the party machines in selecting peers can be a menace. Above all, at a time of sweeping constitutional reform after the Scottish referendum vote, it is simply not possible to argue that everything else should be reformed and that the Lords should not. There will clearly be a very significant overhaul of our system of governance, with something close to devo-max in a Scotland having its own financial powers, and probably something similar in time for Wales and Northern Ireland. There is also growing support, from Conservative and Labour local authorities, for a form of devolution in England based on either regional or local/urban government. As Robert Hazell's Constitutional Unit has well written, England has hitherto been 'the black hole of the constitution', a monument to Anglo-Saxon inertia. Legally, it is not much more than Metternich's description of Italy as 'a geographical expression'. That will surely change now. The Smith Commission on fiscal devolution for Scotland in November 2014 will in its course take the process of change a good deal further, and, I hope, will be followed by a similar reform for Wales which can no longer be allowed to trail behind what is happening elsewhere. The United Kingdom that emerges, therefore, will be in profound ways more diverse and less unitary. Its structure will approximate to a federal one, or at least confederal as in Canada or Australia. The massive predominance of England in wealth and population cannot hold the process back.

Within such a systematic overhaul, the Lords must play its part. It is the obvious link mechanism for keeping the union of our country in place. As in federal countries overseas, it could play a vital constitutional role in regulating and managing relations between the different legislative bodies in these islands. A revising body with a different composition – including non-party figures, with distinct representation from different parts of England, Scotland, Wales and Northern Ireland, exercising oversight on what is specific to particular areas and what is generic to the United Kingdom as a whole – would be invaluable. The Supreme Court would retain its present role of mediating in any possible disputes between the regions and nations. While preserving precious national identities, including very much in Wales, the reformed upper chamber would help to show that (to coin a phrase) we are indeed better together.

I opposed Scottish independence mainly because I favour a reform of our traditional structure within the union. A codified, written constitution should be drawn up to replace our present hit-or-miss arrangements based on custom, convention, precedent – and ultimately stand-pat conservatism. This matters to all of us, not just the Scots alone, invigorating, even inspiring though their debate was at the time. It will mean a new kind of House of Lords, not one ham-fistedly cobbled together after a coalition agreement, as in the bill of 2011, whereby individual Lords could sit unchallenged for fifteen years in the name of democracy, with nothing being said about the Lords' powers. It would rather be elected on far more rational lines, directly or indirectly, ideally after a reasoned constitutional convention as was held in Scotland in 1990, to differentiate and underpin its role. It could also be renamed the Senate, as Ed Miliband and David Steel have suggested, and its members designated MS. The undemocratic title 'Lord' should find its way into the fabled dustbin of our feudal past. Very importantly, a new bill should deal specifically with the powers of the House of Lords as well as with its composition, to avoid potential conflict between the two houses. Financial privilege should be cleared up once and for all. The Scottish referendum offers new hope and purpose for the union. So it does for an upper house as a body that can now play its part in defining and reinforcing the idea of British citizenship, as it has never done in eight centuries before. The body in which I have been pleased to serve thus far during this millennium could, and should, move on from a contradictory past to a constructive future.

Chapter Nine

Experiences: Travelling

LIKE MANY OTHER young boys, I always wanted to travel. I was captivated by what I saw in my stamp albums, with their brilliant pictorial scenes from many lands in contrast with our stamps featuring the King's head alone. I read avidly accounts of explorers in distant lands – Livingstone in central Africa, Lewis and Clark in the American west, Champlain in Canada – and I used to fantasise, while walking with my father near the source of the river Leri beyond Dolybont, that I was Charles Sturt in nineteenth-century Australia, trying to locate the source of the rivers Murray or Murrumbidgee. But, after the war in 1945, it was impossible to go anywhere. There were strict currency controls (assuming that I had any money in the first instance), while countries like France or Italy had been ravaged and were just beginning to recover from the war. Apart from my brief enjoyable visit to Jersey with my cousin Gwilym, I went nowhere until my vacation visit to Paris in 1953 for a French history lecture course at the Sorbonne, which thrilled me. I went to Germany to stay with my old Oriel friend Robert Woetzel, in Bonn and the Rhineland, in 1957; and, as mentioned, went to Sweden and then Finland for the Congress of Historical Sciences in 1960 at the age of twenty-six. Otherwise, that was it. My children, like most of the younger generation now, had been across the world more than once by the time they reached their mid-twenties. Even my youngest grandsons, one of them a mere two years old as I write, have done better than I did! I have now been to forty-eight countries and to every continent, but I am sure the grandchildren will more than catch me up in time.

The only country in which I have lived for a considerable amount of time is the United States. I spent fourteen amazing months in New York during my year at Columbia in 1962–3, followed by a further two and a half months in 1965, when I taught summer school at Columbia. I travelled all over the country then – the southern route by car, taking in a large detour via Peru on the way, to San Francisco in 1963 (with other trips to Boston, Virginia, Minnesota, Chicago and Nebraska in between); the northern route by plane and, especially, Greyhound bus to Portland, Oregon, in 1965. Since then, I have been to South Carolina and Louisiana, in 1972; to Texas five times between 1994 and 2014; to Southern California with David, in 1996; to New York City again, in 1997, with both children; and to Ohio and Wisconsin, in 2005. I feel I know the United States well and it is certainly the one country that has made much the biggest impression on me.

My early reactions were very much as a resident in New York City, in the heart of the island of Manhattan. The first fairy-tale view of the city that enchants the visitor at the end of an Atlantic boat crossing should warn him or her that the impending experience is a unique one. I hugely relished its range of open and accessible cultural and social delights, from the upper circle in the Metropolitan Opera to the 'bleachers' in Yankee Stadium. There were also many reminders of home – British productions seemed to dominate Broadway, from Shakespeare to 'Beyond the Fringe'. In almost every bar, the music to be heard in the early 1960s was the late Acker Bilk's 'Strangers on the Shore'. In 1965, it was my countryman, Tom Jones, and 'Green, Green Grass of Home'. One especially memorable evening was when I went on the off-chance to Carnegie Hall to see if there was anything on, and they told me that there were only seats on the stage, next to the pianist. When I arrived for the performance, I listened at the closest quarters to a then unknown young Russian called Vladimir Ashkenazy, playing with a fluid majesty I had not even remotely heard before. The rest, as they say, is history. The new Philharmonic Hall in the Lincoln Center had just opened on the West Side, so I had many happy evenings listening to Leonard Bernstein conducting the New York Philharmonic, which cynics called the orchestra of a hundred and ten soloists. On a personal front, I also recall speaking on St David's Day at the Waldorf Astoria to a large gathering of wealthy-looking New York Welsh-Americans – I was told that the top floor was occupied by the aged ex-president Herbert Hoover.

But New York was formidable too. A lot of the city seemed physically squalid, including around Columbia on West 10th Street. A curious phenomenon was for the buildings on the main avenue to form a kind of crust of civilisation and the side streets surrounding them collapsing into decay. There was much crime, or talk of crime, and you had to navigate carefully if you were invited out to dinner. After all, the Jets and the Sharks of *West Side Story* were located in my neighbourhood. I also had to get used to the general roughness, even rudeness, of the population – like the policeman who responded to my asking the way with, 'Do you think I'm paid to answer that kind of question?' (I bowdlerise). Especially someone with a British accent, who spoke correctly and looked vaguely like an intellectual might be abused, or else homosexuality might be implied, in a city where much was made of the cult of masculinity. But you got used to this kind of thing. Far more positive, I felt, was the vitality gained from New York being a city of minorities, where the Italians, the Poles, black Americans (called Negroes then) in the slums of Harlem near Columbia, even the poor Puerto Ricans on the Upper West Side, made their own distinctive cultural contributions. From the faces of the people sitting opposite you on the subway, you could discern the secret of New York – a city of immigrants, a standing tribute to the richness of the immigrant experience. From my time in Columbia, I was particularly struck by the distinction and quality of the Jews of New York, like dear Gerry Stearn. Heavily Democratic, the Jews gave the city much of its liberal political quality: they provided many of its voluntary social services, a kind of welfare state in miniature; they made up a 40 per cent proportion of the student body, and many faculty members, including the two professors of American history, at Columbia University; they attended in large numbers the Metropolitan Opera and Carnegie Hall, and often sponsored the productions put on there; they kept the theatre in Broadway going; and they largely made the city into the intellectual and literary capital of America from the *New York Times* downwards. They were a civilising and stimulating force in the community and beyond, much as the Huguenots from France had been in many lands two centuries earlier. Their influence helped me to feel that this pulsating, turbulent place was home.

When I left New York, other cities like Boston (which seemed highly anglicised to me), Minneapolis (where I spent Christmas in 1962), and even 'the second city', mighty Chicago, seemed quite to lack the peculiar aura of New York, being almost provincial in comparison. Some other parts of America, in the meantime, Kansas or Nebraska for instance, seemed hardly to offer anything at all. The South in 1962–3 was a considerable shock, with overt racism and segregation in its beautiful cities. As I have already noted, my friend Graham Parry and I were astonished not to be served a Coca-Cola in the refreshment room at the historical museum of Colonial Williamsburg because we had inadvertently sat in the 'Negro' section. This made us very angry and a shouting match ensued, ending with the waiter banging our drinks down hard on the table and muttering obscenities. When we drove through the south from Virginia via Florida to Texas, the difference in quality between the white and black parts of town astonished us – the black areas often lacked pavements or street lights, or even glass in windows, almost centuries removed from the standards in the white neighbourhoods. By 1965, it was clear that, stimulated by Lyndon B. Johnson's Great Society programme, a massive change was under way. By 1972, when I lectured in Columbia, South Carolina and Baton Rouge in Louisiana, the segregation had totally gone. After nearly a century of discrimination, the South had been legally purged and was now delightful again. When David and

Katherine joined me for a visit to New Orleans in 1994 it was totally enjoyable as we munched our goujons of crocodile and had our breakfast in Brenan's, and listened to the blind blues musician in Preservation Hall. The state of Texas stands alone, hard to define as either South or West, with Austin a charming artistic city with much surprisingly picturesque country nearby – notably Lyndon Johnson's home in the Pedernales valley, where his ranch survives. In 1994, it was Lady Bird Johnson's birthday, and there were helicopters parked outside the back door.

The south-west I saw at length in 1963, as we drove the three thousand miles across the country through the magical contours of New Mexico, Arizona, Utah and the many national parks of southern California, was breathtaking. Monument Valley, beloved of western movies, was especially memorable. We gave a lift there to a young Navajo boy who, in the heart of the USA, knew not a word of English. The vastness and variety of America impressed itself upon us always; people appeared astonished that we had even come from as far away as New York let alone Britain. California seemed to me the most stunningly beautiful state of all, with Yosemite supreme amongst the many glorious national parks, which made me feel far more positive towards their early patron, Teddy Roosevelt. I saw the Rockies, Yellowstone and the North-west in 1965, when I made the northern route to Oregon. I was particularly impressed by Montana and Idaho, majestic with their mountains and forests, and gazed down at their mines, which had provoked some bitter strikes from copper and silver miners in their day. The area reminded me strongly of Wales, and I could see why Big Bill Heywood of the Industrial Workers of the World had appealed to the Welsh valleys. In Butte, Montana, I was asked by a waitress if I was British and, if so, had I met Ringo and the Queen. Oregon and Washington state were lovely too, especially the cities of Portland and Seattle. An area which I knew less well was the Mid-West, which I had opportunity to discover many years later in 2005. In Ohio, I was struck by seeing the Stars and Stripes flying everywhere, even over mortuaries. A former graduate student at Oxford had invited me to visit the Rutherford Hayes Library in Ohio, and I looked at that particular post-Civil War president's papers. Rutherford Hayes is commonly dismissed as a mediocrity elected on a bogus ballot, but that judgement is unfair. I noted that he spent much time on two issues, black education and prison reform, neither of which were likely to be vote-winners in 1877. I also enjoyed a ball game watching the Cleveland Indians in a local derby against the Detroit Tigers, and bought an Indians T-shirt for my impending first grandson. I was with dear Philip Allen, my old mate from Oriel, in a Chicago hotel when the news of the birth came through, and we substituted morning coffee with champagne. Afterwards, Philip and his wife Peggy took me to Spring Green, Wisconsin, to see the Frank Lloyd Wright residence at Taliesin, named after the Welsh poet who also gave his name to my father's birthplace. We visited also the shores of Lake Superior, and the small Upper Peninsula of western Michigan, an old logging and mining area.

America went through fundamental changes during my visits, spread over half a century. In 1962, in New York City at least, it seemed to me a more progressive place than Britain. The nation seemed egalitarian in speech and in dress, in ways unknown in our country then. It had few public schools, no landed aristocracy, no established church and, of course, was a republic in which people felt themselves to be citizens rather than subjects. A Democratic government looked like a better version of a Labour one over here. The great exception at that time was the Deep South, which New Yorkers felt to be an obscene aberration and which they were working to reform. When I went again in 1965, as I have said, things had changed very much for the better. The South was visibly changing, with civil rights legislation in 1964 and 1968 transforming the status of the African-Americans and removing the stain of segregation from the statute book and social convention. Lyndon Johnson was clearly having a hugely positive effect too as president, with a tidal wave of emotional goodwill after the assassination of President Kennedy. (We stayed a boring night in Dallas in July 1963, four months before Kennedy's tragic death there.) Johnson's brilliant orchestration of a string of massive reform measures – Medicare and Medicaid, anti-poverty programmes, housing, urban renewal and elementary education (especially important for a former schoolteacher like Johnson) – make him in that respect one of the really great American presidents in my view, and among the most effective. Robert Caro's great biography brings that out brilliantly, as does the marvellous Lyndon B. Johnson Museum in Austin. The effect of change was palpable, even in urban New York. The Columbia campus had been a scene of violence in 1964 when the local black population in Harlem demanded a share of the fine sporting facilities of the university next door. A compromise was reached, and now racial tranquillity was restored. It was also a remarkable period for American popular culture, with challenging folk singers like Bob Dylan, Pete Seeger and Joan Baez (a particular favourite of mine) the protest heroes of the hour. For perhaps a fleeting moment America presented a picture of vibrancy, affluence and optimism which I found almost inspiring, as I told my Swansea students when I got home. I felt we could do with some of the Great Society, and the nation that created it, here in Britain.

Tragically, very sad events soon followed the bitter conflict over the extended war in Vietnam (not very evident in the summer of 1965), renewed racial tension in northern cities and the assassinations successively of Robert Kennedy (whom I had heard speak at the Oxford Union, quite inspiringly) and Martin Luther King. Johnson, the hero of the hour in 1965, had to step down as president in the face of mass protests –'Hey, Hey, LBJ, how many kids did you kill today?' The United States has lost much of its innocence and inner peace subsequently. I would like to have lived in the United States then, especially New York City; I had hugely enjoyed its universities, I had been stimulated by its art and intellectual life and the glories of the Hudson valley. I had even fallen in love there for the first time, with Judith Green, a local Jewish girl. Nowadays, the United States seems sharply different to me. There is a doctrinal neo-liberalism that has swept aside the progressive New Deal liberalism still current in the 1960s, when great figures like Eleanor Roosevelt and Governor Herbert Lehman were still alive. (I remember seeing Herbert Hoover appear in an old newsreel in a local cinema, and the audience as one stood up and booed.) The religious right (almost unknown in 1963, other than in a few parts of the Deep South) is now hugely powerful, including on the choices available to women; inequality has become even more rampant, not only for black people, notably over health care, housing and the basics of social life. American foreign policy, even under Barack Obama, whose election I enthusiastically welcomed, has been rudderless, veering from blind warmongering, as in Iraq, to total inaction during the Arab Spring. Visiting Texas again in October 2014, I was struck by the widespread near-hatred of this liberal, black president, some of it no doubt racist. But the excitement I felt on my first visit has far from deserted me; America still seems to me to have a unique vitality and an infectious idealism and I have loved teaching its history. I am hugely fortunate to have seen so much of it, and met so many of its hospitable citizens. It helped me to grow up both as a historian and a person, and, foreign though I feel it to be, I feel closer to it emotionally than to almost any other country on earth.

I have visited two other countries in the American hemisphere. Peru I saw with two friends in June 1963. I knew virtually no Spanish, but the domination of the local newspapers by the impact of the Profumo case in Britain soon led to an improvement in my reading skills. It was a tough, if fascinating, tour. Peru was hardly tourist-friendly at that time, and travelling on their long-range buses over wild mountain roads was a rugged experience. On the other hand, we also travelled by trains, built by the British in the previous century, which were picturesque in the extreme. We went from Lima on to the attractive city of Arequipa in southern Peru, surrounded by volcanoes; then on to Puno on the shores of Lake Titicaca (whereon sailed an old nineteenth-century steamship built in Greenock); then on to Cuzco, the highlight of our journey; and finally to the fabled lost city of Macchu Pichu, 12,000 feet up in the heart of the Andes. Two things struck me. One was the extraordinary gulf in social and living standards between the favoured Hispanic Peruvians in the coastal towns and cities, and the desperately poor Quechua-speaking Indians high up in the Andes. Simon Bolivar's revolution had clearly been for the former only; the latter sometimes ventured down to Lima, a journey for which their blood composition was not really suitable, and lived on sordid refuse tips in the city. Life expectancy among the Peruvian Indians was very low. In Lima, the conquistador Pizarro's tomb served as a monument to racial subjection. It was not surprising that Indians were flocking to support the Communist protest movement Sendero Luminoso (the shining path), and its leader Abimael Guzmán. In contrast, we attended an authentic Indian folk festival up in the hills, replete with alpacas and vicunas, which was very entertaining and colourful. Among the astonishing sights we saw were the Indian people who lived on floating reed islands, literally *on* Lake Titicaca, their children being taught by a Seventh Day Adventist school. The other feature to strike me was the extraordinarily long-lasting impact of the Inca empire. The Incas appeared to behave rather like the Romans towards the Greeks. They were great warriors, colonisers and road-builders, erecting terrifying fortresses like the battlements of Sacsuahaman just outside Cuzco, and the awesome citadel of Macchu Pichu. The tapestries and jewellery in the Lima folk museum, however, all came from peoples like the Paramongans, whom they conquered. I had never been to a Third World country before; it was tough but unforgettable, especially Machu Picchu, and I wish I had gone again.

The other country I visited in that hemisphere was Canada – or at least Ontario. Canada seemed quiescent compared with the vibrant nation to the south. There was much debate among its academics as to the nature of the Canadian identity. For a historian, much the most fascinating place was Quebec city. A lift took you down from the Heights of Abraham – with its graves of both the generals, Wolfe and Montcalm, following the great battle of 1759 – to the old seventeenth-century city below with its many monuments from the reign of Louis XIV. Canada seemed to me potentially a lovely country, an English core attached to a highly attractive French community, where the language flourished and the food and wine excelled. Unfortunately, the tensions between the two communities, and the friction symbolised by the Parti Québécois has to some degree made Canada a country of internal conflict ever since. The routine arguments about bilingual road-signs were familiar to a Welshman, but there was an undercurrent of terrorist violence in Canada. I was sufficiently stirred (or plain foolish) to write to Prime Minister Pierre Trudeau about Canada's problems, and I treasure the reply that I received from him personally.

Another major country of which I have had some experience is South Africa. As I have mentioned previously, I went there three times through the aegis of my great friend Bruce Murray, in 1997, 1998 and 2000, to lecture at Witwatersrand and other universities. In the course of these visits, thanks largely to Bruce, I saw a great deal of this great country as well, as it emerged from the trauma of the apartheid years. It is a land of extraordinary natural beauty, with the elegance of Cape Town, the splendours of the 'garden route' along the south, the picturesque scenery of the Drakensburg range in the Natal National Park, and its amazing wildlife, notably in Kruger Park, which we visited for three days. The historical monuments were memorable too, as I have described, the battle sites of the Zulu and the Boer Wars in particular. One of the intriguing topics discussed at the Pretoria conference in 1998 was that of the correct name for a war in which the blacks were broadly not involved. On balance, the Anglo-Boer War seemed to find most favour.

But the legacy of the racial conflicts of the apartheid period was inescapable in South Africa. This was made transparently clear on two successive days at the end of my first visit in 1997. On the first, we went to the attractive city of Pretoria to see a rugby match between the home team Blue Bulls and the British Lions. The Lions actually lost that first match, with the Welsh captain, Rob Howley, carried off injured. But what was striking to me was that virtually no one was speaking English – it was an almost entirely a white Afrikaaner crowd at the match. The next day, Bruce had arranged for me to travel with him to the stadium at Soweto to see a football World Cup qualifier between South Africa and Zambia. This time, too, hardly any English was spoken, but that was because Bruce and I were just about the only white people present. It was a totally black occasion and crowd. When South Africa scored after about fifteen minutes, there was huge excitement – fireworks went up into the air and it seemed that shots were fired in celebration. Bruce and I were patted on the back as though we had scored the goal. It seemed almost unbelievable that these two events, and these two crowds of people, belonged to the same country. There was much talk of black crime and burglary: in Pretoria the hotel staff would not let me walk to a nearby hotel cashpoint because it would, they said, be too physically dangerous. When I lectured in Grahamstown, at Rhodes University, there was another ominous experience. Grahamstown looked to me like a plush country town in Surrey, and I assumed it had just a few thousand inhabitants. I was told that in fact 80,000 people lived there, the vast bulk of them black people who lived in a township over the hill. A black man harassed me somewhat as I sat having a coffee in an open-air cafe, and I had to seek help. My hotel room there was subjected to attempted burglary. The hotel building had been designed by the old Boer leader of yesteryear, Piet Retief, who had an interest in architecture, and the old door had been sadly damaged during a burglary attempt, though nothing had been taken. The burglars were captured by the police; my white host shook his head, and said it was all the result of doing away with apartheid – apartheid had kept them under control, he said, and the country had been unsafe ever since it was abolished.

On the other hand, progress was clearly being made. Black students were numerous among my Wits students, and segregation in Johannesburg had virtually disappeared. The mood appeared positive and the economy, boosted

▲ Figure 26 *Speaking at the University of Bordeaux in 1999, with Peter Shore and Anne-Marie Motard.*

◄ Figure 27 *My introduction in the House of Lords, 12 July 2000, with Lord Merlyn-Rees.*

▲ Figure 28 *Celebrating my peerage with David and Katherine.*

▲ Figure 29 *With Prince Charles, Katherine, Sir John Meurig Thomas and Clive*

▲ Figure 30 *With Lord Callaghan to celebrate his ninetieth birthday at 10 Downing Street, 27 March 2002. Sir Patrick Cormack MP is on the right.*

▲ Figure 31 *Speaking at the University of Bordeaux on 'The Special Relationship',*
24 January 2003. I met Elizabeth for the first time after my lecture, and another 'special -
relationship' was born!

▲ Figure 32 *Celebrating my seventieth birthday at home, 16 May 2004, singing 'The Red Flag' with Michael Foot.*

▲ Figure 33 *With my children and cousins and their spouses, celebrating my seventieth birthday.*

▲ Figure 34 *My final meeting with Lord Callaghan, at Upper Clayhill Farm, 3 February 2005. Left to right: (back row) Michael Callaghan; Lord Merlyn-Rees; Lord Healey; me; Baroness Margaret Jay; Professor Michel Adler; (front row) Lady*

▲ Figure 35 *At a gaudy (dinner), Queen's, c.2005.*

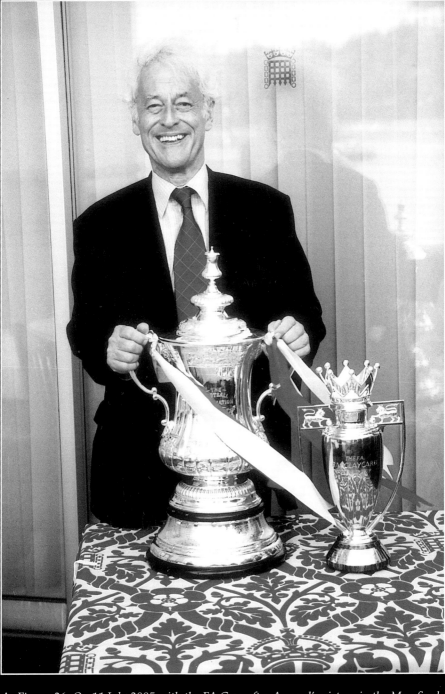

▲ Figure 36 *On 11 July 2005 with the FA Cup, after Arsenal's victory in the May final held in Cardiff.*

▲ Figure 37 *Katherine and me on the Yangtze in August 2006.*

▲ Figure 38 *Interview at Michael Foot's home in Pilgrims Lane for the* Today *programme, with Michael and James Naughtie, 14 March 2007*

▲ Figure 39 *Launching* Michael Foot: A Life *at the University of Texas, Austin, in* May 2007.

▲ Figure 40 *With Ffion and William Hague at the launch of* Michael Foot: A Life *in* March 2007.

▲ Figure 41 *Speaking at an exhibition of socialist classics in the House of Lords, with Lord Sawyer, in 2008.*

▲ Figure 42 *My entry into the Gorsedd of Bards at Cardiff in August 2008.*

▲ Figure 43 *With Elizabeth at Fatehpur Sikri, India, in April 2010.*

▲ Figure 44 *With Elizabeth at Biarritz, after lecturing at the University of Pau,
8 November 2011.*

▲ Figure 45 *With David and my grandson Joseph when Wales took on New Zealand at the Millennium Stadium, Cardiff, 22 November 2014.*

▲ Figure 46 *Receiving my lifetime achievement award from Hywel Francis MP, joined by Elizabeth, at the House of Commons, 18 June 2014.*

▲ Figure 47 *With my grandchildren – Joseph, Clara, Thomas and Samuel – New Year's Day 2015.*

by South Africa's great mineral wealth, seemed to be surviving international storms well. The African National Congress had, in its own way, provided a stable leadership for the first years of the new country; the great Nelson Mandela was alive and well, and living quite near Bruce in northern Johannesburg. I was impressed with the moral support given to the new government by the white academics I met. I spoke to an English medieval historian, not obviously political, in Cape Town, who quietly said to me of the recent past, 'Of course we all had to be activists.' Bruce himself, a member of the ANC at that time, had shown much fortitude at Wits, one of the few reasonably liberal universities then. I could see something of the new strength of South Africa during my last visit in 2000. Before my lectures began, I went with Bruce to Zimbabwe to see Victoria Falls, an unforgettable experience, and I found the walk down from the statue of Livingstone and the beobab trees to the Falls area in itself thrilling. Zimbabwe had been reduced by Robert Mugabe to a state of economic paralysis. The large hotel in which we stayed was virtually empty, as was the boat on which we took a trip down the Zambesi, spotting giraffes and elephants en route. The Zimbabwe currency, extremely visually attractive with animal illustrations, was virtually worthless. It could be used for wallpaper. By contrast, the South African rand, at a large discount against the pound sterling, was a strong currency in Zimbabwe and we used it to pay our bills. South Africa was recovering, and at least it was not Zimbabwe.

The other country outside Europe which I have visited several times is at the other end of the world – Malaysia, in south-east Asia. I have been there five times to look at educational institutions and give historical lectures; some were on biography, of which the Malaysians had a very different idea from mine, opposing any kind of personal revelation. In the official biography of its first prime minister, Tunku Abdul Rahman, the author proudly states that the subject had read it through carefully before publication 'to avoid error'. I first went with Jane in 1992; then in 1993 with David; in 1995 on my own; in 2007 with Katherine; and 2012 in with Elizabeth. Each time, I was invited there through the good offices of the Aberystwyth Old Students association in Kuala Lumpur and its presiding genius, my old friend, Tan Sri Arshad Ayub, himself a proud graduate of Aberystwyth. He was an extraordinary polymath, an educationalist who had founded a university – the technology university MARA – a banker and a businessman, and once a member of the government. His influence is writ large on the history of the fledgling state of Malaysia in its early years. He and his lovely wife, Zaleah, were remarkably hospitable, as were the old students. Twice I had dinner with them on the top floor of what was then the tallest building in the world – higher even than the Empire State Building in New York that I had ascended back in 1962. Twice I met through them the Crown Prince of Perak state, Rajah Muda, a highly intelligent man who was a graduate of Worcester College, Oxford, and apparently a member of its rugby team, and who had attended some of my lectures in the Oxford Schools. I have travelled widely in Malaysia. Twice I have been to Melaka (formerly Molucca), a fascinating historic town with legacies from the imperialist rule of the British, the Dutch, the Portuguese and the Chinese; three times to Terengganu on the east coast; and to the island of Langkawi, now threatened by unplanned tourist development. The most impressive feature of Malaysia to me was its strong emphasis on higher education, at first through contacts with British universities, as with Aberystwyth and MARA; the Minister for Education was the most important member of the Cabinet. I was struck by the fact that the minister I met, a very able man, was Chinese, a somewhat oppressed minority in Malaysia where the Malay majority held the key positions. There were, however, some darkening clouds ahead. One was the growth of Muslim fundamentalism in the east of the country, including in Terengganu on the east coast, where I visited KUSZA (Koleg Universiti Sultan Zainal Abidin), a new college which Aberystwyth was sponsoring for university status. Some of our women alumni in Malaysia told me of their fears for their professional lives over this development of fundamentalism. Another cloud was the difficulty arising from the fact that Malaysia was virtually a one-party state, run by the Malay-dominated UMNO (United Malays National Organization). When I was there in 2012, the trial was under way of Anwar, the leader of the mainly Chinese opposition party. He was variously accused of rape and sodomy, and had been beaten up by the police in gaol, with no action taken. Much public anger was caused when the judges acquitted him after examining DNA samples but, in February 2015, the judges changed their minds and sentenced him to gaol for five years. It seemed to me that Anwar's main crime was to be leader of the opposition.

I had other visits to south-east Asia. I went to Singapore with David in 1993, and enjoyed lecturing at the National University there where it was that I interviewed Lee Kuan Yew. Singapore was fun, if a bit claustrophobic, and David and I enjoyed the theme park on Samosa island with its film of the surrender to the Japanese in 1942. I went with Katherine on a wonderful holiday to Cambodia in 2007, where we both marvelled at the splendour of Angkor Wat in the early morning sunshine. I noticed that Cambodia, unlike its neighbours, made explicit reference to recent political conflicts, and the horrors of the Khmer Rouge regime. There was a revealing if horrific museum of torture weapons, Tuol Sleng, in Pnom Penh, which showed how the Cambodians had endured the horrors of the Khmer Rouge as they had also the bombing unleashed on them by my old interviewee, Henry Kissinger. Katherine and I enjoyed a drink in the Press Club in Pnom Penh, beside the River Mekong, which was owned by a man from Swansea.

These were all visits resulting from lecturing engagements which I was invited to undertake. My visits to India were a mixture of work and tourism. I went there first with Jane for the conference of the Commonwealth Universities in January 1991. I have always liked the people of India; I have had two special Indian friends, Partha Gupta and Bhikhu Parekh. There was a state of emergency in 1991 at the time of my visit, and Jane and I were escorted into the Taj Mahal by armed troops; the Taj Mahal was still magical, a temple of love. The conference in New Delhi, a friendly affair, offered an instructive insight into Indian intellectual attitudes. The many Indian vice-chancellors there told me how they were instructed to assume humility at their high stipends, while millions in their country were impoverished; they were encouraged to undertake a kind of community service, leaving their posts for a while to work in the fields. I described to them how wonderful Jane and I found New Delhi, and how pressed we would be in Wales to match the city at its next hosting. They replied, to my pleasant surprise, that the Wales conference would be the best yet – when I asked why, they told me it would be because the Prince of Wales would be present, and he was. I was the host when they visited Aberystwyth, and they much enjoyed the narrow-gauge former slate train to Devil's Bridge, which could easily have been back home for them in Simla. I saw India last with Elizabeth, a kind of second honeymoon in early 2010, when we hugely enjoyed Delhi, Agra, Jaipur and especially Simla, the old military headquarters of the Raj. We found ourselves obliged to stay on longer than expected though because volcanic ash in Iceland grounded much global air traffic for a while. India seemed to me both economically buoyant but also socially divided to an alarming degree. The wealth of cities like New Delhi seemed even more marked on my 2010 visit, but so did the desperate poverty in rural areas. In 1991, the buildings in the countryside were dilapidated; now, in 2010, they were literally falling down. Elizabeth said it looked like a war zone. It seemed to me that a fairly fundamental social and economic reform would be needed to keep the country stable, lest the gulf between the two nations become unbridgeable. The caste system also, alas, is all too evident.

I went elsewhere in Asia too, but only as a tourist. With Katherine, I had an amazing tour of China in 2006, taking in the Great Wall, Beijing, Xian (for the terra cotta statues), the three Gorges dam, a cruise down the Yangtze, Shanghai, Guilin and the Li river, and Hong Kong. It was all totally astonishing, especially the Great Wall. China was culturally fascinating – witness the Tai Chi exercises undertaken in public parks, with fine choral music, during the mornings. There was adjustment on age grounds, and I particularly appreciated the collective back-rubbing indulged in by senior citizens. The impression was of extraordinary energy and economic activity, but at significant human cost. In Beijing, thousands of simple homes (hutongs) would be destroyed to make way for the stadia of the 2008 Olympic Games, while a pall of poisonous smog could be seen hanging over Beijing from miles away, which was also very apparent as we cruised along the Yangtze. China was also terrifying in its feeling of utter state control. Katherine and I searched the Internet for 'Tiananmen Square'; and 'Human Rights' – we drew a blank each time. Our guides did not seem to have travelled much – one of them said he had been abroad once, by which he meant Hong Kong. We much enjoyed Sri Lanka in 2003, a very pleasant country, at the time enjoying a lull in the war with the Tamils. Kandy and Galle were exceptionally attractive cities; there were lots of elephants, and monkeys who ran off with my swimming trunks left to dry out on a hotel roof. In the Middle East, we very much liked Jordan, especially Petra and the Dead Sea, in 2008. It seemed a most agreeable and tolerant Arab country, with lovely people; in marked contrast was Egypt, which I saw with David and Katherine in 1995. The pyramids and the Great Sphinx were as breathtaking to me now as they had been to my young father during the First World War. Luxor was especially marvellous, with its huge temple at Karnak. The most unfortunate thing about Egypt was the despicable behaviour of some Egyptian males towards Katherine as a 16-year-old girl. We had to give up walking in the streets of Cairo altogether. My father's opinion of Egyptian men in 1917 had not been high either.

I also visited Africa at various times, and found each country on that vast continent instructive, not least for the historian's interest. Tunisia, which I saw with the Lords' Archaeological group in 2003 at the time of the Iraq war, had extraordinary Roman archaeology. The huge amphitheatre at El Jem was breathtaking, as large as the arena in Verona, and the Roman city of Douga was colossal. But most moving for me was the almost empty expanse of what had once been Hannibal's Carthage, destroyed meticulously by the Romans after the Punic wars, with salt put down on the soil to destroy anything that looked as if it might be fertile. It was ethnic cleansing with a vengeance. On that visit, we met the prime minister of Tunisia, a pleasant man whose view of the Iraq invasion was identical to my own. The murders in the beautiful Bardo museum in March 2015 I found most distressing. I have twice very much enjoyed Morocco, with Katherine in 1999 and Elizabeth in 2013; on each occasion, I stayed in Marrakech, a lovely city with glorious palaces and the famous souks. For the British historian, a most interesting place in Marrakech was the Hotel Mamounia, where Winston Churchill had stayed many times and from which he had painted pictures of the Atlas mountains. It was disappointing to us in 2013 that the youthful staff seemed to know little of his connection, and did not even know where his portrait was stored. I had, of course, visited Gambia with David in 1999, and enjoyed its wildlife; and, during my stay in South Africa, Bruce took me through beautiful Swaziland and the apparently derelict little state of Lesotho, formerly Basutoland. On the other side of Africa, there was a jolly trip in 2007 with Katherine to Zanzibar, where the capital Stone Town was particularly interesting. Preserved there as a museum was the house of a heroic Welsh sea captain named Matthews, who had apparently ended the slave trade in Zanzibar, which was at that time run from the date plantations of Oman. Our plane on the way back was held up with some technical problem which allowed us a day in Dar-es-Salaam – not a beautiful city at all, but with a fascinating historical and ethnographical museum which also contained in pickled form the oldest fish in the world, the famous coelocanth. I enjoyed this museum, with its records of the period of German occupation before 1918, prior to the country becoming British-ruled Tanganyika, which itself did not seem to have brought any great economic or social improvement.

In 2001, Katherine took me to Australia, a country she had visited before. We did the usual tourist sites – the Barrier Reef, Sydney and the Blue Mountains, Melbourne, Adelaide and Ayers Rock – all hugely enjoyable, along with a visit to Bowral, the home of one of my boyhood gods, the great Don Bradman. I particularly enjoyed Adelaide, which seemed to me a gracious, very English city. One joy was the bust in front of the university in Adelaide of Lord Florey, the Nobel prize-winning scientist who had appointed me to Queen's in 1966. A much sadder sight was seeing a group of apparently drunken aborigines being rounded up by police in a public park. Australia has many proud claims to eminence and acclaim, but race relations with its appalling treatment of the indigenous coloured community is not one of them. Still, in general, for the tourist in me at least, Australia seemed a very pleasant country with very friendly people – and of course a love of cricket, always a sign of civilisation. I have never visited New Zealand, a bridge too far for a retired man – though David and Katherine have, and both enjoyed it tremendously, especially driving around the South Island. I have always enjoyed the company of New Zealanders, though much less so seeing the All Blacks regularly trample Wales into the turf pallets of the Millennium Stadium in Cardiff – the most recent occasion in a sixty-year sequence being on 22 November 2014, when I went for the first time with my son and grandson Joseph, to watch them play.

The great majority of my overseas trips, of course, have been to Europe. I have always felt instinctively European, even if it is not a 'Europe of the mind' as hailed by the more zealous Europhiles. I have strongly supported British membership of the EU, and believe the populist views of the UK Independence Party to be a dangerous fantasy. One of my very few speaking ventures at school had been to urge British membership of the Schuman plan for a coal, iron and steel community back in 1950. My preference, though, is always for great civilisations. I never favour little countries like Luxemburg, which seem to exist mainly for the purpose of providing a tax haven for multinational corporations, and which exercise an undue influence in the EU through dubious politicians like Jean-Claude Juncker, the architect of his country's tax arrangements; the same goes for Lichtenstein, Andorra and Monaco. For all the wonders of my beloved Wales, small is not always beautiful.

My second favourite European country is Italy, which I have visited often over the years: first in 1961 with a Swansea colleague, the political scientist, Geraint Parry; then several times in the 1980s with Jane and the children; once in 2002, to lecture in Bologna; and latterly for some delightful visits with Elizabeth. David and Katherine have always loved their Italian jaunts – Jane had a Mediterranean temperament, and she blossomed in Italy. I myself appreciated the fact that the women seemed to look like Sophia Loren and that the men were genial and often comic. We once had a funny exchange with a waiter in our hotel near Pisa. He greeted us at the table with the words 'no rush', which I thought a bit strange; it turned out that he meant 'Know Rush?', referring to Ian Rush the Wales football striker who had recently moved from Liverpool to Juventus in Turin – so Wales had made its mark in the heart of Tuscany. My travels have taken me mostly down the well-known tourist trails – Venice, Tuscany, Umbria and, of course, Rome – I do not know Apulia and the far south. Rome is a marvellous compendium of Roman and Italian civilisation down the millennia, and Elizabeth and I have three times celebrated our wedding anniversary there, fantastically on each occasion. The *castelli*, Frascati and the rest, outside Rome are equally compelling. We once had had a jolly family holiday in Sicily, where we discovered that the holiday centre was run entirely by and for French people, with us being the exceptions. I won the table tennis competition, beating an eight-year-old boy in the final; without being falsely modest, I can say that I have always been unbeatable against eight-year-old boys. Our grasp of the French language came on apace, while we uttered scarcely a word of Italian during our entire stay. Sicily was quite an atmospheric place, especially Palermo. I have always enjoyed Lampedusa's famous novel of the island, *The Leopard*, and the book on Lampedusa by David Gilmour, the son of Ian, my dear late dining companion at the *Gay Hussar*.

As a historian, I have always loved the way the Italians treasure and preserve their historical legacy, especially from the Renaissance period. Visiting Italy, only in Venice did the legacy seem physically threatened by both potential and actual flooding. By contrast, Italians seem to have little respect for their present circumstances. Elizabeth and I were amazed in 2012, when we were allowed to observe the Senate meeting in a glorious Medici palace; senators spoke among colleagues reading newspapers, using mobile phones and chatting up secretaries (let us assume that that is who they were). Every standing order that the House of Lords would exercise was being broken at once. Elizabeth noticed that some senators were even dropping litter on the plush red carpets. It was ironic that we entered the senate chamber via a room devoted to the glorious memory of Mazzini, Garibaldi and the Risorgimento; the senators showed total contempt for their legacy, the parliament of a united Italy. It came as no surprise to me that so little notice was taken of the 150th anniversary of Italian unification in 1861; as d'Azeglio famously said at that time, they have made Italy but have yet to make the Italians.

Germany I found fascinating but it jarred, inevitably so for one with my war memories. It was difficult to avoid the consequences of war when I visited the country; in my remarkable first visit to Bonn in 1957, with Robert Woetzel, at a time when London had recovered from the ravages of the Blitz, I was astonished to see great cities like Cologne and especially Essen, home of the Krupps works, still displaying many miles of devastation, the work (as placards constantly reminded us) of the RAF (and 'Bomber Harris' in particular). In city after after city, from Dusseldorf to Stuttgart, it was a picture of cities still rebuilding after the unleashing of Britain's weapons of mass destruction. The great university city of Heidelberg had not escaped. Berlin in 1999, shortly after reunification, bore the legacy of the Holocaust and the role of Checkpoint Charlie. For that reason, it was a bit grim, even though I enjoyed a trip to San Souci at Potsdam, where Frederick the Great had once entertained Voltaire amidst much elegance. More pleasant was lecturing to a group of German and other scholars on post-1918 European reconstruction, at the leisurely spa town of Baden Baden in 1998. I have been a few times to the stimulating seminars on Europe at the Friedrich Ebert Stiftung at Freudenstadt near Stuttgart, arranged by the eminent Scottish historian and my very good friend Chris Harvie, later to be a Scottish MSP, and I have lectured for him in the University of Tübingen, but these were international experiences rather than specifically German. My most interesting moments, perhaps, came in 1957 when a general election was taking place. I heard the Chancellor Konrad Adenauer, speak in Bonn, where he was well received despite being in the socialist stronghold of North Rhine Westphalia. Robert Woetzel and I also went to a rather violent meeting of the far-right Deutsches Reichs Partei. In retrospect, the most significant result of that year's election was the decision of the Socialists, in their Bad Godesburg programme, to ditch the remnants of pre-war Marxism, a move much appreciated by Hugh Gaitskell and the Labour centre-right in Britain. The Social Democratic Party in Germany was heavily beaten in 1957, but its time was to come in the 1960s under powerful figures like Willy Brandt and Helmut Schmidt, whom I was later to interview.

Austria in 1968, as I have said, was not a success partly for personal reasons, though I enjoyed driving through Carinthia and Styria in the south-east, which felt Balkan. There was, however, a macabre fascination in driving over the border into what had once been Hitler's Eagle's Nest at Berchtesgaden, high up in the Bavarian Alps. It was here that Lloyd George had visited him in 1936, and afterwards disastrously written of him as 'the George Washington of Germany'. The Netherlands I have always enjoyed – Amsterdam four times and Utrecht once. Apart from the incomparable art, I especially cherished my first visit there with Jane in 1973, travelling by train in that small country to enjoy the glories of Delft, Leiden and the Hague, along with Zandvoort on the coast where we ate soused herring by holding it from the tail and somehow managed to share consecutively one swimsuit without indecency. Belgium, as I have mentioned, was remarkable for its divide between Flemings and Francophones – Katherine reported that among the EU staff when she worked in Brussels, the only tension was between the two Belgian linguistic groups. But I much enjoyed two visits to see Katherine there; I took her to the Grande Place to have a drink in the building where, in 1848, Marx wrote the *Communist Manifesto*, which, as a non-Marxist, I have always found inspirational. Auden has immortalised the *Musée des Beaux Arts*, and rightly so. On my second visit, David came to join us for his birthday, which we celebrated by seeing the battlefield at Waterloo. I had read much about it at school, and recalled how General d'Erlon had marched up and down without engaging in battle at all at Quatre Bras. The farmhouses and woodlands came back to my mind as I gazed at the battlefield from the Butte de Lyon. A notable feature of the memorials there was that, contrary to everything I had read previously, the battle of Waterloo was apparently won by Napoleon. In Scandinavia, as I have said, I found social democratic Sweden most interesting, especially Stockholm harbour, with the good ship Vasa, which sank in 1628 but is now raised up from beneath the harbour waters, and the city of Uppsala with the tombs of the Vasa kings and the great botanist Linnaeus's charming garden. Finland was a wonderland of its own.

Southern, Mediterranean Europe, other than Italy, I have not found so appealing; I am an irredeemable northerner. I visited Greece in 1961, and found Athens repellent. The incomparable glories of the Parthenon and the other buildings on the Acropolis were being worn away by traffic pollution and vibration. At the time, I felt the Greeks did not deserve to inherit these historic monuments, often used as a quarry in the past. Now there is a fine purpose-built museum to house the projected return of the Elgin Marbles, though I am inclined to keep them where they are. Relocating such priceless exhibits to their habitat of origin would lead to chaos. My most memorable day in Greece was spent in Mycenae, a unique archaeological site and a magical landscape. I could well understand how excited the German archaeologist Heinrich Schliemann became when he gazed upon the legendary tombs of Agamemnon and Clytemnestra. Latterly, Elizabeth and I have visited Crete, which we greatly liked, especially Knossos, the great discovery of the Oxford archaeologist Sir Arthur Evans. Spain is not one of my great countries either. Katherine took me to Granada to recover from my car crash in 2005, when I feasted on the glories of the Alhambra, but thought the city drab and overpopulated by people of religion. I much prefer more relaxed Catholic countries like France, where faith is not oppressive and where there is not a superabundance of priests and nuns. As regards the Alhambra, I recalled the sardonic remark made to me by a Spaniard at Oxford that medieval Spain had been graced by two peoples – the Jews and the Moors – and the Spaniards had got rid of them both. My one visit to Madrid took me to see the glories of the Velasquez and Goya paintings at the Prado, a thrilling privilege. I did not greatly care for Lisbon, other than the eighteenth-century areas rebuilt after the massive earthquake of the 1750s, though I much enjoyed seeing the tomb of Vasco da Gama (some years later, the driver who almost killed me in a road accident was Portuguese).

Finally, I had a few forays to eastern Europe, to the former Communist or Soviet satellite states. I had never any wish to see Russia, which I felt would be oppressive and a bit grim, though many friends have told me how marvellous Saint Petersburg now is. In Croatia, as I have said, the walled city of Dubrovnik, once Ragusa, was utterly beautiful. I could well imagine how Michael Foot had fallen in love with the place, and had campaigned in his old age for international support for Dubrovnik when it was attacked by the Serbs – as Gladstone had similarly done in his old age for the massacred Armenians. I have also twice visited Montenegro, a most beautiful mountainous country, though still not reconciled with Croatia after the war. I could see why it had been the setting for Lehar's 'Merry Widow'. I enjoyed a visit to Prague with Katherine in 1996, though we noted that the atmosphere everywhere seemed quite quiet, so few years after Wenceslas Square. It was particularly memorable to go through the old palace high above the Vltava river, where took place the famous defenestration of May 1618 which had led to the Thirty Years' War that I had much studied as a student. We greatly enjoyed an evening at the lovely baroque opera house, though I would have preferred Czech opera, ideally Smetana, even to the beautiful Italian opera we heard. An evening in Riga's graceful opera house was also a delightful highlight of a lecturing visit to Latvia with Elizabeth in 2014.

A few years earlier, I had gone to Bratislava during my time at Aberystwyth. The Slovaks did not seem to like anyone very much, especially the Czechs from whom they had recently broken away. When I lectured at Comenius University, my remarks on Lloyd George's critical view of the Czech president Eduard Benes at the time of the treaty of Versailles and also around the Munich crisis –'that little swine Benes' – went down particularly well with my Slovak audience. I recall also marvelling, as I spoke in a riverside café in among the jukeboxes, at the Danube fast flowing below. I was talking about nationalism, and I felt that the river of nations was surging on beneath me as I spoke. A young Scottish woman from the British Council took me to see Brno, the old capital of Moravia, a lovely historic city inside the Czech border, which meant making taking a train from Bratislava. At the border of the two countries, all the personnel changed – the engine drivers, the guards and the ticket collectors – equally bad-tempered in both countries. The Slovak ticket collector abused everybody else but decided, for some reason, that I was the only passenger in the compartment who had the right ticket – heaven knows why – so I escaped censure.

In this Baedeker of my travels, I have left until last my most important and favoured overseas country. That was, of course, France, which I must by now have visited close upon a hundred times. I first went to France as a student, to Paris, in 1953. It seemed then in a drab, bleak state after the war, and things were not improved by a general strike breaking out. But it was still the most beautiful city I have ever seen, especially the area around the Sorbonne, where I have had the privilege of addressing audiences in recent years since marrying a French wife. I know, and love, almost all of the country – Normandy, Brittany, the Loire, the south-west, Languedoc, Provence, Burgundy, Picardy – almost everywhere except Alsace and Lorraine (though I have been to Strasbourg). France always sounded an exciting country to a young British man after the war, with recordings of Edith Piaf, Les Compagnons de la Chanson, Maurice Chevalier and Charles Trenet very popular (even though some of them had been accused of being 'collabos' during the war). My own favourite was an absolute non-collabo, Juliette Greco, a left-wing Bohemian friend of Jean-Paul Sartre and Jean Cocteau. French films, with stars like Arletty and Jean Gabin, always seemed to be exciting, more intellectual and artistic than British films at the time, and very popular with undergraduate audiences in Oxford at the Scala cinema in Walton Street. I am still an enthusiast, while a highlight of every day is my morning's read of *Le Monde*, the most intelligent newspaper I know.

I have always been struck by France's regional variations. When I first went to Paris, I met in my hostel some Breton boys, who were very excited that I could speak Welsh and that we could therefore have quite decent conversations in the Brythonic Celtic tongue. They were strongly nationalistic, carrying around a petition to free some Breton poet who had been jailed for being a collaborator during the war. They got me to go with them to the final stage of the 1953 Tour de France in a Paris Stadium, which was actually won, in those far off days, by a fine French rider, Louison Bobet. But we all wore caps supporting the Breton cyclist, Malléjac, who came in second overall. I had some very happy times with those Breton lads, including rowing on the Lac Supérieur in the Bois de Boulogne, the first time I had ever done such a thing, and I have frequently wondered where they might be now. There was also much Basque culture in evidence when I spoke at Pau in the south-west. I much enjoyed a visit with Elizabeth to Pau castle, with its mementoes of Henry of Navarre who changed his Protestant religion to become King Henry IV, France's finest ever monarch.

There was some sense of Languedoc identity, though not the Occitan language, around Narbonne, reinforced by the migration of Spanish republicans after the Civil War, while in Arles there were processions playing Provencal music and celebrating the poetry of Mistral. I am told that Alsace is noticeably Germanic. I could well understand the argument in Eugen Weber's great book *Peasants into Frenchmen* that the Third Republic felt the need to try to impose a sense of identity on all the regions and districts after 1875. As President de Gaulle famously observed, how can you govern a country which has 246 different cheeses? The solution was to impose what I consider to be far too rigid a Napoleonic centralisation and sense of direction from Paris, especially in education at all levels up to unversity. It is partly for that reason that French teachers of all kinds, often on the left, have so frequently gone on strike or demonstrated against a government which appears to ignore or override their views.

But I love it all. I admire France's colourful and brilliant history. I adore its beautiful cities like Rouen, Rennes, Dijon, Angers, Montpellier, Aix-en-Provence, Nimes, Arles and Nice; its wonderful mountains, including such unique places as Cézanne's beloved Mont Sainte-Victoire in Provence; its beautiful coastline and its magical rivers. The south-west I especially adore. Emotional, spontaneous, rugby-loving and *gauchiste*, the people of Aquitaine, Languedoc and the Basque lands remind me of the Welsh and I feel at home there. I enormously enjoyed visiting Aquitaine in 1967 with Malcolm Vale, an authority on medieval Gascony; with Jane in 1973, on a blissful honeymoon; and with Elizabeth in 2014 on a delightful holiday which took in various *bastide* towns and such picturesque castles as Biron and Lanquais.

It is a cultural as well as a personal joy that I have found my wife there, a proud beautiful Huguenot from Bordeaux. That has always been a handsome city, and it has been improved further still recently by the admirable transport and planning policies of its right-wing mayor Alain Juppé, who, in the French way, has combined being its mayor with being prime minister and later foreign minister of France – and is currently being talked of as a possible future presidential candidate. The nation could do much worse: I would vote for him. The *Grand Théâtre* in central Bordeaux, with its stunning façade, is a fine example of eighteenth-century neo-classical architecture, while handsome parks and fine restaurants abound, including my absolute favourite, Le Noailles, where it was that I decided I could not live without Elizabeth. The riverside along the Garonne is wonderful too. For a historian of my persuasion, Bordeaux generated two of the very greatest Europeans. Michel de Montaigne in the sixteenth century, apart from being an important mediator in the religious civil wars, wrote his wonderfully laconic, penetrating essays, with their subtle insight into personality and their dispassionate sympathy for humankind. The estate around his château is very atmospheric; it commemorates the great man with the great Sauternes, Château d'Yquem. Montaigne's tomb, in the Musée de l'Aquitaine, is always a place of pilgrimage for me. I can well understand his appeal for Michael Foot, even though dispassionate is hardly a word one would attach to Michael himself. And Montesquieu, that *philosophe par excellence* is a prince among jurists, anthropologists and political philosophers. His *De l'Esprit des Lois*, with its emphasis on environmental factors for instance, seems amazingly contemporary, while his influence upon the world is writ large in the constitution of the United States. If I go to see Elizabeth in the Bordeaux Law School, it is comforting to see the statue of the great man half-smiling at you as you ascend the stairs. He makes me feel safe. I also greatly enjoyed seeing his beautiful home at La Brède, ten kilometres from Bordeaux.

For a Francophile like myself, the present condition of France is not reassuring. I rejoiced with Elizabeth at the election of François Hollande as president in 2012 (for whom she had voted) and was applauded by the left-wing *Anglicistes* teachers at a conference at Limoges, where I was guest speaker, when I quoted Hollande's campaign slogan 'Le changement c'est maintenant'. But the outcome has been very disappointing. This is partly due to Hollande himself, who has been a far from commanding figure, derided for his absurd woman troubles, while his Socialist party is much divided, as the left so often is in government. In 2012, I had always preferred as candidate Martine Aubry, mayor of Lille and the daughter of Jacques Delors, a far more credible socialist. Fortunately, Hollande's standing rose sharply in early 2015 after his statesman-like response to the *Charlie Hebdo* assassinations and his role in arranging the ceasefire in the Ukraine. More profoundly, the French economy is flat, the debt is vast, the budget is unbalanced, unemployment is high, and there is an endemic need to promote dynamic change and cuts to some public spending. Too many vested interests push the other way and, as a result, France does not punch its weight either in the European Union or the world. Every time I go there now, I sense a widespread malaise. In particular, there is an acute feeling of social division and dislocation, with growing youth unemployment, disillusion in the provinces, racial feeling directed against both the Jews and the large Muslim minority, and the emergence of the racist and anti-European Front National as the leading party in the polls. Marine le Pen, as a young single mother, may be more personally sympathetic than her father, but she still peddles an appalling doctrine, populist, prejudiced and neo-fascist. It seems to have particular resonance in Provence, perhaps because of heavy migration from north Africa and the Maghreb. I hope that France eventually rejects her message. At least the initial French response to the atrocious murders of journalists by Islamic fundamentalists in the office of *Charlie Hebdo* in January 2015 appeared to be the reassertion of community values and republican solidarity rather than racial or religious war, but the future remains ominous.

There are historical long-lasting political and social antagonisms in France, which live on to poison the present. The impact of the sixteenth-century religious wars, which shed so much blood on St Bartholomew's Day and on other occasions, still has some legacy, at least in the south-west. Elizabeth tells me she still believes there is discrimination against the Protestant minority. The 1789 revolution and its successors bequeathed fierce ideological divisions between a monarchist Catholic right and a republican anti-clerical left. The Dreyfus case in the 1890s added to this volatile mixture the virulent force of widespread anti-semitism. The Popular Front in 1936 stirred up political bitterness, in which men of the right cried 'Better Hitler than Blum!' These latest conflicts have inherited all these and added their own virulent forms of inward-looking nationalism and protectionism.

And yet, at the same time, the French have also inherited, more powerfully than almost any other people, a passionate commitment to democracy, popular sovereignty and a belief in human rights. They are the nation of Montaigne, Descartes, Montesquieu, Voltaire, Victor Hugo, Jaurès, Blum and Mendès-France, the last the best French prime minister, even if only briefly, in my lifetime. I have faith that this great, inspired people will reclaim their better past and overturn the cheap demagogues who are currently undermining it. I particularly hope this proves the case in attitudes towards the educational system. This brilliant people does not at present have the schools and universities it deserves. The system is vastly over-centralised with insufficient autonomy for French universities (only two rated in the world's top two hundred) and the academics poorly paid and shabbily treated. I am glad that I spent my career in the British university system; but in France of all countries, a recovery in the mind will mean a recovery in the spirit, and I feel sure it will happen. I retain my affection and admiration for everything fundamental to the country. It embodies what I understand by civilisation. My heart sings every time I go there. And I gather that, after being married to a French person for more than five years, I can claim French citizenship; that would indeed be an honour.

But it is still in Britain that I wish to live. My life has been enormously stimulated by travel worldwide, especially in my years of retirement since 1995. My work as a university teacher has given me many professional opportunities to teach and research overseas, and the enrichment of many cultures is something for which I am deeply grateful. But by instinct and temperament, I am an outward-looking British person, wedded to the union of our nations. The older I become, the more attached I feel to the mountains and rivers of the Wales from which I come, the London where I presently work, and the rolling gentle countryside of west Oxfordshire, where I have made my home and many of my friends. The more I have travelled, the more I have appreciated Britain. Above all else, as I have written in these memoirs,

191

it retains its indomitable sense of personal liberty and tolerance of individuality and eccentricity, stronger than in any country I have seen, despite recent governmental attempts to whittle it down. I would not put things quite as strongly or emotionally as Orwell's famous celebration of our country in the *Lion and the Unicorn* or *Homage to Catalonia* – that has too often lent itself to plagiarism or pastiche. I would not be quite so enraptured as Orwell (or John Major) by old maids cycling to church. But, especially after a lifetime of being on the move, I like it here.

Chapter Ten

Experiences:
Old and New Labour

OR AS LONG AS I have been an adult, I have been a member of the
Labour Party. At least, that is the belief of the keepers of the party membership records, and who am I to challenge them? I joined the Wood Green
constituency Labour Party in the summer of 1955 at the age of twenty-one, just
after taking my BA examinations at Oxford. As recorded, there was a wobble,
indeed rather more, in 1968 and another, more serious, at the time of the Iraq
invasion in 2003. But I rejected the path of deviation then and, at present, am
in my sixtieth year of continuous recorded membership. It has, however, been
anything but a serene sixty years. There have been many difficulties and disap-
pointments. Labour has been fighting an uphill battle for much of that time,
facing a predominantly right-wing press, and has in fact been in government
for just twenty-four of those sixty years – thirteen of them in one continuous
run after 1997.

At the time of writing in 2014, Britain was confronting a coalition government which had heaped years of severe austerity upon the populace, and
a harsh squeeze on wages and living standards, the worst this country had
known since 1865. Yet Labour's prospects looked as unpromising as during
any period in my long years of membership – this despite having received
some fortuitous bonuses. At the May 2015 General Election, after the Liberal
Democrat intervention discussed previously, Labour had had the good fortune
of the retention of the old constituency boundaries that favoured them by up
to thirty seats. Scotland had chosen to remain in the union to offer (theoretically) some of its seats to boost Labour's tally; it would be almost impossible to
achieve a Labour majority based on England and Wales alone. As the Clacton
by-election in October 2014 spectacularly demonstrated, UKIP was likely to
cut into the Conservatives' vote in their heartlands. But then the Heywood by-
election on the same day in October showed how vulnerable Labour is to UKIP

in England too, while an electoral tsunami from the SNP in Scotland became overwhelming since the Scottish referendum vote, threatening to wipe out virtually all of Labour's seats there. Failing another unpopular coalition being formed, the polls currently suggested that the best Labour could hope for was to form a minority government in a hung parliament. The party seemed to have neither vision nor a sense of purpose – it lacked a narrative. It was not what I anticipated or hoped for back in 1955. In fact, the May 2015 General Election, when Labour gained only 30.5 per cent of the vote, showed that things had become far worse, with Scotland irretrievably lost.

After I joined the party in 1955, it was just beginning to show some signs of a truce in the ongoing civil war, left versus right, Bevanites versus Gaitskellites, which had torn Labour apart since Aneurin Bevan's resignation from the government over the 1951 Budget, and the consequent charges imposed on the National Health Service. There were pugnacious personalities involved to stir up the acrimony, not the least of them being Michael Foot who, in the time I was writing his biography, seemed to regard Hugh Gaitskell with more bitter hostility than he did any Conservative, living or dead. Gaitskell and Bevan then moved closer together, however, and formed a strong partnership from 1957 when Bevan was Shadow Foreign Secretary. They worked well on the Polish Rapacki Plan for a nuclear-free zone in central Europe, for instance, to mitigate the stark geographic divisiveness of the Cold War in Europe. As a 'keep calm' man, I had always believed that on domestic issues Bevan and Gaitskell were not far apart anyhow. They were both revisionists in their way. Attacks on Bevan as an egotistic wrecker, or on Gaitskell as a non- or anti-socialist, both seemed to me wrong. Labour won some by-elections such as Carmarthen, and the one that I took part in at North Lewisham. Anyhow, it seemed incredible that a government responsible for the debacle of Suez could hope to survive the next election. Labour had been searching for a new social democratic programme to succeed nationalisation and the policies of its high noon in 1945–51; in truth, at least on the economic front, I think it has been doing so for the whole of my lifetime.

The big idea in the late 1950s was that Labour was about equality. This great principle, voiced during the Peasants' Revolt back in 1381, enshrined in Tawney's great book which I read as a schoolboy, had been proclaimed anew by the West Indian economist W. Arthur Lewis. It was the central argument of Tony Crosland's *Future of Socialism*, which claimed that the economic argument about capitalism was effectively over in a new age of consumer affluence, and that the new priorities were social issues and the quality of life. Equality had a strong ancestry across the party spectrum. Even Roy Jenkins, in the *New Fabian Essays* of 1952, had linked the idea of equality with financial redistribution and had actually argued for a capital levy. In the General Election of October 1959, the election in which I have taken the most active part, Crosland and others put heavy emphasis on the idea of equality, notably through comprehensive schools and a redistribution of wealth as well as income. But it did not seem to cut much ice with the electors, who placed a higher value on their growing affluence as upwardly mobile consumers, and tended to see equality as meaning levelling down. This was a disappointing experience for me. Labour seemed out of touch with the electors and lost heavily. Close to home, Labour lost Swansea West. After the election, the party reacted badly. Gaitskell made the proposal that Labour get rid of Clause 4, the old clause in the party's programme of 1918 committing it to the nationalisation of the means of production, distribution and exchange. I thought this a good idea, but that the timing was hopelessly wrong. Douglas Jay suggested that the name Labour Party be jettisoned. The sociologist Mark Abrams declared that generational change and the contraction of the traditional industrial working class meant that Labour might never win office again.

At this bleak period in 1959, the party went into one of its internal convulsions, as it did later after 1979. The Campaign for Nuclear Disarmament combined its basic demand of getting rid of nuclear weapons with a general assault on the leadership, Gaitskell in particular. The 1960 annual party conference saw a CND motion carried against the leadership and Gaitskell pledging himself to 'fight and fight again' to reverse the decision. I could not support or join CND, though; while it seemed to me totally inconceivable that we could ever use nuclear weapons and there was an absurdity about pouring out money on weapons we would never deploy, an emotional mass movement like CND was not the way to get rid of them. CND was dominated by eminent veterans like Bertrand Russell, J. B. Priestley and Canon Collins of St Pauls, who did not think politically at all, while many others were motivated by spite against Gaitskell as much as anything else. My main objection, though – as one of its great figures, Alan Taylor, candidly admitted – was that CND was inspired by a kind of moral imperialism, which claimed that if Britain made a unilateral renunciation of nuclear weapons, everybody, including the Russians, would be so impressed that they would follow suit. I still hold that view. Michael Foot seemed astounded that I wrote in my preface to his biography that I had not joined CND even though its members included some of the people I most respected in public life. I had to point out that among the others who took my view ('naked into the conference chamber' and all that) was his hero, Aneurin Bevan. He was on my side.

By 1964, CND was clearly in decline and Labour looked forward to a strong majority in the election. In the event, that majority was only three. By that point, the idea of equality was losing its primacy as Labour's version of 'the vision thing' – many of Labour's new voters were part of the property-owning democracy, more concerned with consumer choice and fearful of the possible emergence of enforced equality of outcomes. In effect, the notion that Labour was about equality died with Hugh Gaitskell in January 1963. After that, the party tried to give democratic socialism, so far as that was Labour's fundamental philosophy, a new direction. The re-emergence of equality as a priority after the year 2000 focused on somewhat different themes, attaching that concept to women, ethnic communities and sexual minorities.

By the election of 1964, when I was far more restrained in my partisan activity by my work for the BBC and the book for Nuffield College (discussed in chapter 3), Labour had acquired another big idea. This was planning, an idea revived from the late 1930s when it was variously espoused by younger socialists like Jay, Gaitskell and Durbin, as an attempt to merge social democracy with Keynesian-style economics. It was part of the cult of modernisation popular at the time with all parties. Harold Wilson, an outstanding leader of the Opposition, gave it much currency with his celebrated speech at the Scarborough party conference in October 1963, when he linked Labour with science and the 'white heat' of a new industrial revolution. He skilfully embodied this in person, portraying himself as a classless Yorkshireman from a state grammar school, in contrast to the Conservatives' (admittedly astonishing) choice of the old Etonian patron of the grouse-moor, the Fourteenth Earl of Home. This did not cut too much ice with the electors though, partly perhaps because Home himself proved a more skilful leader than had been anticipated, partly also because people were still well aware of the big improvement in living standards and household budgets that the thirteen so-called 'wasted' years of Conservative rule had meant. They had never had it so good.

Wilson's tiny majority in 1964 (which, in fact, played to his tactical strengths as leader) was greatly boosted in March 1966 when it rose to ninety-seven. In Wood Lane, on the election programme on television, I watched with inner enthusiasm as the 'swingometer' operated then by the great Robert McKenzie (and later by Peter Snow) showed regular lurches to the left. But after that, I did not think that Planning was effective as a big idea either. There were attempts to modernise institutions, partly successfully with the civil service through the Fulton Report, but totally unsuccessfully in the case of the House of Lords proposal which was scuppered by Michel Foot in alliance with his private pal Enoch Powell. But Planning did not come across as a central instrument of reform, mainly because it did not work. It was associated with some ventures that seemed almost cruel – the tower-blocks to which many poor people were relocated in local authority housing programmes appeared almost as a parody of the supposedly humane values of 1960s socialism. It was beaucratic and inhumane. When in later years I would go canvassing often elderly people at the top of such buildings, where the lifts frequently broke down, I wondered how they could survive such a caged existence. I am afraid that in many instances the answer is that they didn't.

So far as regenerating the economy was concerned, under the successive chancellors Jim Callaghan and Roy Jenkins, Planning did not operate with positive effect. A particular error in 1964, which Tony Blair avoided in 1997, was to divide economic direction between two masters, Jim Callaghan at the Treasury and George Brown at a new Department of Economic Affairs. It was suspected this was Wilson's way of giving key positions to the two great rivals immediately beneath him. The division of power never worked. The system was spelt out in a Treasury'concordat'at the very start of the government, actually written by Peter Jay, Douglas's son and a very bright Treasury official at the time. It laid down that the Department of Economic Affairs would deal with the long term, but that that did not exclude the short term; and the Treasury would deal with the short term, but that that did not rule out the long term. Even with two ministers less combustible than Brown and Callaghan, this would have made for confusion. It was impossible for the DEA to carry out its role satisfactorily while the Treasury operated such a vital instrument as the control of interest rates and took key decisions in relation to the value of the pound. In the end, the rate of growth which aimed at 25 per cent over six years was less than half of that between 1964 and 1970. Gross domestic product rose by an average of only 2.3 per cent a year compared with an annual 3.8 per cent in the previous six years of Conservative government. The DEA limped along and finally disappeared in 1968.

In the personal contest, Jim thus triumphed over George, but it was a pyrrhic victory because Jim was forced to devalue the pound, a move he and Harold had resisted for three years, under pressure from the Bank of England and much of the civil service. Jim was left demoralised and his civil servants told me of his low spirits when he went to the Home Office. However, he soon bounced back and was skilful enough to avoid much of the flak for devaluation, which landed instead on Harold Wilson who had rashly told the viewers that 'the pound in your pocket is not devalued'. Jim's journalistic allies like John Cole in the *Guardian* made sure that he made no such error himself. In fact, devaluation was helpful to the economy, but that bonus was restricted because Roy Jenkins was slow to take the necessary deflationary consequential action when he succeeded Jim at the Treasury.

I myself never fancied Planning as an exciting governing idea. It was a drab, value-free notion, divorced from ideology or moral force, which owed much to Wilson's own experience of wartime technocracy as an assistant to Beveridge. Perhaps it also owed something to his enthusiasm for the policies of the Soviet Union when he was at the Board of Trade, which apparently attracted the interest of MI5. His volume of speeches in 1964, *The New Britain*, spoke of'Labour's

Plan', listing in detail Labour's plans for the economy, housing, employment and Commonwealth Trade. His foreword to that volume linked socialism to the scientific revolution:'That is what socialism means – a unity of direction for all the decisions the government has to take.' It told you nothing of the kind of society that Labour wished to create. It also disappointed its practitioners. Professor Patrick Blackett, the Nobel prize-winning scientist, brought into government by Wilson, left early in disillusionment. The one minister, interestingly enough, who seemed to respond was the centrist Minister of Technology, Tony Benn. By 1970, the idea of Planning as the route to socialism seemed threadbare. Ben Pimlott's fine biography of Harold Wilson rightly describes the void at the centre of Labour's ideology henceforth.

I was by the end of the Wilson government disillusioned in the extreme. While I warmly appreciated the prime minister's friendly and human qualities, his government's main policies had failed. There was a paranoid culture in Downing Street which spoke of conspiracies, leaks and moles. When the memoirs of Marcia Falkender and other aides came out afterwards, that culture was even worse than we had thought. Wilson's last stand of 1974–6 proved to be little improvement, and the 'lavender notepaper' with proposals for titles for personal cronies, some of whom went to gaol, seemed symptomatic. As with Lloyd George, Wilson fatally exposed himself with a questionable honours list. This disillusionment, I am sure, underlay my unsuccessful attempt to leave the party in 1968; it was the tone as much as the policies of the government.

At the same time, this government had many positive and even idealistic achievements. It was admirable that Wilson had stood up to the Americans (which I read about in Lyndon Johnson's papers in Texas) and declined to send British troops to Vietnam. He showed far sounder judgement than his successor in 2003. In my own profession, it was the start of a golden age for higher education, though the main credit in this regard must go to the Robbins Report, published some time before Labour took up office. Many fine new universities were created, the student population was much increased, and social mobility improved. Interestingly, there was not much emphasis on developing science, which had been the background to the setting up of the Robbins Committee in the first instance, and of which C. P. Snow had written influentially in *The Two Cultures.* Jennie Lee proved to be a dynamic minister of the Arts, as Patricia Hollis's admirable biography of her shows, while Harold Wilson himself deserves enormous credit for creating the Open University. It made brilliant use of the then new concepts of part-time study and distance learning, and was genuinely innovative. The prime minister's staunch support was a major reason for its great success. It is perhaps a progressive social achievement equivalent in value to Nye Bevan's National Health Service. I was privileged to lecture several times at the Open University summer school at Keele University and to make, with Arthur Marwick, their first foundation film, 'The Historian at Work'. The passionate enthusiasm of the mature students for their studies was something I have never quite experienced elsewhere, and I found it very moving.

And, of course, Labour responded brilliantly to current demands for more 'permissiveness' – or plain freedom – in leading one's personal life. This owed most of its impetus to Roy Jenkins alone. The censorship of books and plays by the dead hand of the Lord Chamberlain and others was substantially undercut. The abortion of unwanted foetuses became legal through support for David Steel's private members bill, despite reactionary opposition from the Catholic church and other religious groups. The two great liberal reforms which we had discussed as undergraduates both came about: homosexuality was decriminal-ised, and a huge injustice which had destroyed the careers and even the lives of many blameless victims (Alan Turing, to name perhaps the most eminent) thereby overturned; and the barbarity of capital punishment was brought to an end permanently in 1969. Jim Callaghan was rightly supposed to be far less enthusiastic about 'permissiveness' than the more intellectually vigorous Roy Jenkins. With Jim, the influence of the Portsmouth Baptists, whom he had long ago left, ran deep. But he did carry through the abolition of hanging. He had always been a courageous abolitionist, including challenging Herbert Morrison directly during the passage of the Criminal Justice Act in 1948. That will always be a shining achievement of his political career, also one much associated with the campaigns of Sydney Silverman, the father of my school friend Paul. If Labour with its socialism seemed ineffective as a party of economic planning, it shone for its humane social reform. The Wilson government was a key phase in making Britain a more civilised society, even if this was the product of a coa-lition of different views across the political spectrum.

I knew that Labour would lose the 1970 election. I listened to Harold Wilson speaking at Ninian Park in Cardiff at the start of the campaign; there was a large audience and it was a glorious sunny evening, but the meeting was flat – Wilson seemed tired and the speeches failed to kindle any enthusiasm. Ted Heath, a moderate man, I felt deserved to win his uphill struggle, and I was glad he did so. Labour's continuing search for a big idea lurched into the 1970s when the global economy plunged into a time of massive inflation when all the parties had somehow to find a credible formula for recovery.

Labour's new watchword now was the Social Contract with the then mighty trade unions, a recipe for industrial harmony which Labour alone, through its composition and its history, could provide. It was negotiated pri-vately between the TUC and some of Labour's leaders, including Jim Callaghan, a former trade union official who had almost brought the government down in 1969 over 'In Place of Strife'. When Callaghan was appointed Foreign Secretary under Wilson in 1974, civil servants noted how close he felt to the union world.

He allocated time every day to see key figures in the labour movement and cultivated a kind of trade union bargaining style in day-to-day business. I got my interview with Helmut Schmidt on that basis. The Wilson government of March 1974 marked the high point of trade union involvement in politics. They had never been more powerful, with their membership rising to over thirteen million, and a rebellious mood among the shop stewards who directed union policy from below. The contract consisted of a grand bargain in which the unions emphasised their support for the government and their moderation on industrial action. In return, the government would consult the unions on their forthcoming social and economic legislation, and try to tailor their measures to meet the unions' views. Chief of these would be repeal of the Heath government's Industrial Relations Act, which had led to massive ill will. An immediate portent was that Michael Foot, passionately pro-union, went to the Department of Employment in his first venture into government at the age of sixty. He began his duties by settling the miners' strike wholly on the miners' terms, as the Wilberforce inquiry had indeed recommended. For the next two years, union-government relations were exceptionally close, with Jack Jones (a great industrial statesman whom I liked) and Hugh Scanlon key figures. This reached a climax in the summer of 1976, when Jack Jones saved the government's bacon at a time of acute pressure on the pound by skilfully devising and pushing through a flat rate £6 pay increase all round, which both gave a check to wage inflation as well as being highly redistributive and egalitarian.

But I was very doubtful about the Rousseauite-sounding social contract, sympathetic though I was to the unions. I did not like the elected government of the day acting at the behest of an outside pressure group, however powerful, while several of the more hawkish members of the TUC General Council did not inspire confidence. A man like Alan Fisher of NUPE seemed hardly to think of the wider community and the national interest at all, and ignored inflation. The general public was turning against the union leaders, and there was press talk of Jack as 'The Emperor Jones'. The Labour Party was already showing signs of turning from being a broad-based national movement into a nexus of self-interested client groups like public sector trade unions and the residents of council houses who provided them with most of their votes. Further, a contract needed both sides to agree to make it work. But, at a time when the oil price explosion had led to a terrifying increase in inflation worldwide, the unions pursued a series of massive pay claims, almost trying to keep pace with each other. The rate of inflation rose to over 25 per cent which was not sustainable for very long. Union leaders seemed willing to be driven by opinion on the shop floor as interpreted by shop stewards. I sympathised with the plight of the low-paid, but some of the militant unions like oil tanker drivers were anything but low-paid. With the balance of payments looking sickly and the pressure on the pound leading to talk of a possible further devaluation, in the spring and summer of 1976 the government lurched along barely in control. It was at this stage that Jim Callaghan succeeded Harold Wilson, whose final term in office (when his own health was deteriorating) was fraught indeed.

Jim Callaghan's government illustrated precisely the frailty of the social contract as Labour's big idea. It consisted of three phases. The first was marked by terrifying financial pressures on the economy, ending with the fraught negotiations for the loan from the International Monetary Fund. Callaghan succeeded because he conducted an impeccable exercise in collective Cabinet government, winning over minister after minister and seeing off the sniping of Benn from the wings. He well recalled the disastrous division of the second Labour government in 1931 when he was a young man. He, at least, would not be another Ramsay MacDonald. The second phase, a period of around twenty months from January 1977 to October 1978, a phase often forgotten by the historians later, was remarkably successful. The government, boosted in its Commons majority by the Lib-Lab pact negotiated with David Steel, had continuous success in its economic policy – the balance of payments improved, the pound strengthened, and international confidence returned. Callaghan himself, with his close links with Carter and Schmidt, built up a reputation as a world statesman, ran well ahead of Thatcher in the polls, and was widely expected to be returned again next time. There was much disappointment in party circles that he did not call a general election in October, which might have seized that opportunity. In fact, after looking at the materials in his papers, I felt I would have taken the same decision as Jim did, since there was no certainty at all of an overall Labour majority even in October. The West Midlands were especially unpredictable, and Jim did not fancy another period of minority government or a new Lib-Lab pact.

The final phase saw the unions plunge, one after another, into the near-chaos of the winter of discontent. Jim told me later how depressed he had been; Kenneth Stowe told me of how the Prime Minister had spoken of letting the country down. Even grave-diggers went on strike. A kind of *ennui* or *anomie* settled over a gloomy Downing Street. Jim had been betrayed by the unions he had defended so stoutly in 1969. Jack Jones's successor as general secretary of the Transport and General Workers was Moss Evans, who proved a minnow by comparison and who ignored the facts about inflation and showed no statesmanship of any kind. What a pity that Jack could not have stayed on for a year or two. The strikes ended with a near-meaningless and toothless St Valentine's Day compact with the TUC. The Labour government fell soon after, and the social compact disappeared into the history books as another grand but failed idea.

It was accompanied by something equally worrying to me – socialism reinvented as nationalism. Benn and supporters such as Stuart Holland urged the need for Britain to claim its sovereignty, by stopping the outward flow of investment, by imposing import controls and by conducting a siege economy of planning agreements and directives. It was Labour's version of Stalinism, of socialism in one country. It was totally impractical, assuming the voters would ever have accepted it. It visualised a sovereign country detached from the world economy and able to ride the storms on its own. Earlier in the 1970s, there was another manifestation of this nationalism when Labour swung strongly against the European Common Market, which it had attempted to join in 1967 before being rebuffed for the second time by President de Gaulle. Neither of my future biographees distinguished themselves here. Jim Callaghan, for internal party reasons, made some distinctly anti-European speeches including a deplorable effort at Southampton in 1971 when he responded to an alleged French attempt to downgrade English ('the language of Milton and Shakespeare') by using terrible cod French – 'Non, merci beaucoup'. Michael Foot was implacably anti-European, and seemed to regard Brussels as a threat to the sovereignty of the British parliament comparable to that once posed by Charles I, whom he saw as rightly having been executed. Fortunately, both changed their views in time. Jim renegotiated (or claimed to have done) our terms of membership of the Common Market with much skill in 1974–5, and ensured that the referendum on Europe was comfortably won. As Prime Minister, he became much more sympathetic to Europe through his friendship with Schmidt and Giscard d'Estaing (both of whom, fortunately, spoke good English), and even flirted with the idea of joning the Exchange Rate Mechanism to avoid Britain's constant sterling crises. Michael in his old age became strongly pro-Europe; he now saw the European Union as the embodiment not of de Gaulle but of Delors and his Social Chapter. But in the 1980s, socialism as nationalism was another non-runner.

Labour in the 1980s had no big idea; indeed it had hardly any time for ideas at all. It was a time of a fight for control, a clash of faiths, a battle for the party's soul. The period of fratricidal in-fighting between the mainstream centre-right and the hard left is still painful to look back on. It was time of immense internal bitterness. I attended just one party meeting and found it so deeply personal and unpleasant that I never went again. The next meeting of the West Oxfordshire party meeting I attended was in 1997. There was on the one hand a remote and uninspiring leadership, which was not winning new support and which left such hollowed-out constituency parties as that in Bermondsey, where Labour chose an unelectable candidate and lost the by-election to the Liberals by a record swing. That kind of thing encouraged a popular call for 'participation'. But what happened was something much worse – a kind of bogus 'participation' conducted by far-left entryists of whom the Underhill report, ignored by the National Executive in the 1970s, had already warned. The press wrote of 'bed-sit Trots' in the constituencies; they were reinforced by old Marxists looking for a home since the Communist Party had imploded in 1956. Jim Callaghan even confronted them in his own Cardiff constituency in 1982, where their main spokesmen were university lecturers – a profession towards which, as a non-graduate, he was always somewhat ambivalent (other than in his dealings with me perhaps). The Trotskyist Militant tendency sought to impose a socialist programme on the Party far more extreme than it had ever had before. Militant tendency was in broad alliance with many groups within the trade unions, some of which (such as NUPE) had hard-left officials well to the left of the membership.

Tony Benn gave his malign encouragement to all these groups, encouraging every strike and every protest movement, no matter how undemocratic or violent. I cannot understand why he is seen now as some benevolent national treasure whose wisdom should be reclaimed. Jim Callaghan and Michael Foot both found him utterly disloyal, liable to say, when challenged about a week-end speech, that he gave it as a member of the National Executive not as a minister of the Cabinet. I thought him selfish and deeply vain; it was somehow appropriate that in his later years he toured the halls giving readings from his diaries. His books demonstrate that he was no political theorist. Despite his attempts to encourage a Levellers march in Burford, he had no sense of the Levellers' history, which he saw as some kind of nonconformist sect; and he had no interest at all in the arts, no hinterland. It was a mercy that he failed to win the deputy leadership against Denis Healey in 1981. Interestingly, the vote was not as narrow as it seemed, because those unions who held proper ballots invariably backed Denis. This was true of NUPE with its many women members, but whose secretary Alan Fisher, nevertheless, voted implacably for Benn. The latter's unpopularity with working-class voters I saw for myself in Oxford East in 1983. In my view, his divisive, doctrinaire approach was perhaps the major reason for eleven years of Thatcherism. Much the best Benn I have met is Hilary.

Michael Foot, the unfortunate leader of the party in 1980–3, at least played a far more honourable role, even if in defeat. He had the historical insight to see Labour as a coalition, a pluralist body of political socialists and trade unionists, of left, centre and right, which needed mutual comradeship to keep going. In a valuable pamphlet in 1981, *My Kind of Socialism*, he wrote of how the pioneers had created a party in 1918 with divided sovereignty within it, the parliamentary party and the membership at conference: 'Neither will bend the knee to the other.' In this he took the same wise view as Keir Hardie in 1907, when there were party disputes about women's suffrage: 'There should be free play

Kenneth O. Morgan

between the sections.' Fortunately, it is the Foot/Hardie and not the Benn view
that has prevailed over the years. Solidarity has prevailed over sectarianism. The
ending of the Cold War was to give the process momentum; socialist dogma
collapsed like the Berlin wall. Michael Foot himself was too old and too gentle
to impose discipline over the warring comrades, though he did begin the process of expelling a few members of Militant Tendency. But it was too little if not
too late. Michael's great achievement in party terms was to detach the so-called
'soft left', including people like Neil Kinnock, John Silkin and Joan Lestor,
away from the hard left, and to get them to back the leadership. That way recovery beckoned.

The leadership of my friend Neil Kinnock was a glorious phase in
Labour's history. He plucked up the party from dark pits of despair to make it
again forward-looking and electable. He had a tough start with the year-long
fight of the miners in 1984–5, a hard choice for a man from the Welsh valleys
whose father had been a miner. I was somewhat torn myself. I had immense
natural sympathy for the miners as a community, especially after teaching
in south Wales in the early 1960s when the mines were still going strong. I
remembered the good people of Pontyates, where I took my extra-mural class,
their charm and their culture. I gave money to the miners picketing Didcot
power station near Oxford. A wealthy woman named Sarah Rothschild,
whom I once met at Oxford, brought to Didcot pickets food supplies, only
unfortunately it consisted of hampers from Fortnum & Mason, when the
miners would have much preferred fish and chips. One of the people who
came well out of the strike was David Jenkins, my old colleague at Queen's,
now installed as Bishop of Durham. His attack on Ian McGregor, the elderly
American brought in by Thatcher to run down the coal mines, went down
well on the left.

I wrote a number of articles on the strike, sympathetic to the miners but
also showing awareness of the economic facts of life which meant that the
mines were ultimately doomed. There was one amusing sequel when Christine
Ockrent, of Antenne Deux TV in France, rang me up to do an interview in
French. It turned out that my interviewer, later to become a good friend, was
Michael Crick, whose French was even less strong than mine. Twenty seconds
before the camera began rolling, he posed me an urgent question – 'What's
the French for miners?' I offered *mineurs*, which is what we used. Labour came
out of the strike better than it might have hoped, which is more than can be
said for the miners themselves, especially after the kamikaze leadership of the
Communist Arthur Scargill. After his activities, the South Welsh coalfield collapsed from twenty-eight pits, employing over 20,000 men, to just one; and
that, the cooperative Tower colliery kept going by Tyrone O'Sullivan, has now
gone too.

204

Thereafter, the main theme was Neil's leading us towards recovery. There was no philosophical reflection about the process, but Labour, with the aid of so-called policy forums, removed mass nationalisation, unilateral nuclear disarmament and opposition to Europe from its programme, and I welcomed seeing the back of them all, both in themselves and as assistance to Labour some day getting back into power. It was not a time of doctrinal speculation – in fact, the party had not produced an important work of theory since Anthony Crosland's *Future of Socialism* appeared in 1956 and, frankly, none has appeared since. The left has no Tawneys or Laskis nowadays, though latterly it has found inspiration abroad from the brilliant left-wing French economist Thomas Piketty. Domestic novelties like 'Blue Labour', with their UKIP overtones, have been non-runners. Roy Hattersley, at least, did produce an interesting if long-forgotten book in 1987, *Choose Freedom*, which aimed to fuse collectivist democratic socialism with ideals of personal liberty, drawing on the philosophical writings of John Rawls, which suggested a possible way forward.

The main need for Labour, as in its struggle with the Liberals in 1922–4, was to assert itself against the Social Democratic Party as the main challenger to the Tories. I was never tempted to join the SDP, though good friends like Robert Maclennan and David Marquand (for a time) did so. I was too inescapably Labour, while I felt the SDP was too irredeemably bourgeois; a kind of middle-class waiting-room in which the members debated rather than decided. I was not impressed by the books produced by leading SDP members, and I was not surprised when the party began to disintegrate after the 1983 election, which proved to be its high point. Like the Liberal Democrats under the 2010 coaliton, the SDP could not decide which way it would move on such key issues as the role of the state, taxation and welfare. It proved to offer a useful outlet for protest votes in by-elections, but now the travails of coalition have taken away that role. There are now variously UKIP, the Scottish Nationalist Party and the Green Party to play that role as an outlet for anger towards the Westminster élite. It was Labour, which still claimed a mass working-role vote, which survived in 1983 and 1987, and ultimately inherited the prize of power.

I was very disappointed on both personal and political grounds that Neil did not make it to Number 10 in 1992, but the party, after that disappointment, showed every sign of reaping the benefit of his work. It may have been Neil's good fortune that Labour lost because otherwise he would inevitably have been stereotyped as yet another Labour Prime Minister who devalued the pound. The extraordinary disintegration of the Conservatives under John Major, a decent, honourable man who deserved better, showed how unstable the party had become after the shock therapy of Thatcher, who was anything but a reassuring conservative force. Europe made the internal party divisions unbridgeable, and I realised while I was in Aberystwyth that I would be going into retirement under the aegis of a Labour government, probably with a very large majority. I welcomed the sadly brief leadership period of John Smith, a fine man, strongly committed to devolution and to Europe, two of my main principles. For some time, I welcomed warmly the advent of Tony Blair in 1995. He created an image of dominant leadership much needed after the disunited rabble that the party had been at annual conferences and NEC meetings for years past. I welcomed the decision to abandon the ancient Clause Four, though the words inserted in place of the original conveyed hardly anything at all. Blair and New Labour were profoundly right to try to appeal to all parts of the United Kingdom, and not to regard seats in traditional areas of southern England or rural constituencies as no-go areas. Thus, in 1997, Labour was to capture unlikely seats in Kent, Sussex and even Dorset. Labour would try to straddle the classes more effectively and give far more prominence to women (whose Labour representation soared to over a hundred) and ethnic minorities. Blair also brought a new professionalism and technical expertise to the way the party was run. What Harold Wilson had once called 'a penny farthing in the jet age', where our members despised the modernist gimmicks of Saatchi & Saatchi, was now a high-tech machine in Millbank where an old Victorian organisation now surfed the internet. Electronic devices kept the comrades on message, should they show any inclination to think for themselves.

There was also a swinging of the axe on old party shibboleths, perhaps to a frightening extent. Nationalisation, universal welfare, full employment, redistributive taxation, and sociological approaches to law and order all went like the autumn leaves at Vallombrosa. Some of these rather alarmed me (especially with regard to unemployment, which had now been replaced by inflation as the economists' main source of concern), but the need for a totally fresh start in policy-making seemed to me beyond dispute. I cheerfully canvassed the voters with Alastair Parker on the Blackbird Leys housing estate in Oxford East, and found the returns as positive in 1997 as they had been depressing in 1983 when the political dark ages were beginning. I watched the results on television with David and Judith Marquand, and was duly amazed. I was one of those 'still up for Portillo'. I came back home at around five in the morning to find my daughter Katherine awake and waltzing around the house in sheer joy; she had spent her entire sentient life as one of Thatcher's children – she described how she had spent years sitting next to me on the sofa watching the television news, and every time That Woman appeared on the screen I would always shout. I shared her joy at the passing of the Conservatives, but (and this is the privilege of the elderly) I warned her that disillusion, like prosperity, was always just around the corner.

The remaining thirteen years of new Labour went some way to confirming that melancholy prediction. The government was certainly a bracing change in very many ways. Blair was a commanding, charismatic leader, the strongest ever, the first Labour Prime Minister not to face a destructive challenge from the far left. There was no Lansbury, Bevan or Benn to upset the applecart – the only prominent left-winger at the time was Ken Livingstone, and he was safely esconced as mayor of London, where I approved of the great bulk of what he was doing. Blair had a powerful chancellor in Gordon Brown, who inherited a strong balance of payments position from the Conservatives' Kenneth Clark. For the first time, we had for ten years a Labour government which was not plagued by financial crisis. Labour, for the first time, had won a higher reputation for economic competence, a title which the Conservatives had relinquished in the chaos of the ERM crisis in 1992. There was greater public spending, notably on the National Health Service by Gordon Brown (with whom Michael Foot regularly communicated), while individual consumer spending went up, notably in making the housing market buoyant. For a brief period, British economic growth could be said to outstrip that of Germany. Socially, for several years, it was a time of social peace. There were no great strikes, no winter of discontent, no peasants' revolt against the Poll Tax; even Northern Ireland, with its timeless tensions, was engaged in a plausible peace process in which Ian Paisley and Martin McGuinness, incredibly, shared office in the government. The only challenge came from the Countryside Alliance, variously over issues ranging from petrol taxes to fox-hunting, and it could easily be contained. There were few racial clashes, and the National Front was minute. There was nothing at all like the upsurge of the Front National in France, where Jean-Marie le Pen made it to the final run off in the 2002 presidential election, and his daughter Marine made the party stronger still and heading the opinion polls. Britain seemed a country for the moment at peace with itself, within a broad liberal consensus. The harmonious meetings of the Parliamentary Labour Party, which I regularly attended, certainly under Blair and at first under Brown too, showed the same consensual atmosphere.

The government's more specific policies had brought many advances. There was a welcome reduction of 600,000 of children in poverty while, linked to that, the Sure Start scheme gave children from low-income families a valuable educational send-off in life. There were strong programmes of urban renewal, and museums were free once again. On the income side, the Blair government could claim to have carried out an old socialist promise, that of instituting the minimum wage, through its acceptance of Delors' (and Hywel Ceri Jones's) Social Chapter; while the tax credits, on which Katherine worked in the office of the Paymaster-General Dawn Primarolo, were a substantial programme of redistribution towards the poor. Educational standards in the schools showed a dramatic improvement, as monitored by my old Queen's student Sir Michael Barber. It all seemed more stable and potentially longer-lasting than the programmes of earlier Labour governments, even that of Attlee in some ways. In its international policy, the government showed signs at last of being at the heart of Europe, though providentially resistant to monetary union and the Euro.

For the historian of the Labour Party, there were three outstanding novelties in the New Labour programmes, all of which I enthusiastically supported. First, it became the party of devolution and carried this principle through for Scotland and Wales, and later for Northern Ireland. This was a huge contrast with earlier years. Pioneers like Hardie, MacDonald and Lansbury had been staunch supporters of Scottish and Welsh home rule (and, of course, for the whole of Ireland as well). After the First World War, though, Labour had become strongly unionist, with the unions in particular stressing the solidarity of the workers throughout the United Kingdom in fighting back against unemployment and recession. Attlee's government did nothing much for Scotland and Wales, while consolidating the greater power of the Scottish Office, secured during Churchill's wartime coalition by Tom Johnston. A book like Crosland's *Future of Socialism* contained no hint that policies might vary at all in either Scotland or Wales. The Callaghan government had pressed on unenthusiastically with separate bills for Scotland and Wales, but it was in debating the issue that the government was brought down by one vote in 1979. In 1997, however, devolution swept through in Scotland and got home by a whisker in Wales (when, as noted previously, I prophesied the result correctly on Channel Four). The achievement of devolution, initially with Labour-led governments in both Edinburgh and Cardiff, was therefore a huge landmark for the party, and led in time to a significant extension of power for the governments of both nations, all the more so after the dramatic Scottish referendum in September 2014 and its aftermath.

Second, Labour became much more obviously the party of democracy with a raft of other constitutional reforms, including of the House of Lords, and the crucial passage of the Human Rights Act in 1998, a great civilising measure worthy of the land of Magna Carta. It was all a remarkable legislative achievement for Derry Irvine, as Lord Chancellor, at a period when Tony Blair showed little interest. At the same time, it was all very piecemeal, even incoherent. Gordon Brown took considerably more interest in these matters and when I served on the Joint Select Committee of the Constitutional Reform Bill in 2008 we discussed the merits of a written, codified constitution, which I had myself always favoured. It looked as if, after the Scottish vote in 2014, that we were advancing more strongly along this path, and that there might emerge something akin to a federal or confederal Britain in the aftermath of the Westminster politicians' pledges (or 'vows') during the Scottish debate. From the historians' viewpoint, the idea of Labour leading the way on constitutional reform was a considerable novelty. The Attlee government, along with the Wilson government, had offered almost nothing on this front. Now, constitutional reform was being seen as a vital component of social as well as political democracy.

Third, Labour became the party of personal freedom as it had not been earlier. In its formative years, it had almost been a puritanical party, through its emergence from the nonconformist chapels and the traditional moralism of male-dominated trade unions. I noted that Jim Callaghan, of working-class background, took a broadly traditional view in being unhappy with 'permissiveness' (in conversation with me, he found me rather too libertarian on such matters as US troops of both sexes sharing tents in the desert in the Middle East). By contrast, the bohemian *litterateur* Michael Foot was far more relaxed. However, Roy Jenkins had carried through a brave programme of radical reform in the 1960s, dealing with literary censorship, abortion and homosexuality among other issues, with a boldness that did him enormous credit. The Blair government now carried this on, in the sphere of gender equality, race relations, and sexual preference. We voted strongly for gay adoption, while in 2013 it was Labour votes that were the bedrock of the Lords majority for gay marriage, larger than that in the Commons. It was ironic that in the sphere of civil liberties, as already noted, Labour's zeal for personal freedom was far more restrictive. But the policy generally was an important step towards a more humane and tolerant society. In this area, at least, Ed Miliband had every reason to praise his party's commitment to One Nation, even if commentators attributed this phrase to Disraeli rather than to the less flamboyant Stanley Baldwin. All this, along with a stronger policy of involvement with Europe, made for a bold progressive agenda. We would not have had any of it with the Tories, especially with Thatcher at the helm. With her, we would have kept capital punishment and scrapped sanctions on South Africa.

But, as the New Labour years ground on, Labour doctrine and policy began to look less appealing. One fundamental problem was that my party seemed to have no doctrine, either socialist or anything else. Roy Jenkins, no less, had committed himself to the view, in *What Matters Now*, a book of speeches in 1974, that 'a working-class party without a Socialist philosophy would be a front for vested interests'. Some party apparatchiks made this lack of ideas a virtue, and advocated a focus simply on professional competence in office. As a result the party of progress came to seem a managerial clique, with no philosophical inclinations, and expressed itself in a barbarous form of semi-literate Newspeak. As Orwell's Winston Smith put it in *Nineteen Eighty-Four*, 'the whole aim of Newspeak is to narrow the range of thought … In the end we shall make thoughtcrime literally impossible because there will be no words in which to express it'. The message, when it did come through, increasingly failed to command trust. Labour's technical control of information too often turned into 'spin'. Iraq made this problem much worse. For Tony Blair, the essence of Labour's ideology appeared to be the cult of youth, which he hammered home time and again in his early years in office. His first speech as party leader in 1995 included the word 'young' no fewer than thirty-seven times. For Gordon Brown, the key word was 'change' – which featured seven times at the start of his first prime ministerial address. The self-contradictory, loosely expressed doctrine of the 'Middle Way', of which I could never make sense, has been rightly described by John Rentoul in his highly sympathetic biography of Tony Blair as 'a 'blanc-mange of generalities'. It was this vagueness that contributed to the public's sense that politicians were all the same, all of them professionals who had no other experience in life, with their leaders all PPE graduates from Oxford, of the kind I had myself lectured to down the years. It is perhaps a sombre legacy.

This lack of a philosophy led to another problem, a jumbled union of opposites. New Labour, in its anxiety to bring together a range of interests, social classes and regions in one portmanteau body, tended to contradictions. It found itself at the same time advocating devolution and command-and-control centralism (notably in Gordon Brown's regime at the Treasury), it yoked together consumer choice and governmental control, it seemed at various times to be both for and against greater European integration, it waffled about immigration. There were two more fundamental issues. In its anxiety to steer clear of the economic direction which Labour had so rigidly advocated in the recent past (notably in the notorious 'longest suicide note', the 1983 election manifesto), in effect it swallowed economic Thatcherism whole. Its economic policy was neo-liberal and based on market choice. Tax rates were kept low for the wealthy and for overseas businesses. Britain was almost a tax haven for international capitalism and urged the cause of deregulation and business freedom in the European Union, when its partners, even those led by right-wing governments, preferred a more directive policy. A sinister group of international capitalists, Russian oligarchs and others, began to buy major property in west London, using it as a negotiable form of currency rather than somewhere to live. As a result, house prices were driven up for everybody else, including would-be first-time buyers. Labour, more strongly than the Conservatives, advocated the privatisation of public assets, the reduction of taxes on wealthy people and corporate interests, and the state promoting a policy of 'free' markets. Labour deprivatised nothing, not even the railway companies which became a by-word for technological underdevelopment, and effectively subsidised by their customers through ever-rising fares. The only virtuous exception was the publicly-owned East Coast line.

Similar policies were pursued over the water companies, the gas and electricity industries. The prices and markets were rigged, and the executives allowed to help themselves to huge remuneration at a time of a financial squeeze for everybody else. Public-private partnerships (PPI initiatives, so called) were disastrously introduced for the London tube. In the case of air traffic control services, Labour went on impetuously with privatisation on their own account, and came close to doing the same over Royal Mail. Labour's old faith in public ownership, public service and the public realm has been shredded. When, at the time of the credit crunch in 2008, Labour had finally to nationalise Northern Rock and some other financial institutions, it did so reluctantly, almost apologetically. There were those of us who viewed taking a badly run bank into public ownership with undisguised joy. As a result, New Labour's commendable efforts to advance in other social areas have founded upon the entrenched inequality brought about by neo-liberal economic policies. The demoralising austerity of the past few years, which has depressed social expectations for so many people, including in London itself with its many pockets of real poverty, should be replaced by far bolder, expansionist policies in which public spending has a key role.

The other great weakness of New Labour's time in office I have already alluded to, and will repeat only very briefly. The party of Keir Hardie, George Lansbury and Nye Bevan also became the war party. The disastrous invasion of Iraq in 2003 was only the most serious part of a series of wars, from west Africa to the Balkans, in which Tony Blair's government engaged. The sequel is admirably set out in *Blair's Wars*, written by another of my former pupils John Kampfner, an editor of the *New Statesman*. It is extraordinary how careless that government was in committing both air forces and ground troops to distant war zones. None of them had any first-hand experience of war themselves, which may be why they were so casual in their responses – unlike old soldiers like the wiser Denis Healey, who had seen horrors at Anzio and knew all too well about the pity of war. Perhaps they were influenced by Labour's long reputation of being weak, even unpatriotic, on foreign and defence issues. Apart from the moral inadequacies of such a policy – with 'liberal intervention' the new mantra for western invasions – the invasion was directly harmful to Labour's electoral chances. The 2005 election saw the majority fall by a hundred, and Tony Blair awkwardly challenged in his Sedgefield constituency by the father of a young soldier killed during our invasion of Iraq. Ed Miliband won a good deal of support for his disavowal of support for the Iraq invasion, which he said was a mistake. His brother, David, lost the Labour leadership election in consequence. Since then, there has been anguished internal debate in the party as to whether they chose the right Miliband.

However, in September 2014, it was sad to see Labour (other than around thirty dissentients in the Commons) fail to challenge or question the government's decision to bomb Iraq again during the campaign against Isis Muslim fundamentalists. All the same, the usual post-imperialist errors were still apparent. An uncertainty as to whether to go beyond air strikes, an absence of clear military objectives for the forces to follow, a Pavlovian response to the American view that it is our role to act as policemen of the world, and a blind refusal to see that a western invasion like this only turns angry young Muslims into terrorists, threatening our security in British cities, and encouraging some British-based Muslims to travel to join their co-religionists in combating the west – all these are present again as in 2003. In defence policy as in economic, Labour too often cleaves almost unthinkingly to the conventional wisdom. The prospects before us are not encouraging in either case. It is bleak to see our party, once seen as the last best hope of progressives and internationalists across the world, lapse into acquiescence in a lawless, vengeful world. I only hope my grandchildren and their contemporaries do not suffer from the consequences.

You would gather from the above catalogue of past experiences, that I am a somewhat disillusioned and battle-weary member of the party – and you would be right. There have been so many miscalculations, perhaps even crimes, over the years. At the same time, I expect to remain Labour until I die. I have never seriously contemplated joining another party. I have much in common with the libertarian instincts of the Liberals and now the Liberal Democrats and the patriotic passions of Plaid Cymru. Party differences are far more blurred than they were and it would be possible to visualise working with either in a parliamentary pact, of the kind that worked well for Jim Callaghan in 1977. I have never been blindly tribal, even if this book conveys the opposite. Still, for all its past and present weaknesses, Labour seems to me the only party capable of confronting the social divisions and imbalances in our country and, now and again, of doing something about them.

It would be good to see a much bolder, more confident approach to current issues. We totally lack 'the vision thing', as the 2015 election showed. It is remarkable how defensive Labour has been in proclaiming more radical features of its record as with tax credits or the use of nationalisation to preserve our banks in 2008. It has been far too passive in allowing the Tories and their Liberal Democrat associates to place the blame for deficit on the Brown government – in fact, Brown saved the British, and perhaps the world, banking system, and the economy was actually growing just before the 2010 general election. As an internationalist party, Labour should be open and honest in proclaiming the value of immigration and membership of Europe, and not try to lead a race to the bottom in truckling to UKIP. Our economic problems are not the fault of either immigrants or Europe; in fact, both are highly positive factors for our economy. The party also needs some of Jim Callaghan's wise judgement in committing itself to new reforms. Rash, off-the-cuff pledges on such matters as freezing energy prices or a mansion tax have had a habit of unravelling as soon as they have been announced. On the mansion tax, it would be far better to revise the existing Council Tax bands instead. There is a callow amateurishness about the Labour front bench; Tony Blair's obsessive cult of youth has gone too far, and there is a lack of authority. We lack the Healeys, Croslands, Jenkinses and Williamses of yesteryear.

As a historian, I would also like to see this traditional party, an Edwardian survival, show more regard for its history. This could have been a welcome result of Jon Cruddas's revisionist review led by a man of keen historical understanding. Tony Blair had no feel for history at all; history was dead stuff, the past, inseparably linked with Old Labour which everybody knew was out of date. Hence the casualness in the handling of complicated mechanisms of governance and the 'mess' (in Anthony King's words) created out of constitutional reform; hence the unthinking attack on Iraq in 2003 without reflecting on the historical circumstances in which the Sunnis, Shias and Kurds were yoked together in Mesopotamia in 1919, the force of Arab nationalism throughout the Middle East over the decades, or the continuing animus against western imperialist aggression ever since the Sykes-Picot treaty. The Anglo-US belief that 'democratic' Iraqis would throw up their arms in joy after being bombed and thousands of their citizens killed, and immediately embrace the form of democracy advocated by the western invader, is sheer fantasy. It is to be hoped the long-running Chilcot Inquiry may reflect on these matters; two fine historians were members of that inquiry – Lawrence Freedman and Martin Gilbert, the latter sadly dying in early 2015.

In fact, in spite of the deeply disappointing outcome of the 2015 election, I think that Labour made some progress under Ed Miliband after 2010. It stayed broadly united, unlike in 1951 or 1979, which were other periods of electoral defeat. It looked more positive than the governing Socialists in France, with their poor leadership, false promises and subsequent political collapse. Over here, Labour's processes of revision helped to redefine and reinvent the party. Cruddas's policy review could lead to a long overdue change of emphasis. In effect, the democratic socialism of which Tawney wrote, not to mention George Orwell, is being vindicated for its democracy and, to a limited degree, for its socialism. Labour is ceasing to be a party of centralisation and rigid attachment to the union, with the gentlemen from Whitehall always seen as a fount of wisdom. Scotland has already shown its passion for full local control and direction, and the SNP has drawn up its own prospective written constitution. I was glad to see the report of the Smith Commission on fiscal devolution and to hear Ed Miliband's positive reaction to its recommendations. Wales, much more cautiously, is moving in a similar direction. England, of course, is a far larger and wealthier partner, but a form of regional devolution there is perfectly conceivable, based perhaps not on artificial 'regions' but on familiar, existing structures of local and urban government. It could help to redress the profound inequality between different parts of England. Localism will be a new watchword of our time, a determined reversion to the greater pluralism of the years before 1914. Historians will have their role as pathfinders by judiciously appraising the evidence (I will never say 'the lessons') of the past. As Nye Bevan once said, after emerging from the mists on the summit of the mountains above Tredegar, you cannot know where you're going if you don't know where you've been.

The modern Labour Party, heavily shaped of course by the 'economism' of the trade unions, is broadly a fusion of two socialist visions. There is the structured, positivist model of the Fabians, central and local government enmeshed, with much use of experts, and complex administrative interaction; an important component of the creed of 'national efficiency'. That positivist model was sometimes (falsely) accused of not having a philosophy at all. At its worst, it reminds one of Orwell writing about a state held together by reference clerks and tele-programmers, though there was of course a much better side as well. Edmund Burke, who I do not really see as the founder of modern Conservatism but rather as a social philosopher on whose ideas Labour should reflect, had a deeper sense of society than Fabian pioneers like Sidney and Beatrice Webb. The Conservative MP Jesse Norman's brilliant book on Burke should be read by all would-be socialists. For Burke, society was a partnership of the dead and the living, an evolving corporate whole which lived through its organic spontaneity and naturalness. Alternatively, there is in our past the much more pluralist model of Keir Hardie and the ILP, based on an ethical socialism, communal solidarity, localised power, the kind of close-knit organic democracy that there was in his Merthyr Tydfil, with its chapels, co-ops, choirs, brass bands and football clubs. That was a society with which people could readily identify. It linked socialism automatically with the idea of participating citizenship. That is a concept that has been mislaid these past decades, and needs reviving now. This truly new Labour would reflect a diminished commitment to older institutional models, including the Westminster parliament, not to mention liberation from the ancient class divisions which gave the party birth. The committed historian could try to recreate and redefine the moral components of that earlier world. Burke famously appealed to the New Whigs to draw wisdom, in their reflections on liberty, from the Old Whigs in the past. The values of Old Labour could be resurrected to give hope and inspiration for the New.

Chapter Eleven

My History

WITH ONE OBVIOUS appalling exception, my life has been endlessly happy and fortunate. I have spent it writing and teaching history, a vocation and a joy rather than a job. I have found writing books, chapters and articles on historical matters to be deeply pleasurable, the fulfilment of what I always wanted to do, and not too many people can say that. In addition, I have spent my time teaching the young, and their sense of curiosity and frequent irreverence has always been deeply enjoyable. I have taught them in a variety of wonderful universities – Swansea, Queen's, Oxford, Columbia, Witwatersrand and now King's, London – each of them perfect for someone of my temperament, surrounded by fascinating and highly intelligent colleagues. I have not been particularly well paid by comparative standards, even as a Vice-Chancellor (my current successor earns three times my final salary in 1995), but the quality of life I have known has been far more rewarding. It has given me the opportunity to travel widely, to lecture in countries from Malaysia to the United States, and to enjoy the culture of many remarkable nations. Before that, I was the beneficiary of wonderful schooling in Aberdyfi and in Hampstead alike. In my personal life, I am a child of the post-1945 Welfare State who enjoyed the enormous benefits of free education and a National Health Service. As a result, I have reached the age of eighty without so far suffering any major illness. I have also avoided disagreeable alternatives, notably managing not to do national service and going on instead to work at Swansea, a hugely stimulating and civilising experience, the essential foundation for my work as a scholar.

Personally, I have married two remarkable and beautiful women – one cruelly taken from me, the other with me now to provide warmth and inspiration. One was dark, tempestuous, Mediterranean; the other is blonde, graceful, Nordic – it has been like being successively the husband of Maria Callas and Grace Kelly. I have had two glorious children, of great talent and supreme loyalty, all twelve months of the year, and now four lovely grandchildren, while my Welsh cousins and their spouses are lovely, warm people who have sustained me in good times and bad. This memoir, therefore, is the contented chronicle of a very lucky man, and I have never ceased to forget my obligations to all those who helped to make my life so happy and fortunate.

The writing of history is the main activity with which I have been identified, and I have always found it intellectually and personally absorbing. It is necessarily a very private and solitary activity. Looked at in the abstract, it was not perhaps the ideal way of embarking on retirement as an ageing bachelor, but it provided the most stimulating form of renewal of the zest for life. As E. H. Carr, with whom I do not often identify, suggested, if you want to understand history, look at the historian. I respond to exploring past events and ideas in an atmosphere of total privacy. The one time I wrote a book with someone else, I found it a slightly awkward experience, even though I was married to my co-author. I saw around me as a vice-chancellor pressures from research councils for scholars to work in teams on group projects. I am by instinct a team player – although an only child I have never been a loner – and always enjoyed working intimately with others, from trying to be a loyal departmental colleague in various institutions to taking the Labour whip in the Lords rather than opting for the comparative isolation of the cross benches. But my professional approach has always been to work alone – certainly to learn from others in seminars and group activities, but ultimately to work on historical conundrums in my own way at my time of choosing (usually the morning). The most important necessity in writing history books – perhaps any kind of books – is the sense of momentum, not labouring in intense detail on solitary issues in single sentences, but keeping up the flow and thereby sustaining that continuity which is what history is about. One of my worries about the Research Academic Exercise introduced to assess the quality of university research work in the 1980s (a very necessary reform in my own experience, bearing in mind the casualness and indolence of some of my own tutors), is that it tends to marginalise the individual and the individualist, the solitary scholar, the idiosyncratic or even eccentric teacher, from whom, in my own life, so much insight and intellectual excitement has actually come. The RAE, with its rigid criteria and formal institutionalised procedures, tended to exclude the marginal man. Alan Taylor was a maverick who published enough but broke many of the formal rules, but I learned more from him than from whole battalions of the organisation men. Writing and teaching history, in my view, should reflect not only your abilities as an intellectual professional but your qualities as a human being.

My approach to writing history, therefore, has been on the whole traditional. My method has been broadly that of the Venerable Bede – without his English nationalism. Like Alan Taylor again, I would classify myself as 'an old-fashioned hack historian', and proudly so. I believe that the essence of history is the sense of movement, change and sequence, and that demands a narrative framework. In that context, I am firmly of the view that history is a form of literature which should be as readable as possible, written neither in officialese nor in journalese. Its essential magic lies in the fact that it appeals to everybody because everybody has a sense of the passage of time. So I have always thought it important to talk to schools, extramural groups, and that splendid body the Historical Association. I have never refused any invitation from their branches in any part of the country – even if it meant addressing ten men and a dog on a wet night in Manchester, those ten men (and perhaps even the dog) wanted to be there, and it is their lay enthusiasm that keeps our subject alive and is the life-blood of an informed democracy. I have always tried to make my writings lucid and never to shower them with masses of statistics, partly no doubt because my own technical command of such material is not one of my stronger points. I regret that too many economic historians now seem to see their subject as akin to mathematics rather than opting for the great analytical interdisciplinary sweep of some of their predecessors in the past – R. H. Tawney, to name one. So many economic historians now seem to have given up writing in sentences. I no longer read the *Economic History Review*, for which I used to write book reviews. At the same time, within a narrative context and methodology, the approach should be analytical, opening up conceptual themes and showing their wider significance.

I was greatly influenced as a young scholar by a wonderful book from my old mentor in Aberystwyth, David Williams, a historian influenced by the French *Annales* School. His *Rebecca Riots* (1955) appears at first sight to be the story of unremarkable local working people in west Wales in the 1840s, knocking down toll gates as a means of protesting against the poverty of rural life and those who directed it. But, in fact, he universalises his theme, depicting the local, social, cultural and religious pressures that made this a community in crisis. In due time, these riots led on to a wider democracy, political as well as social. It is this ability to draw out wider, deeply important ideas from apparently limited local materials, without artifice or self-promotion, that inspired me, and I know that the breadth of this quiet Pembrokeshire man's culture hugely impressed major scholars like Richard Cobb and Christopher Hill when they were his colleagues at Aberystwyth and at Cardiff respectively. With his Voltaire's bust by his side, David contained multitudes. He dedicates his book to his forebears, 'sons and daughters of Rebecca'. I would like to think that my own books reflect something of my own ancestry among the rural working class of Aberdyfi and Dolybont. After all, they gave me a truly privileged background.

In my own lesser way, I have tried to follow David's example, and to draw out wider conclusions. In writing about Keir Hardie, I tried to illuminate the mosaic of different groups which made up the labour and socialist movements in Britain, and by inference the composition of other radical movements as well. In writing about the Lloyd George coalition after 1918 or the Attlee government after 1945, I tried to bring out wider processes of post-war change, social and cultural. In my book on Wales from 1880 to 1980, I was concerned with far wider themes of democracy, social equality and the idea of nationhood. In writing biographies of such notable people as Jim Callaghan and Michael Foot, I aimed at writing a 'life and times' volume, rather like the Victorian tomes of such as Moneypenny and Buckle, setting my biographees against the context of wider movements to which they responded and often tried to transform, rather than focusing simply on the personal minutiae of their lives, fascinating though both of them were as men. Two historians who greatly influenced me as a young man were Asa Briggs, notably his *Victorian People* and *Victorian Cities*, and Eric Hobsbawm, particularly his *Primitive Rebels* and *Labouring Men*, with their genuine internationalism of outlook. In each case, I admired their popular sympathy as much as their scholarship. Asa, for instance, a synoptic scholar of great power, was also a marvellous historian of the humdrum. He once wrote a marvellous little essay on Victorian pins. It was astonishing and sobering to me that, in the summer of 2014 on Waterloo Day, I should follow these two giants of my profession in receiving a parliamentary award for lifetime achievement, presented by my dear friend Hywel Francis. Like my old Queen's colleague, Geoffrey Marshall, when he trained at Blackpool with the legendary Stanley Matthews, I felt privileged to be on the same strip of turf as Asa Briggs. Three other historians who greatly influenced me were, significantly, all French. My old history teacher at UCS, Reg Rands, encouraged me to read (in translation), Élie Halévy's *History of the English People in the Nineteenth Century*, a powerful and deeply moving synthesis of the idea of liberalism. I much admired François Bédarida's subtle analysis of social change in Britain in the industrial era and greatly appreciated the chance to meet the great man himself in Oxford in the 1980s. An exceptional book for me more recently is Pierre Nora's *Les Lieux de Mémoire*, which brings out for me the relationship between history and memory in a most exciting way. But I have always found the academic curiosity and personal sparkle of French academics most appealing; perhaps it is not surprising that in the end I married one of them.

Like all other historians, I have found stimulation in working on sources of all kinds, manuscript, printed, oral, visual and physical. Architecture I have always found deeply illuminating for my subject as well as a joy in itself. My more recent forays into contemporary history and biography have meant my drawing increasingly on oral history, always a challenging and enjoyable form of research, never dull, but inevitably needing especial care in meeting the objective and critical tests to be applied to all forms of historical evidence. But the staple of my research has tended to be manuscript material of the most traditional kind, the most revealing and dramatic evidence of all, especially when contained in a brown envelope headed 'not to be opened'. Nothing in my life exceeds the excitement that gripped me when I first looked at the Gladstone Papers in the old British Museum; or the many boxes of late-nineteenth century politicians in the National Library of Wales in Aberystwyth; or the Lloyd George papers in the Beaverbrook Library; or the records of the Labour Party in the party offices in Walworth Road or before that in Transport House (where they were brought to me on a tea trolley); or going through Jim Callaghan's communications with other world leaders in his flat in West Square. Particularly compelling could be the surviving fragments of pioneers in the labour or socialist movement, where quite poor and ill-educated people carefully preserved the surviving papers of their relatives or close colleagues. Keir Hardie's career proved particularly fascinating for me in that particular way. The Public Record Office (now the National Archives) has been a treasure-house of its own, ever improving, a model of how modern technology can assist the scholar. It follows that the archivist or director of an archive is an absolutely indispensable ally and colleague of the working historian. Men like Stephen Bird in the Labour Party archive or John Graham Jones in Aberystwyth were almost as irreplaceable as the manuscripts over which they presided. The Parliamentary Archives and History group rightly sees the two professions as inseparable from one another.

It is an intriguing thought to me that two of the great historians whose stamp on my own life was in different ways so profound – Alan Taylor and Richard Hofstadter – were not themselves great delvers into manuscript archives. Alan really only worked continuously on archives when he ran one (the unforgettable Beaverbrook Library), while Hofstadter is on record as expressing some disdain for what he called 'the archive rats' who gnawed away in the basement on obscure details. In each case, their mastery in drawing knowledge and wisdom from printed sources more than redressed the balance. But I have to say that I have been, for six decades, very much an archive rat myself.

The other point to be made about writing history is that you do not undertake the public activity of producing books simply for them to be read by other scholars alone. While specialist journals, covering all the variations of our subject, are essential for the advancement of knowledge, ultimately the audience is potentially the whole of humankind. I once heard the great art historian Sir Kenneth Clark say that 'because history is hard to write, that does not mean it should be difficult to read'. Some historians seem to write almost perversely in a deliberately arid, arcane fashion. I do not admire them for that, nor do I feel it is a sign of intellectual depth. I do not feel theirs is the way to stimulate the sense of historical inquiry within our society, let alone make it a force in the making of public policy – an admirable objective, which historians are now valuably taking seriously, not least the mighty British Academy which has assumed new roles in promoting and protecting the humanities and social sciences. In my own case, I feel my sense of history has been much improved by doing other things, although adjacent to history in many ways. I benefited from ceasing to be a day-to-day college tutor, admirable though that vocation was. In serving for nearly seven years as Vice-Chancellor, my managerial and executive role gave me a wider insight into the world, new and uncomfortable experiences of making choices at a time of severe financial constraint, maintaining morale and achieving a balance in attaining one's objectives, promoting the public image and attending to public relations. Academics can sometimes be unreasonable or too confined in approaching these matters. Michael Foot once told me that he would have written a somewhat different life of Nye Bevan after experiencing himself five years of the pressures of Cabinet office. In a far, far humbler and more parochial way, the experience of power when being a Vice-Chancellor gave me some sense of what I was trying to do when I wrote about a prime minister – after all, Edward Gibbon wrote that his brief part-time experience in the Hampshire Grenadiers was helpful for the historian writing about the legions of the Roman Empire.

Equally, I have benefited in my later life in becoming a member of the Lords. It is a limited experience. Nobody elected me, although I suspect that in 2015, with a major remodelling of the British constitution in prospect after the Scottish referendum, the composition of the upper house will undergo the same major surgery that the rest of our political institutions will experience. But to hear at first hand debate and argument on the key themes of our society, and those of the world, and even to be able to participate directly in those debates, adds an essential dimension to the understanding of our times that goes far beyond parliament itself. It has made me a more complete human being and thereby, I hope, a better historian.

I have spent almost all my life in universities, of course. They are, therefore, uniquely precious components of our society as far as I am concerned. In retrospect, I am most fortunate in the timing of my career. I began teaching around the time of the 1963 Robbins Report, which greatly added to the strength and security of our universities, and introduced the first time (a cynic would say the only time) that the British took their universities seriously. I was struck, both as a historian and as a Vice-Chancellor, by how many of the values of the Welsh national movement of the later nineteenth century were focused on education at all levels, with the crowning glory as I saw it being the national, federal University of Wales. It is thus saddening to me that, since my time, the university has largely broken up and is a shadow of its former greatness. It seems that the quality of Welsh life, perhaps of Welsh civilisation, has thereby been damaged, although the recent advance of my former university of Swansea as a separate institution, is exciting and encouraging. Universities must be sustained. All major nations in the modern world have seen them as central to their culture. When totalitarian regimes under a Hitler or a Stalin wished to liquidate the remnants of the old order, the universities were foremost among their targets, their libraries pillaged or even destroyed. In Britain, for centuries our universities have enjoyed enormous international esteem and are models for many other countries to follow. At the present time, several of them appear in the world's leading twenty higher educational institutions. Governments regard them as supreme among Britain's agencies of 'soft power'.

It is, therefore, deeply concerning for me as for many other academics that British universities now face threats and challenges which could damage their very existence. Symptomatic of those worries is that our universities have been removed from the domain of the Department of Education and have been relocated in the Department of Business, Innovation and Skills. Equally, overseas students have been dealt with not as an aspect of education but as part of the concerns of the Home Office, and have perversely been included among the statistics for immigration. It is as though universities are no longer seen within a seamless educational system, as part of a comprehensive public good; it is all very different from my earlier experience as a university teacher, from 1958 down to the mid-1980s. When I began work, universities were seen as major cultural institutions, which were essentially run by academics with light regulation at a distance by the University Grants Committee. This latter body oversaw the administration and funding of higher education, and had been set up in 1919 by Lloyd George's Coalition government under the aegis of H. A. L. Fisher, the distinguished historian who served at the Board of Education. There was an atmosphere of autonomy and freedom – and of youth. There were many lively young academics in post then. I played in the Swansea staff cricket team around 1960, and it was competitive; there were enough of us to form two cricket teams. It was sad, when I was invited as Vice-Chancellor to attend the University of Wales annual cricket dinner in Aberystwyth thirty years later, to find that most of the teams seemed to be able only to summon up around nine players. The fun had gone. Government cuts and low morale had taken their toll, even on the field of play. In retrospect, that university world of the 1960s, in my youth, looks like a long-lost golden age.

In total contrast to my early years, in the latter part of my career, from the mid-Thatcher period onwards, universities have been under pressure. They have been treated as essentially commercial institutions dictated by the alleged priorities of the market as in the policies of Thatcher herself. The change in nomenclature tells us everything. Would-be students have become customers universities are seen as governed by the principle of consumer choice like supermarkets; deans and pro-vice-chancellors have become line managers. I was largely shielded from these developments as a fellow of an Oxford college, perhaps too much so. But I encountered them in full force when I joined a pompous self-regarding body, the Committee of Vice-Chancellors in 1989, which included no polytechnics at that time but was dominated by rather right-wing managerial chief executive officers from the older 'provincial' universities. The language they used was quite unfamiliar to me as a university scholar (which, unlike many other vice-chancellors, I still regarded myself as being). Sometimes the vocabulary was military with talk of 'strategy' and 'targets'. At times it was curiously sporting with references to 'level playing fields' and 'moving the goal-posts'. But the dominant language was always business-oriented, concerned with the creation of wealth, and the Committee of Vice-Chancellors and Principals deferred to it. I am not surprised that vice-chancellors now, with grossly inflated salaries at a time of supposed financial stringency, make so little effort to resist the transformation of their precious institutions. They do well out of things as they are. It is not surprising either that the major inquiries into university administration and finance have been led by major businessmen – Jarrett of Reed International, Lord Browne of BP – and that their commercially driven analyses have been self-reinforcing. The economic premises of their doctrines, such as that the unfettered market leads to innovation, genuine competition and free choice by informed consumers (the last in fact usually poorly-informed young people aged around seventeen), are never questioned, and the commercialisation of our universities continues remorselessly. It is part of the wider process of the privatisation and corruption of the public realm which David Marquand has highlighted in his *Mammon's Kingdom*, a process begun by Thatcher but carried through with equal zest by the Blair regime. There can hardly be a more valuable or vulnerable victim.

It is for that reason that, at the invitation of an eminent Oxford historian colleague Sir Keith Thomas, I have become active in the Committee for the Defence of British Universities set up in 2013. It aims to protect our celebrated university system, long held in the highest international respect alongside such institutions as the BBC or the British Museum. The challenges now are manifold. There is a financial/social crisis resulting from the abolition of the old block grant and the reliance (almost totally so in the cases of the humanities and social sciences) on student tuition fees. This is a highly unstable base for university finance, apart from being obviously a bonus for the rich. The politicians have been woeful. The Conservatives, like so many grocers, see the issue solely in terms of customers paying the right price for what they choose. The Liberal Democrats, of course, completely broke their election pledge on tuition fees, and have suffered grievously in terms of public trust. Labour, in late autumn 2014, still had to arrive at a policy, though there was a pledge to reduce the basic tuition fee from £9,000 to £6,000, which would be a great help. (The only party that has come honourably out of the issue is the Scottish National Party, in government, which has retained Scottish Labour's abolition of tuition fees and gained much popular credit for it.) The outcome in the broadest terms is that the student loan system actually loses rather than saves money, since much of it is not paid back, and yet provides universities with no secure financial base for future planning. There are also important issues of university autonomy to be resolved; at a time when politicians have talked of rolling back the state, the encroachment by central government over them has become ever more oppressive. University teachers, therefore, have a duty to reassert the traditional freedoms of their calling. They should call for more freedom to attract their own students (including overseas students much disaffected, notably in India, by Home Office policy). They should have freedom in determining the balance of their disciplines and their academic staff. They should be free to determine their own priorities as regards resources, instead of measuring everything by an alleged market return. They should be assisted more in creating a strong science base. They should certainly be free to decide what should be taught and how. Michael Gove's observations on the teaching of history quite rightly emphasised the element of continuity of historical change, but also came perilously close to triumphalist celebration by a non-historian of the heroics of our 'island story'.

I am, therefore, anxious at the current threats to commercialize our universities, to cheapen the intellectual substance of what they do, to focus on 'wealth creation' and training 'skills' rather than their real role in training minds and generating an inquiring culture through which a nation can live and prosper. But I am not terminally depressed about it. If I were a young man in my early twenties today, I would still hope to become a university teacher – partly, no doubt, because I have never shown any talent at anything else. Our universities and colleges are still centres of free inquiry and the pursuit of truth, of fundamental value for a creative society. Compared with universities in other countries, despite the disparity in funding compared with a country like the United States, British institutions still show up strongly not only in the various formal league tables but in world discourse among creative people in the arts and sciences. When I taught in the US, I was struck by the vitality and brilliance of the younger faculty, but also by the hierarchical system of administration which kept senior and junior faculty at arm's length. British universities seem to me far more democratic, with their departments and faculties and academic senates – this was especially marked in Oxford in my experience, where colleges were run by teaching scholars rather than a cadre of professional administrators, and the most senior and junior fellows had equal status. It was time-consuming, but it made for academic freedom. French universities, with their undisciplined mass entry (and exodus) of sub-standard students, their casual treatment of academic staff and their extreme Bonapartist centralilsation, seem to me both less enjoyable and less academically distinguished, apart from a handful of élitist *grandes écoles*. I would not like to have taught in a continental university, and rejoice in the fact that the humane institutional systems of British universities still serve as models for many countries across the world.

There are many things amiss with our universities, especially their finances and the difficulty they have in outreach to less privileged students, of whom I was one. It would be wonderful to see a political party campaigning for universities, once again, being financed from general taxation. The cost of the redundant Trident, for example, could cover that. But that is evidently a total pipedream. Still, they remain proud, unique institutions, emphatically worth fighting for. They have given me a marvellously stimulating career for which I am humbly grateful and I hope many, many others may enjoy the same in the future.

My lifetime as a historian has, of course, been a time of exceptionally violent historical change, indeed the period of most revolutionary upheaval in the history of mankind. Britain itself has transformed itself beyond measure in the eighty years through which I have lived. In my childhood, obviously during the years of world war but also the years that followed, most people never seemed to go anywhere much, and certainly not overseas. There was nowhere really to go, and not too many had the money to do so anyway. I went abroad for the first time at nineteen, and did not do so again for several more years. Now I have been to almost fifty countries around the world. Everything looks and feels different. There have been extraordinary transformations in science which bear down on everyone's lives – the coming of nuclear power, the information revolution in electronics, and immense advances in medicine, which among other things have enabled me to write this book at an age which, in 1934, would have had people seeing me as half way into the crematorium.

In Britain, the core has been ripped out of city centres; placid country towns have been undermined by traffic congestion, ring roads and out-of-town supermarkets. In Wales and elsewhere, glorious hillsides have been scarred by wind turbines. Churches have become almost totally marginalised, pressured reluctantly into reform over women bishops and gay clergy. In 2014, Britain hardly seems a Christian country any more – and the bane of my childhood, the traditional, pre-war Sunday, is mercifully no more. Family life has been in retreat since the 1960s; only a bare majority of households are now founded on married couples of opposite gender, while Britain leads Europe in the proportion of marriages that end up in divorce. The population has been transformed – Conservative ministers say 'swamped' – first by Commonwealth immigrants, and then by Eastern European peoples like the Poles (630,000 migrants to

London in 2004–7). London is also said to be the sixth largest French city. This fosters nativist protest from ethnic Britons and has fanned the racist propaganda of UKIP even though, to my mind, immigration and diversity have been strongly beneficial to our economy and our culture.

The institutional symbols of Britishness have been revolutionised too with the constitution being reinvented, the Lords losing almost all their hereditaries, the Common law incorporating the legal traditions of continental Europe, Brussels looming as large as Westminster or Whitehall in the governmental system. The Scots could well go their own way, and the Welsh and Northern Irish follow their own distinctive paths. In September 2014, the unity of the United Kingdom hung by the thread of 10.5 per cent of the Scottish voters. Only the Queen survives as an enduring focus of loyalty, and even here the deferential religiosity towards the Crown during my childhood has long since disappeared. The eventual reign of King Charles III may be an unsettled time. In Scotland and in Wales 'God Save the Queen' has almost disappeared as a public refrain, while in England the flag of St George rivals the Union flag. There has been almost envy at how selected popular landmarks drawn from both world wars could make a popular unifying impact – there were ample signs of this in the unsubtle patriotism linked with the commemoration of the First World War, that obscene bloodbath, in August 2014, with many soldiers and the younger members of the royal family on frequent public display. In May 2000, when there was celebration on both sides of the channel to mark of the 60th anniversary of the evacuation of British forces from Dunkirk (an event seen in France as an act of disloyalty), some observed that a revival of the essentially isolationist 'Dunkirk spirit' might be of value.

It is the duty of the historian to try to make sense of these changes, and to respond to them in his or her work, both in the themes described and from the author's standpoint. It is not easy for historians today – indeed, perhaps it is harder now than at any time since their craft began millennia ago. My lifetime, a time of comparative peace within Britain in formal terms, has been an era of continuous violence, apart from the two world wars. The *Guardian* noted in early 2014 that it was the first time since 1914 that Britain was not at war with anyone, and that we were commemorating the First World War to make up for it: since the *Guardian* made its comment, we have once again, and for the third time, bombed Iraq. We have seen how terrorists abroad, from Ireland to the Middle East, can bring appalling violence to our own land. We have not experienced anything as extreme as the disaster of 9/11 in New York, which so grieved me as a former resident of the city, but that one event claimed sixty-seven innocent British casualties, while the London bombing of 7/7 led to fifty-two deaths, not all British. These tragedies show bleakly how the world has been both more interlinked and more divided by recent technological and political developments. If globalisation has enabled us to communicate more rapidly and to work together more easily (often at huge economic and social cost), it has also enabled us to kill each other more efficiently and ruthlessly, and to witness the result online or on screen. As a historian, it has been valuable, if dreadfully sombre, for me to have lived through a world war in which I saw some of the physical effects at first hand, and to have lived in the United States in the 1960s and witness the racial conflicts and seen on screen the assassinations of that troubled era, and to have felt directly the threat of annihilation. A highly formative experience for me, as a human being and indeed as a historian more indirectly, was to be in New York during the Cuban crisis in October 1962. It felt terrifying at the time, and the records since have confirmed how close we came to world catastrophe. The world owed so much, in my view, to the rationality and calm of President Kennedy during those thirteen days of supreme crisis. Cuba certainly changed me as a humble resident of Manhattan. The sense of violence and destruction, perhaps bringing with it an end to our world, left with me a sense of apocalypse now, valuable for any would-be chronicler of our times.

In looking at this tormented record, the historian has to try to observe from a variety of perspectives. Only through a divided consciousness can the ambiguities of our world be fully understood. My perspectives are not only my own. There were the perspectives of my parents after the First World War, my father a fortunate survivor of that conflict. My parents grew up in a world of mass unemployment and intense social cleavage in the interwar years. Mass unemployment was for me, though not for many others, totally unknown. I have not known one day without paid work since I left university, and this continues in my eighties. If you are a historian, unlike a scientist, to continue meaningful work after your retirement requires neither lab space, nor expensive equipment, nor research funding, but simply trying to keep your wits and to ward off Alzheimer's. In 2011, at the age of seventy-seven, I acquired a new job, a visiting professorship at King's College, London. My seminars there with Andrew Blick and Vernon Bogdanor give me endless renewed joy, and my work with Professor Robert Blackburn on a codified written constitution (in which I deeply believe) was totally fascinating; it produced the important document *A New Magna Carta?* As I have said, I have been a lucky man, luckier than my father, though certainly not abler than him.

My parents' perspectives can be balanced against those of my children, David and Katherine – forward-looking, vibrant, totally free from older people's prejudices about class, race and sexuality, at ease with changes in a more technical world in a way that I certainly am not (they have taught everything I know about computers, including the ability to write this book), and at ease also in their personal relations with each other and with young people of either gender. I am deeply proud of them and know they will transmit their humane idealism to Joseph and Clara, Thomas and Samuel, my dear grandchildren, in all their futures. I am similarly proud of the perspectives of my wife, Elizabeth, a serious constitutional law academic with her own divided consciousness; half Scottish, half French/Swiss Huguenot. I learn so much from the joy of living with her, the values and challenges of being French, of being an Anglophile, of being a member of a small religious minority in a Catholic country where these things still count, three hundred and thirty years since the bigoted Louis XIV revoked the Edict of Nantes. Her ancestral memories are a part of my consciousness and, as a non-Christian, I rejoice when she wears her Huguenot brooch on public occasions. I hope it will not go the same way as the Muslim niqab (*le voile*) so brusquely condemned by many of her fellow-countrymen.

My own consciousness exists on many levels. I am a hybrid of reformist radicalism and a love of historic continuity, perhaps of tradition. I press for change, and I live for order and peace. On a formal level, I am a product of three identities, all of them important to me. I simply do not accept UKIP-style stereotypes of exclusive national identity. Recently, I wrote for a distinguished French periodical, *Entre Deux Mondes*, and I felt that the title was highly appropriate for me: *Entre Trois Mondes* would have been even better. I am proud of a Welsh identity that is deeply important to me and makes me what I am. I speak a different language from the English and I see things differently from them in fundamental ways. I come from a different place, with few public schools and no established Church, more democratic and classless, with its own popular culture. I have written extensively on the modern history of Wales, and found it helpful to view it side by side with the history of England. In the twentieth century, as at the time of Glyn Dŵr in the fifteenth, their histories are significantly, subtly different. A key difference to me is the existence of the Welsh language, which is a beautiful, lyrical medium that enhances world culture by expressing thoughts and values in unique ways. I was not a partisan of Cymdeithas yr Iaith Cymraeg (the Welsh Language Society) in its campaigns, which seemed to me aggressive and even Anglophobe at times, but I could respond to the force behind them. I was as angry as them when George Thomas, as Secretary of State for Wales in 1968, shouted at us through the television camera, 'Remember – *you* are the minority'. I shouted back at him from my living room sofa, 'Not where I come from, you sanctimonious hypocrite!' Wales to me would not be Wales without her language, and I pray that the Welsh schools that have sustained it continue to flourish.

It gave me enormous pride to be made a member of the Gorsedd of Bards at the National Eisteddfod in Cardiff one sunny day in August 2008. My grandchildren loved the music and flower maidens, the great horn and the mighty sword wielded by Robin McBryde, the former hooker of the Welsh rugby team.

I cherished that day the sense of communion I felt with the teachers, black-smiths, farm labourers and fishermen from whom I sprang. Elizabeth has been with me since at two *eisteddfodau*, at Bala in my ancestral Merioneth, and at Llanelli, close to the immortal Stradey Park of 'sosban fach' fame, and she loved it each time. Maybe we will go to the pan-Celtic *eisteddfod* at Lorient in Brittany one day. Another humbling event shortly after the Cardiff eisteddfod was being awarded a gold medal for lifetime achievement by the Honourable Society of Cymmrodorion, to whom I had given my first-ever public lecture back in January 1959, and of which I was by 2008 a vice-president. Yet another touch-ing occasion came when I received another such award at the 'Welsh Politician of the Year' event held in Cardiff City Hall in December 2014, surrounded by family and friends. I appreciated the fact that a Welsh historian of politics could be considered alongside its practitioners. Certainly, the Welsh historians of my generation and younger, by emphasising the continuities of their nation's past, have helped to change their world.

But my Welsh consciousness is not in the least Anglophobic. My par-ents, both first-language Welsh speakers and proud patriots, loved England and English people, taught them and lived among them. Ethnic nationalism is the last refuge of bigoted minds, and I could never respond to such a thing anywhere. I have lived most of my life in England, the last twenty of them in retirement in west Oxfordshire, which I adore. I love the beauty of its villages with their Tainton stone and their Stonesfield slate roofs, the magical serenity of its parish churches, its streams, its willows and elms and its green meadows, not to mention the majesty of Oxford itself where I still have the privilege of working as an honorary fellow of Queen's and Oriel. I love my neighbours, their informality and simple decency, the humane courtesies of English village life. More important still, perhaps, I revere the sense of freedom and tolerance, of a basic sense of fairness deep-rooted in the instinct of the English people. As I have written earlier, English people have an understanding of the eccentric and the individual unmatched by any other nation on this earth. They are alien to the idea of *raison d'état*. It is something to celebrate anew with the 800th anniversary of Magna Carta, an event that could be honoured also by overturn-ing the remaining oppressive legacies of the recent counter-terrorist acts. I am a passionate Welshman who salutes the very idea of England – and of course, therefore, someone who profoundly wishes the union of the nations of the United Kingdom to stay intact, which I believe it will.

Equally, I feel very attached to the union of Europe. As I have stressed before, I had a strongly developed European consciousness long before I mar-ried a woman from France. I have always responded to a multicultural con-text, just as I celebrate a multi-cultural Britain from which I, my children and grandchildren gain so much. I felt a kind of primitive kinship with Europe as a boy. I was desperately shy at public speaking at school, but I do recall saying something in a debate in 1950, when I supported Britain's joining the Schuman Plan for a western European coal, iron and steel community. The Attlee government kept its distance – Ernest Bevin was never keen on it, and Hugh Dalton felt it had echoes of cartels, even of the Vatican. My only argument was that our socialist comrades in France and Germany wanted us to join. It was no doubt facile, and I knew no economics, but I think the instinct of that sixth-form boy was right. But in 1950, the Dunkirk spirit of isolation was abroad in the land, and we kept aloof from Europe until 1975, twenty years too late. Now we gain enormously from membership of the European Union, especially in trade and cultural exchange. Millions of jobs depend upon our membership, and we would be isolated outside with difficult and expensive prospects for re-entry. Our membership of the European Court of Human Rights at Strasbourg seems to me essential for the land of Magna Carta and the Petition of Right and the Bill of Rights. I am appalled at the irresponsible casualness of David Cameron paving the way for a British exit, and the spinelessness of the supposedly pro-European Liberal Democrats in failing to resist him. The Labour Party is wobbly, and dithers over referendums, but appeared to be standing firm under Ed Miliband. At least it looks from the polling evidence as if the British people have more residual sense, despite the xenophobic impulses of UKIP, and that a referendum in 2017 might see our country vote to remain in. As a vice-chancellor, I saw the enormous potentiality, in student exchange, research projects and funding and general cultural stimulus, of the European link for our universities. Now that I am in the Lords, I have spoken and voted consistently for the European idea; as Dylan Thomas wrote in a different connection, 'I'd be a damn fool if I didn't.'

My history book of my own history is almost closed. It is the record of a world of many frightening changes. But as a person I feel myself to be that same shy yet enthusiastic boy who went to school in Aberdyfi to sit at the feet of Miss Egwys Jones, that proud daughter of Llanegryn. The world has changed. My own philosophy towards it has not, at least not fundamentally. My own values and philosophical assumptions are much the same as they were when I was a teenager. If anything, in what Gibbon called my state of 'autumnal felicity', I am an example of a man who, as he grew older, moved more to the left. I certainly feel my instincts to be more radical now than, say, forty years ago, particularly because, as an Oxford don, a Welsh vice-chancellor and a member of the Lords, I have seen the frailty, often accompanied by straight deceit, that characterise those who claim to govern our world. I have also seen how apparently progressive changes can cover up something far more sinister. Thus we are far less deferential in our society than we used to be, but certainly not more democratic. We do not enjoy a proper sense of citizenship in this country (indeed that is also a major weakness in the European Union with its democratic deficit). In Britain we are more classless in speech, dress and leisure activities, but the class divide is more paralysing than ever. Major sociological studies have shown how the dead weight of class, in terms of resources, opportunities, housing, environmental quality and expectations in life, creates a huge imbalance in our society, where rooted inequality diminishes the quality of life for everyone. Inequality has swept in apace over the decades since 1980, under Conservative, New Labour and Coalition governments alike, most acutely since 2010. Much of our society and its most precious institutions have become a casino for the super-rich. They generate massive crises through their own irresponsibility and greed, as in the 2008 credit crunch, but serenely evade all the social consequences and re-emerge more irresponsible and greedier than ever. Right-wing governments pander to their needs with one-sided tax concessions on a mammoth scale, while the pay of ordinary working people slumped for many years, more so than in other European countries, despite the alleged conomic recovery. Worse still, our predatory capitalists are now no longer home-grown but form an international celebrity caste above the law, beyond the Inland Revenue, and with close links to our political élite. In London, they use expensive property as a form of pocket money and drive prices up for everybody else. Their empty homes in west London are a form of currency, not somewhere that anyone would wish to live in. I shall spend my remaining days or years campaigning relentlessly against all that.

Despite this, my core values remain impregnable. I would describe my religious views as basically humanist, a doctrine of good fellowship with no supernatural overtones, since I regard them as unproven. At the same time, my views are very close to the secular side of Christianity. I am struck by the fact that Elizabeth, a Reform Protestant Christian, and I, non-religious, take exactly the same view on all day-to-day issues including such controversial matters as gay marriage where we are both on the side of tolerance. That is as it should be. I have sympathy with the great Victorian non-believer, George Jacob Holyoake, who preferred the term 'secularist' to 'atheist' which he thought conveyed the same form of bigotry and proselytism as did the more intolerant forms of Christianity. I have no sympathy with crusading atheists who stir up ill-will between different faith communities in a way reminiscent of Muslim fundamentalists. I celebrate the fact that the Labour Party was from the start a coalition of faiths and beliefs, secularists like the Webbs and many of the Fabians, with non-denominational Christians like Keir Hardie and Philip Snowden, Catholics like John Wheatley, Anglicans like George Lansbury, the broad mass of working-class nonconformists from which the party sprang in the West Riding, Lancashire and south Wales. Unlike the French and German socialists, the fledgling Labour Party was not an anti-clerical party (a point I remember once discussing with the Christian Socialist Gordon Brown), and it has been the healthier for it.

Close to my humanism has been an essentially ethical socialism. I have always felt capitalism to have a moral emptiness and in its less regulated forms to be savagely cruel. Labour sprang up in this country from a Liberal background; in Wales, through men like Jim Griffiths, it took on a strongly national identity. It thus has clear affinities with the Liberal Democrats and Plaid Cymru today, and I could imagine supporting one or other of them on occasion. But Labour, with its distinctive ethic, tries to confront, as others do not, the blatant class division and social injustice which the capitalist economy has created over very many decades in our history. It is also willing to adopt the public realm to minimise those divisions, wield power in overcoming them, and thereby civilise our society. I also feel that on a whole range of issues – race relations, feminism, the trade unions, capital punishment and penal reform, public support for the arts, censorship, moral reform, cultural tolerance – Labour is more likely to have the right values and instincts, though too often it fails to assert them. They are the values that have lain behind my history and that inspire my life, and they are why the Labour Party, especially as it emerged from the value-free managerialism of New Labour, has been important for me these past sixty years. They are also why I have felt a broad-church Labour party to be the most effective opposition to the malign dogmas of Communism, a creed resulting in the crushing of liberty, including among free trade unions. Like Keir Hardie, for me 'socialism is not a doctrine of economics'; attempts to define Labour in terms of efficiency or planning have not attracted me and, as in the 1960s, were often proved plain wrong. Socialism for me transcends the Labour Party of 2015, a colourless amalgam which seems to have lost its self-confidence and its zest for power. It is a creed of fraternity and humanity, a partnership of individuals and classes embodying the dignity of labour and the brotherhood of man.

The other guiding star of my core values has not done well these eighty years: that is the cause of peace. I have not been an outright pacifist, as I have explained: I felt a movement like CND was too emotional and too mixed up with other motives. The Second World War had to be fought to protect mankind from the poison of racist tyranny. But most of the wars in which we have been engaged since 1945 have been unnecessary or even malign. In the 1950s and 1960s, most of them were occupied in unsuccessful forays in coping with the remnants of empire. Since then we have had a series of engagements in or around the Middle East, using traditional tactics of imperialist aggression in a postcolonial world. There can be established a logical case for humanitarian international involvement, but all too often this has been tarnished by moral inconsistency, unstated capitalist objectives (such as oil) or, as in the case of the Iraq invasion of 2003, plain hypocrisy and serial lying. The case for going to war, the most ominous action that can be taken on behalf of a state and a nation, needs the most precise justification (far more so than either Blair or Cameron has shown any sign of undertaking), clear public approval in parliament and the country, and evidence that it is proportionate and, to the extent that it is possible, benevolent in intent by protecting defenceless minorities, women and children. Not many of our recent wars, if any, have passed that test. There is also the endless danger of what the Americans call 'mission creep', when an allegedly limited, short-term objective transmutes into something more sinister, messy and prolonged. The ten-year war in Afghanistan, for instance, which cost over four hundred and fifty brave British lives, is such an engagement which has proved to be ruinously unproductive and made both central Asia and this country less safe as a result.

I hate the glorification of war, and find the commemorations of the First World War in 2014 unsettling. If not, mercifully, a celebration of militarism, they have become military displays which served to endorse current operations in Afghanistan and Iraq, as well as giving the tabloid press the chance to pronounce on the latest expensive hat worn by the Duchess of Cambridge (for whose personal lifestyle one can feel only sympathy). To me, the First World War should be remembered not in ostentatious state and royalist pomp and circumstance, but in private acts of mourning by bereaved individuals and families throughout the land. In this spirit, I think now of my father's dear friend, Ivor Morgan, a farm lad from Glanfred, Llandre, north Ceredigion, who fell in Palestine just over a month before the war ended, and is buried in Ramleh war cemetery in Egypt. My father wept when recalling his death around 1958, and I, born many years after poor Ivor died, weep for him now. In contrast to many other good, sincere people, whom I would not dream of condemning, I preferred to steer clear of the 880,000 ceramic red poppies massed beside the Tower of London in August 2014 (no dead foreigners are recorded). Better instead to study and learn about the muddled, ambiguous origins of that war in history books by Colin Clark and others. The right response to such a colossal tragedy is that of Wilfred Owen's poetic judgement. It was, he wrote, 'Obscene as cancer'.

I did, however, find myself deeply moved by one commemorative event in July 2014, when the Parliament choir, in which Elizabeth is an enthusiastic soprano, took part in a joint performance in Westminster Hall with the choir of the German *Bundestag*. That, along with a moving, humble speech by the German ambassador, did seem to convey exactly the right message, and felt like a genuine festival of reconciliation. We need more of it.

War and other tragedies make my lifetime a dark period. But, for myself, I retain my sense of optimism and hope. There have been so many desperate conflicts in human history. In the immediate past, terrorist violence, including in Britain and France, has posed fearful new threats to the lives of many harmless individuals: indirectly, they have affected my own life in recent months. Despite them, more comforting conclusions can be drawn, especially in Britain. In so many ways, my lifetime, and the things of which I have sought to be the chronicler, have shown progress and improvement, starting with the post-war Attlee government. My parents lived their latter days in increased comfort and with hopeful prospects of health care, thanks in great measure to the legacy of one of their champions, Aneurin Bevan. We bring up children more sensibly and treat the elderly more humanely (as I have good cause to know myself). We are more tolerant on variations in sexuality, ethnic issues and opportunities for women. We no longer hang or flog. We are better educated and, in a digital world, better informed. The world beyond has been constantly troubled, but it has seen the power of the human spirit prevail in ending racial segregation in the United States, in winding up the evils of apartheid in southern Africa, in bringing independence to India and almost all our former colonies, rapidly so in about twenty years of my lifetime and in many cases peacefully so. Even in Northern Ireland, the peace process has yielded results. More important still, the Cold War has ended, and along with it the Soviet Union. I have witnessed the emergence of democracy in several of the countries the Soviet Union controlled, from the Czech Republic to Latvia, and stayed in Berlin in the Unter den Linden, close to where the Berlin wall and Checkpoint Charlie stood and where the Nazis once celebrated their mass burning of books. Fifty-two years after the Cuban crisis which so terrified me at the time, the US and Cuba have resumed normal civilised relations. Despite the climate of fear that terrorism creates, ours is in many ways a better world than when I entered it in 1934. My past is not another country but a real one in which I am content to have lived, and which I have tried my best to improve and to understand, or at least explain to others. Despite everything, I retain my idealism and my belief in humanity (or most of it). Alan Taylor concluded his history of *England 1914–45* (in his anglocentric way) by saying that in 1945 men no longer sang 'England arise', and yet England had arisen. And so has my beloved Wales, all the same.

Main publications by Kenneth O. Morgan

David Lloyd George: Welsh Radical as World Statesman (University of Wales Press, 1963)

Wales in British Politics, 1868–1922 (University of Wales Press 1963; 3rd edn 1980)

Freedom or Sacrilege? The History of Welsh Disestablishment (Church in Wales, 1966)

Keir Hardie (Oxford University Press, 1967)

The Age of Lloyd George (Allen & Unwin, 1971; paperback 1972; 2nd edn 1978)

Lloyd George Family Letters, c.1885–1936, editor (Oxford University Press and University of Wales Press, 1973)

Lloyd George (Weidenfeld & Nicolson, 1974; paperback 1984)

Keir Hardie: Radical and Socialist (Weidenfeld & Nicolson, 1975; paperback 1984)

Consensus and Disunity: The Lloyd George Coalition Government (Oxford University Press, 1979; paperback 1986)

Portrait of a Progressive: The Political career of Christopher, Viscount Addison, with Jane Morgan (Oxford University Press, 1980)

Rebirth of a Nation: Wales 1880–1980 (Oxford University Press & University of Wales Press, 1981; new edn in paperback 1998)

David Lloyd George 1863–1945 (University of Wales Press, 1981; Japanese edn 1992)

Welsh Society and Nationhood, joint editor (University of Wales Press, 1984)

Labour in Power, 1945–1951 (Oxford University Press, 1984; paperback 1985)

The Oxford Illustrated History of Britain, editor (Oxford University Press, 1984; most recent edn 2009; translated into French, Italian, Russian and Chinese)

Labour People: Leaders and Lieutenants, Hardie to Kinnock (Oxford University Press, 1987; paperback 1992)

The Oxford History of Britain, editor (Oxford University Press, 1988; many subsequent editions, one million copies sold)

The Red Dragon and the Red Flag (National Library of Wales, 1989)

The People's Peace: British History 1945–89 (Oxford University Press, 1990; 2nd edn 1998; new edn retitled *Britain Since 1945*, 2001)

Academic Leadership (University of Wales, Aberystwyth, 1991)

Modern Wales: Politics, Places and People (University of Wales Press, 1995)

The Young Oxford History of Britain and Ireland, editor (Oxford University Press, 1996)

Callaghan: A Life (Oxford University Press, 1997; new edn in paperback 1999)

Crime, Protest and Police in Modern British Society, joint editor (University of Wales Press, 1999)

The Twentieth Century (Oxford University Press, 2000)

The Great Reform Act of 1832 (Reform Club, 2001)

Michael Foot: A Life (HarperCollins, hardback and paperback, 2007)

Ages of Reform (I. B. Tauris, 2011)

David Lloyd George, 1863–1945, editor (Liberal History Society, 2013)

Revolution to Devolution: Reflections on Welsh Democracy (University of Wales Press, 2014)

Index